Running for Good

Chicken Soup for the Soul: Running for Good
101 Stories for Runners & Walkers to Get You Going!
Amy Newmark & Dean Karnazes

Published by Chicken Soup for the Soul, LLC www.chickensoup.com

The publisher gratefully acknowledges the many publishers and individuals who granted Chicken Soup for the Soul permission to reprint the cited material.

Front cover photo of Dean Karnazes courtesy of Fitbit
Introduction, back cover, Chapter 3 and Chapter 4 photos courtesy of Victor Magdeyev; Chapter 1 and Chapter 9 photos courtesy of Tyler Ford; Chapter 2 photo courtesy of Serpentine Running Club; Chapter 5 photo courtesy of Elias Lefas; Chapter 6 photo courtesy of Topher Gaylord; Chapter 7 photo courtesy of The North Face Santiago; Chapter 8 photo courtesy of Paragon Sports NYC; Chapter 10 photo courtesy of The North Face Italy.
Photo of Amy Newmark courtesy of Susan Morrow at SwickPix

Cover and Interior by Daniel Zaccari

Distributed to the booktrade by Simon & Schuster. SAN: 200-2442

Publisher's Cataloging-In-Publication Data
(Prepared by The Donohue Group, Inc.)

Names: Newmark, Amy, compiler. | Karnazes, Dean, 1962- compiler.
Title: Chicken soup for the soul : running for good : 101 stories for runners & walkers to get you going! / [compiled by] Amy Newmark [and] Dean Karnazes.
Other Titles: Running for good : 101 stories for runners & walkers to get you going!
Description: [Cos Cob, Connecticut] : Chicken Soup for the Soul, LLC, [2019]
Identifiers: ISBN 9781611599909 | ISBN 9781611592900 (ebook)
Subjects: LCSH: Running--Social aspects--Literary collections. | Running--Social aspects--Anecdotes. | Walk-a-thons--Literary collections. | Walk-a-thons--Anecdotes. | Charities--Literary collections. | Charities--Anecdotes. | LCGFT: Anecdotes.
Classification: LCC GV1061.8.S63 C45 2019 (print) | LCC GV1061.8.S63 (ebook) | DDC 796.42/02 361.7/02--dc23

Library of Congress Control Number 2019937408

PRINTED IN THE UNITED STATES OF AMERICA
on acid∞free paper

25 24 23 22 21 20 19 01 02 03 04 05 06 07 08 09 10 11

101 Stories for Runners & Walkers to Get You Going!

Amy Newmark
Dean Karnazes

Chicken Soup for the Soul, LLC
Cos Cob, CT

Changing your life one story at a time®

www.chickensoup.com

Table of Contents

❸

~Camaraderie & Community~

❹

~Doing It for Myself~

5

~One Step at a Time~

6

~That Marathon Mindset~

7

~Oh the Places I've Been~

8

~Family Ties~

9

~Committing to Life~

10

~It's Therapy and More~

Introduction

The storm hit without warning. The morning had been warm, oppressively warm, as it had been for the past several days, with temperatures hovering near 90 degrees Fahrenheit and precious little shade. Even at noon the skies had been clear. And then, as if some imaginary switch got flipped, the skies darkened and an ominous crack of thunder shook the high heavens.

Soon, rain was falling—a cold, penetrating rain that seeped through my thin windbreaker and quickly soaked my skin. I didn't have the right gear, and it was my own fault. How could I be so stupid? Temperatures in Central Asia have been known to fluctuate by up to 75 degrees in a single hour, and I knew this. And here, in the mountain passes of Kyrgyzstan, I was warned that storms could materialize quickly on otherwise warm and sunny days. This was such a day.

The higher I climbed up the pass, the colder the rain became. I tried moving as quickly as possible—in an effort to generate more internal body heat—but when the rain turned to frozen crystals of hail it became a losing battle. No matter how quickly I moved valuable body heat was being drained faster than it could be generated. I began shivering, the early signs of hypothermia, so I clenched my arms in front of my chest for warmth and protection, and I wrapped the ends of my lightweight jacket over my fingers.

But it was no use; the elements were too much. Even with my arms cinched tightly to my chest and my fingers hidden, the cold and wet were overpowering. I'd gotten myself into a bad situation and there were no clear solutions on how to get out of it. But I knew stopping would only make things worse. So I kept going.

Off in the distance, I spotted a small billow of smoke rising through the raindrops. As I drew nearer, I could see that the smoke was emanating from a small structure of some sort. Closer I drew, trying to better discern what it was. By now my teeth were chattering and my entire body was drenched, from soggy hair to sopping wet feet. I came alongside the structure and stopped, my knees knocking together.

Looking down I could see there was a family standing on the porch. They were looking up at me from under the protection of a tin awning, staring. I stood shivering and looked at them. In that moment of silence a universal conversation took place; we communicated without words and I knew what to do.

Slowly I made my way toward them. I felt welcomed somehow, like a stray dog finding a loving home. As I drew nearer, one of the children, a little boy, came out to greet me. He held out his tiny little hand for me to hold. I unclenched my arms and peeled back the sleeve of my jacket to reveal my fingers. They were blue.

"*Salam*," I managed to say (hello). It was one of the few words I knew in Kyrgyz. They all chuckled. I'm sure I mispronounced it.

The little boy took my hand and led me inside their house, their yurt. The yurt was warm inside, and dry, and smelled earthy and alive, like a fresh garden. The family came in behind us and quietly went about their business. Soon a cup of warm tea was placed in my hands and the man, I presume the father, draped a blanket over my shoulders. I sipped the tea. "Mmm…" I sighed. It was warm and comforting. The children smiled.

There were four of them, three boys and a girl. They all sat attentively looking at me. It wasn't awkward, though. The silence was somehow bridging the distance between us, between our separate worlds. There was no need to say anything; they wouldn't understand English, and besides, most communication is nonverbal anyway.

As the feeling finally came back to my fingers, I decided to try and explain why this alien figure had been ambling past their house. They'd probably met very few foreigners in their time, and certainly no runners. I must have appeared as a strange caricature, an apparition clad in futuristic sportswear and strange cushy shoes.

I began miming my appreciation for the cup of warm tea with a simple thumbs-up. They smiled and nodded in approval. Thumbs-up is a universal symbol, I've learned. Next, I held up my hand palm side down and began waving my two big fingers back and forth in alternating succession, hoping to represent two legs running. They looked a little puzzled. Then I spoke.

"Tashkent… Bishkek… Almaty." Now they looked *really* confused.

Nevertheless, the father seemed to be processing what I'd said. He pointed to me as if to ask, "You? You did this?"

I nodded my head, "Yes, yes," and began slowly running in place, simultaneously jutting my legs up and down and swinging my arms.

Now they all seemed to understand the gist of my message and stared in amazement. The three cities I had mentioned were the capitals of Uzbekistan, Kyrgyzstan and Kazakhstan. They knew this. They also seemed to know that hundreds of miles separated the three, and I was indicating that I was covering this distance on foot, running. The path I was following was the ancient Silk Road, one that nomadic peoples have traveled for thousands of years.

Sipping more tea, the one emotion I didn't detect in their stares was, "Why?" Why would anyone do such a thing? Perhaps the nomadic spirit was part of their DNA and the idea of wandering the land didn't seem entirely foreign to them. We just smiled at each other and there seemed to be an acceptance of my peripatetic roaming as nothing too unusual.

In time the patter of rain began to abate. I finished my second cup of tea and felt the urge to continue onward; there were still many miles left to cover. They sensed my intentions and assembled to walk me out the entrance. "*Rakhmat saga*," I said (thank you). It was the only other phrase I knew in Kyrgyz. Once again they chuckled, and once again I was sure I'd mispronounced it.

The children followed me from their home up to the roadside. We shook hands, their eyes squarely meeting mine. I nodded and grinned, and began to run. They waved, saying nothing. A little ways up the road I turned back. They were still standing there, watching me, observing; they weren't giggling or running around chasing each other, just quietly watching me run off into the distance, a man slowly becoming a stick figure, and then a stick figure slowly dissipating into nothingness over the horizon. They just watched me go.

I didn't know the word for goodbye in Kyrgyz. It was just as well; they've never left me. That family and those children live on within me, to this day. And I hope that a little part of me lives on within them. Running had brought us together; running had made this beautiful encounter possible; running had created this good.

As I reflect on my life as a runner, running has created much good. I have run for charity, for fitness, for friendship and camaraderie, and I have run to unite people. Running and walking have a profound power in this way. The simple act of putting one foot in front of the other can transform individuals; it can transform lives. Running and walking can hurt — running a marathon or walking your first 5K isn't painless — but they can also heal.

The stories you are about to read are a testament to the profound goodness running and walking can bring about. You will read of courageous acts by people who have overcome seemingly insurmountable obstacles and prevailed against all odds. You'll read about how getting out there — and moving your body — creates camaraderie, confidence… and calm. We have countless stories from people who found that running (or walking) helped them overcome not only the obvious issues, like obesity or lack of fitness, but also stress, depression, lack of confidence, and loneliness. You'll read about parents who used running to bond with their children, couples who ran together and repaired their marriages, and people who ran their way right out of jobs they didn't like and into new careers that stoked their passion for life.

Some of these stories are rather miraculous, too. We start the book with a story by Sara Etgen-Baker, who decided to confront her poor eating habits and her lack of fitness by establishing a walking routine. She could only walk 15 minutes initially, but over two years she transformed herself from an unhealthy 300-pound woman to a 130-pound runner. As if that weren't enough, Sara was then chosen from hundreds of thousands of applicants to be a support runner for the 2002 Olympic Torch Relay. The miracle continued when one of the official torchbearers had to drop out and Sara was randomly selected as a replacement and ran the Olympic flame through Santa Fe, New Mexico on its way to the games in Salt Lake City.

The miracles of resilience and fortitude abound in these pages. Brian Reynolds, for example, lost both his lower legs at age four but became an athlete anyway. He opens his story as a grown man at the 2018 Chicago Marathon, where he's trying, for the fifth time, to complete the 26.2 miles. Brian runs on blades, and everything's going great until Mile 22 when his right blade gets caught in a pothole and is torn off his leg. He hits his head, but despite his dizziness when some spectators help him to his "feet," he pulls that blade back on and completes the race, in agony. And you know what? He set a new double amputee world record that day.

I'd venture to say that virtually every story in this collection involves the miracles that come to those who get out there and run or walk their way through our beautiful world. Peter Neiger, for example, returned from serving in Afghanistan and found himself reliving his missions there through recurring nightmares for the next five years. In his dreams he was always running away from terrifying danger. During the day, however, Peter was far from a runner. He was out of shape and had gained 60 pounds since he came back from his tour of duty. Finally a friend convinced him to start running, promising it would help. Peter was skeptical but he bought a pair of running shoes and went for a run. That night, he collapsed into his bed, and the nightmares didn't come. He's run hundreds of miles since then, and he reports that his dreams are happy now.

We titled this book "Running for Good" for a special reason—because we're not only showing you how you can use running for the *good* of your physical and mental health, but also because running (and walking) are so intertwined with doing *good* through races that benefit nonprofits. You'll find that a large percentage of the contributors to this book participate in anything from 5Ks to 100-mile ultramarathons to raise money for various causes. Kristin Knott writes that she was overcome with emotion after nine of her friends joined her in Toronto for a two-day walk to raise money for The Princess Margaret Cancer Foundation. Kristin was in the middle of her breast cancer treatment at that time and was going in for surgery just weeks later. But the support that she felt during that walk was so empowering that she was giddy by the end of it. Raising money to support good causes through running or walking not only does us good, but it challenges us to be the very best we can be.

And that's how I feel about running overall. It challenges everyone. It's the great unifier. It bridges differences, and it's a universal language. Since the days of ancient Greece, mankind has understood the significance of running and what it means to be a runner. It's the ultimate test for us, and it brings out the best in everyone—including those four adorable children standing in front of their yurt in the mountains of Kyrgyzstan.

I'm so proud of the stories we have for you in these pages. I worked with Chicken Soup for the Soul's editor-in-chief Amy Newmark to provide you with motivation and inspiration and plenty of "how-to's"—while still entertaining you. I'm sure you'll find yourself laughing at times, getting teary-eyed at times, and calling someone to share the stories that you think will resonate with them. I'm absolutely certain you'll find yourself lacing up those running shoes with new enthusiasm and resolve, whether you're an aspiring 5K walker, a marathoner, or a crazy ultramarathoner like me.

Happy reading… and I'll see you out there!

—Dean Karnazes—
March 24, 2019

SILK ROAD
ULTRAMARATHON
525
25

Getting Started

Finding My Light

An empty lantern provides no light. Self-care is the fuel that allows your light to shine brightly.
~Author Unknown

"Pick up the pace!" coaxed my husband.

"But I can't!" I said, my heart pounding hard inside my chest. "I can't go any faster!"

"Yes, you can! You're not fat anymore."

There it was, the "f word" and label that defined me for 30 years. I was a plump, pleasant little girl, and then a charming, chunky teenager. By the time I entered college, I was a spirited—and stout—young woman. Six years later, I was an obese college graduate with a promising counseling career ahead of me—a career that failed to take off.

But I was blind to my own obesity, unaware that it was at the core of my unemployability until a potential employer shared his reason for not hiring me. "Your credentials are sound, but your level of obesity tells me you have emotional issues that will diminish your effectiveness as a counselor."

His candor opened my eyes to a hard truth: I was addicted to food. With that realization came responsibility: I had to shed what no longer served me, confront my addiction, and prevent it and my obesity from overshadowing and defining me. Breaking my addiction was hard. It required honest self-examination, altering my thinking patterns, and making different choices. Slowly, I modified my eating habits, eating only when I was physically hungry instead of eating when I was emotionally hungry.

Although I could barely walk down the stairs of my apartment building, I began walking to improve my mobility and awaken my atrophied body. Initially, I could walk for only 15 minutes at a time. My arms and legs rubbed together, chafing and then scabbing over. But I pushed myself every day, walking five minutes longer than I did the day before until I walked for an hour and eventually two. For two years, I committed myself to healthy eating choices and maintained my walking regimen, slowly and painstakingly changing myself from being an unhealthy 300-pound woman to a 130-pound healthy one. At that point, I traded my walking shoes for running shoes and became an avid runner.

My journey motivated my husband. In March 2001, after seeing a commercial inviting Americans to nominate an ordinary person who inspired them to bring the Olympic flame to Salt Lake City, he nominated me to be a torchbearer. The odds of being selected were low (210,000:1), but I was no stranger to overwhelming odds. I believed my story would inspire others and strike a chord with the selection committee.

Running taught me the importance of training for a race. I pictured myself running a race and crossing the finish line. For months, I ran through my neighborhood carrying a broken-off broom handle with a three-pound weight on it in my right hand, feeling the weight of the torch. I waved at my neighbors, pretending they were cheering bystanders. I printed a picture of a torchbearer wearing the white uniform, replaced the face with a picture of mine, and taped it to my refrigerator door. Every day, I visualized myself as a torchbearer. I was in training to participate in a historic running event.

On September 26th, while on my daily run through my neighborhood, an express package arrived. My hands trembled as I opened it and read:

> *You've been selected as a "potential" support runner for the Salt Lake 2002 Olympic Torch Relay… A nationwide search was conducted for ordinary individuals who've inspired others to be*

both torchbearers and support runners. You've obviously touched those around you. Although all the torchbearer spots have been filled, you're eligible to be a support runner. A support runner serves as "guardian of the flame" and accompanies torchbearers carrying the Olympic Flame along its journey… Congratulations!

Although I wouldn't be wearing the white uniform and carrying the torch as I had imagined, I wasn't disappointed. My dream of participating in the torch relay was coming true! Given the odds, I was delighted to be a support runner and "guardian of the flame." I completed the required physical examination, submitted the forms, and waited, knowing that the letter clearly stated I was a "potential" support runner. Months passed without any word, but I continued my training runs through the neighborhood. Finally, on December 20th, another package arrived. It contained my official blue support runner uniform along with instructions for my segment of the relay.

"Bill," I ran inside the house screaming, "I'm officially a support runner! We're going to Santa Fe, New Mexico!"

For the ensuing weeks and despite winter's bitter cold, I bundled up and ran every day through my neighborhood, clutching my makeshift torch in my gloved hand. On January 12th, a bitter cold day, my husband and I stood outside the Torch Relay collection point in Santa Fe. "One of today's torchbearers can't run her segment," announced the relay organizer as she dropped folded pieces of paper into her hat. "One lucky support runner will become a torchbearer. Select a number from this hat as it's passed around."

I removed my glove and reached into the hat, my numb hand trembling. I closed my eyes, stirred the contents, nabbed the first piece of paper that stuck to my fingers, and waited.

"Number 32! Who has number 32?"

I opened my eyes and unfolded my piece of paper. "Me! Oh, my God… me!"

I was whisked inside where I changed into a white torchbearer uniform and boarded the shuttle bus with the Olympic theme song blaring over the loudspeakers. The bus drove down streets lined with balloons and banners, filled with throngs of people waving American flags. At segment 32, I stepped off the bus and positioned myself to receive the flame. The cold air, alive with spirit and excitement, took away my breath. *Hold it tightly,* I thought, as the flame in the torch carried by the runner before me lit my three-pound torch. A rush of emotion surged through my body. I turned around and ran down the street, just as I had envisioned and practiced all those months.

The world vanished. I ran without my feet ever touching the ground. I waved and smiled as I floated past the bystanders, and for an instant I thought I saw Konstantinos Kondylis, the first modern-day Olympic torchbearer, in the crowd. "The lampadedromia is not about you," he murmured. "It's about sharing the Olympic spirit, and giving the flame of strength and inspiration to others."

Like Konstantinos, I was an ordinary person participating in an extraordinary running event — one that had little to do with me. Yes, I was carrying the Torch, but more importantly, I was carrying the Olympic spirit. I still run, inspired to live, work, and behave with the Olympic spirit in my heart, doing my part to strengthen and inspire others.

— Sara Etgen-Baker —

Time for Health

For me, running is both exercise and a metaphor.
Running day after day, piling up the races,
bit by bit I raise the bar, and by clearing
each level I elevate myself.
~Haruki Murakami

Anyone with five kids will agree with me: It's easy to find excuses to skip workouts. Back when Laurie and I were dating, I told myself, "I have a serious girlfriend. I want to spend all my time with her." While we were engaged, all my spare time went into wedding prep — or emotionally supporting Laurie while she did all the wedding prep. Once we were married, I wanted to be home with my new wife. Then we started having kids, and spare time disappeared quickly.

In the blink of an eye, I was in my mid-thirties with five kids and I hadn't worked out in over a decade. I didn't consider myself overweight except at my annual physical when the doctor told me an average male of my age and height should weigh about 40 pounds less. "How would I lose this weight?" I wondered as I left these visits. I was almost relieved when, a few minutes later, I got a call from Laurie and got distracted by one or more of our kids needing to be picked up somewhere or needing a few things from the grocery store.

I justified my health and being out of shape with a sense of pride. I was a devoted husband and father who wanted to spend his time and money on the family and not on himself. Then I got a job at an office with a personal trainer, Rose, who gave group sessions during the lunch hour in a conference room that had been converted into a gym. There were treadmills, elliptical machines, and a set of dumbbells. So, with money and time no longer issues, I started working out two days a week.

It started slowly. I spent the session walking on the treadmill because I found it less grueling than lifting weights. After a few weeks, Rose adjusted the speed and incline so I was forced into some light jogging. I might have pushed back and lowered the settings, except she was so encouraging. If I had a good session, she said, "You're doing great." If I had a lousy session, she said, "Don't get discouraged. Just keep showing up."

I wanted to impress her, so I told her I wanted to beat a 10-minute mile.

"That's a great idea!" she said.

On a dry-erase board, she tracked the time it took me to complete a mile each day. I memorized the speed settings and increased every day by a few seconds. A 15-minute mile became 14. Two minutes of jogging became four. At each session, Rose greeted me with a big smile and said, "How much are you gonna beat yesterday's time by today?" I got inside 11 minutes and planned exactly which day I'd finally beat 10 minutes. When that day came, I felt so anxious I could barely eat breakfast or concentrate on work all morning. At the session, Rose gave me a big high-five. "Today's the day!" she said.

I felt terrible throughout the run. It must have been my nerves. But I powered through. When I got to the final fraction of the mile, I accidentally pulled the emergency stop pin. Rose, my workout partners, and I all shared a collective groan. "Well," Rose said, "you can try it again at our next session."

Two days later, I couldn't wait to hit the treadmill. I was ready. I was hungry. And when I hit the mile marker at 9:59, the gym erupted. I was so amped up I could have run another mile. Rose let me enjoy my victory for the rest of the session. Then at our next session, she said, "So how long will it take you to beat a nine-minute mile?"

"Are you insane?" I asked.

"Nope!" she said. "You can do it. Just keep training like you did for the 10-minute."

I soon beat the nine-minute mile, and then the eight-minute. Perhaps my proudest accomplishment was that I continued to improve after I got a new job and stopped training with Rose. Laurie encouraged me to find a gym close to my new office and continue to work out during my lunch break. I frequently texted Rose my progress, especially when I beat a seven-minute mile, and ultimately a six-minute mile.

During this entire time, Laurie encouraged me constantly. She bought me Dri-FIT clothes and little workout tools to use at home. She noticed if I went more than a couple of days without a run. "Your mood is dropping," she said. "Why don't you go for a jog? You'll feel better when you get home."

Running and working out also became a way to bond with the kids. I took them with me to boot camps regularly. When I played football with my sons and the neighborhood kids, my boys told their friends to line up against me. Their friends clearly saw my gray hair and thought I wouldn't be a problem, so I surprised them when I kept up. They told my sons, "Dang, your dad's fast."

"Yeah, he beats us all the time," my sons said.

At my most recent physical, the nurse took my pulse and blood pressure. "I'm just curious," she said. "Are you a runner?"

I was stunned. "Yes. How did you know?"

"Both your pulse and blood pressure are very low."

I was so excited that I felt lightheaded. As soon as the nurse left the room, I frantically texted Laurie the news. "That's great!" she responded. "You should treat yourself to something. Oh, you should get yourself something at the grocery store because we need a few things for dinner tonight."

— Billy Cuchens —

Through Anything

You have to push past your perceived limits, push past that point you thought was as far as you can go.
~Drew Brees

"I'm not a runner, and I never will be." I spoke those words — bragged them, really — at any mention of this torturous exercise. My single attempt at running a decade earlier had ended with me doubled over and panting at barely a quarter-mile in. I didn't discriminate against running, though. I hated all exercise and physical activity.

I was blessed with a high metabolism — no exercise required — until I hit my twenties, had a baby, and never lost the weight. For 10 years, I carried a few extra pounds. They bugged me, but 20 pounds weren't enough to motivate me to give up my convenient life.

Then my entire world shifted. I finished graduate school, left an unhealthy marriage, and found myself with new freedom — the perfect recipe to stir up change. I learned about nutrition and discovered an intense, CrossFit-style gym. I became obsessed with exercising. Stress and anger were my motivators, and I sweated them out as peace took their place. I slept better, focused better, and all around felt better. I became the fittest, healthiest, happiest version of myself I'd ever been.

Two months into my newfound love for exercise, a group of coworkers invited me to join them in a 5K run. I laughed and said, "I'm not a runner." But when I discovered the event was The Color Run, I reconsidered. Once, after seeing a poster of a happy runner doused in colored powder, I'd commented, "If I ever did a run—which I wouldn't—it would be a Color Run."

When I didn't die by the end of my trial jog, I signed up for the race and trained for eight weeks. I felt intimidated by my five co-workers, who were experienced runners, sure that my form looked weird and that I ran too slowly. I worried I would embarrass myself in front of them and my daughter and mother, who'd come to cheer me on.

However, the day of the race, I not only kept up but I led the pack. All those box jumps and squats I'd repeated until my legs became jelly had strengthened my quads and calves and built endurance.

I had become a runner, despite believing I never would.

Not two months after my initial 5K, a friend invited me to run a half marathon. Whoa. This wasn't a little three-mile race we were talking about. Could I really run for more than 13 miles? Run for more than two hours? It seemed daunting, but I recalled something that had happened a while back.

For two days in early May, Pittsburgh shuts down so thousands of runners can pound the pavement in a variety of events from a toddler trot to a full marathon. I happened to be staying in a hotel near the starting line and found the breakfast room packed with runners. Off-handedly, I said to my daughter, "I'm going to run a marathon someday." I was still anti-running then, but the desire must've lain dormant in my bones.

Here was my chance. It might not be a full marathon, but I could run half of one, something I hadn't thought possible for me just one year earlier. I signed up and started training in March when the weather warmed up. Then I learned that running six or seven miles was no joke, and I was out of practice.

The May event date loomed, and I panicked. Thoughts plagued me. *I can't do it. I'm not trained. I can't run more than seven miles, and that's only halfway. I'll let my friend down. I'll mess up her race.* Two days before the race, I came very close to bowing out. But I'd paid no small fee for this race and figured that if I had to walk I would. I would just tell my friend to go on without me.

The night before the race, I only slept four hours. In the morning, I downed an energy shot — probably a bad idea, but I needed to wake up. I ate my favorite protein bar, but had no concept of running fuel. My friend handed me an energy gel — my first ever — and we were off.

The beginning few miles — usually the hardest for me — passed easily as I took in the sights, read the signs of the spectators cheering us on, and enjoyed the event atmosphere. At mile 5, my friend needed to walk a little. I walked with her but didn't need to. At mile 8, my shins started to hurt, so I popped ibuprofen and kept going. She needed to walk again. I didn't. At mile 11, I was astonished. Full of energy, feeling great, I looked over to my friend and said, "Do you just want to run the whole marathon?" I was joking, of course, and the comment earned me many glares from those around us, but it proved something to me. I'd achieved much more than I thought possible.

Now having been a runner for more than three years, with several 5Ks and four half marathons under my feet, I have more events planned for this year and the goal of a full marathon in the near future.

I've run through cities, parks, and beaches, early in the morning, late at night, and during the most beautiful sunrise of my life. I've run in rain and snow, in far too much heat, and in sickness and in health. I've run my soles smooth and my laces frayed. I've run through shin pain, knee pain, quad pain, calf pain, foot pain, muscle cramps, side stitches, and debilitating despair. I've run with the odds against me. I've run through quitting and restarting, and through all-consuming hopelessness. I've run with too much energy and not nearly enough.

I've run through the stress of a divorce, through anxiety and rage, and then through finding love and watching my boyfriend become a runner as he became my fiancé and now my husband and favorite running partner. We've run three half marathons together so far. And we keep each other going.

I've wanted to give up a hundred times. I've believed I could never come close but pushed through. I kept going. I achieved more than I ever imagined.

And now I know: I can do things that seem impossible. I can

always keep moving forward — no matter what's going on around me or within me, no matter who is or isn't at my side. I can run through anything.

— Denise Murphy Drespling —

The Walking Cure

An early-morning walk is a blessing for the whole day.
~Henry David Thoreau

I never liked exercising. If I could find a quiet place to sit and read all day, I was content. Exert myself? No way. I was a confirmed couch potato.

Then, when I began having marriage trouble, I felt inadequate and depressed. I was simply plodding through my days, putting one foot in front of the other, no longer enjoying anything—not even reading. I met a woman who worked at my husband's business, Linda, who helped turn things around for me. She invited me to go for a walk after work. I liked her right away, so I said "yes."

That was the beginning of a daily walking routine. It was also the beginning of a lasting friendship. While we walked, we talked. We shared our problems, fears, and hopes. We became each other's parenting coaches and marriage counselors during those increasingly lengthier walks. Before long, we were managing five miles a day. Soon, my depression lifted, and I was able to laugh again.

During the years that followed, Linda and I walked in the heat of summer and in the freezing Michigan winters, even in the rain unless there was lightning. When one of us didn't feel like exerting herself, the other one made her go. One time, at my insistence, we started our walk in a gentle mist. A few miles from home, it began raining harder, and then a downpour drenched us. When it began thundering, we ran into an apartment complex. Giggling over our audacity, we knocked on a stranger's door. We must have looked pitiful, dripping from our hair to our soggy shoes. "Could we use your phone to call for a ride?" we asked.

Another time, we donned thermal underwear, heavy coats, boots, and gloves, and slogged over snow-covered side streets on new cross-country skis. We started down what appeared to be a small hill, but I lost control and whizzed down the incline. I landed flat on my back in a snow bank at the bottom. Carefully, Linda made her way to where I lay and reached down to help me up. In her attempt, she also lost her balance and fell on top of me. We lay in a heap, unhurt, but laughing so hard we couldn't even attempt to get up for a quite a while.

We walked and talked through happy times and sad times. No matter what life obstacles we faced, walking helped us through them. When my marriage ended in divorce, we kept walking. When I began dating a wonderful man, we walked. When I remarried, I moved with him to Cincinnati, and our walking days ended, although the friendship continued long-distance.

While Rich was involved in an exciting new job, I was at home, too intimidated by the big city to venture far. My family and friends were hundreds of miles away, and I was lonely. Once again, I felt a budding depression. Although I was happy in my marriage, I missed the camaraderie of a nearby friend.

Rich and I were invited to a gathering of staff and spouses one day. Everyone was polite and friendly, but it was apparent that most of the women had well-established friendships with one another. I was an outsider.

I noticed a young woman standing alone on the fringe of the chattering groups. I wandered over and introduced myself. I discovered her husband was new on staff, and she'd recently moved to the area. "It's hard moving and having to start fresh getting to know people," Cheryl said.

I agreed wholeheartedly. Like me, she was missing her old life. After chatting a while and finding out she lived only a few miles from me, I asked, "Hey, would you like to meet at the park and walk together sometime?"

"Yes, I'd love that."

We began meeting to walk and talk several times a week. This was the beginning of a new friendship and the end of my loneliness.

I'm not sure if it was the walking or the talking that was most responsible for getting me through those tough times — probably both. I think exercise clears the mind and pushes out negative thinking, allowing positivity to enter. That, combined with having the right walking partner, can make a big difference in one's life. And sometimes, if we're lucky, it will result in a new friendship — just when it's needed most.

— Diana L. Walters —

No Donuts for Today

I don't run to add days to my life.
I run to add life to my days.
~Ronald Rook

They were assembling at the starting line—runners of all ages, shapes and sizes—preparing for the first 5K of the spring season. I didn't know this because I was a runner. I knew this because I had stopped at the park's public restroom on my way to buy donuts and noticed the huge banner announcing the race.

For some reason, I decided to sit on the grass and watch the race begin. I was fascinated by the diversity I witnessed. There were teenagers and grandmas, mamas with babies strapped to their backs, and dads with their young sons and daughters in tow. High-fives were happening everywhere amidst good-natured ribbing before the officials signaled for the start.

Everyone looked glad to be there—proud, in fact. I wondered what prompted such enthusiasm. The idea of running for any reason other than chasing down an ice-cream truck had never been appealing to me.

As the runners took their places, I heard exuberant cheering from the bleachers. "Go, Barbara! You got this, Mama!" "Grandpa, we love you! We're so proud of you." A cacophony of enthusiasm drowned out the traffic across the way.

I decided to stay and watch. For some reason, the race became a study in human nature. I was drawn to the heady excitement. Who would cross the finish line first? How long had that person been running? When did he or she become devoted to the sport? For the first time in ages, something captivated me long enough that donuts took a back seat.

To me, everyone looked like a winner. First came the actual winner. He looked around 45. When he crossed the finish line and the ribbon broke, he raised his arms in the air like Rocky. Next up was a woman around 60 who came in within steps of her Rocky counterpart. And then it was a blur of sneakers and heavy breathing, joyful whooping and water cups.

Everyone acted like they felt that way as well. Participants were given T-shirts. Ribbons were handed out in every age division. Phone cameras captured the exhilaration.

On my way to the car, I crossed paths with a runner wiping her brow.

"Congratulations," I said.

"Thank you. I can't believe I actually made it. I almost gave up halfway through the race. I heard my dad's voice telling me I could do it. I raced today in his honor."

I didn't stop for donuts that day. I can't tell you exactly why. I can tell you that something transformative happened that race day four months ago.

Now when I stop at the park to use the public restroom, I also gingerly run the quarter-mile track. Everyone passes me, including the very youngest and oldest. Somehow, that doesn't seem to matter. I'm there. I'm trying. For me, that's a feat to celebrate.

Someday, I hope to hear my family's voices coming from those bleachers when they see Nanny come across the finish line.

—Lisa Leshaw—

The Not-So-Fun Run

What you do makes a difference, and you have to decide what kind of difference you want to make.
~Jake Goodall

"Are you signing up for the Fun Run?" my friend and fellow teacher, Jessica, asked.

I shook my head. "No, races aren't really my thing."

"It's not a race," she said. "It's just a Fun Run."

"The words 'fun' and 'run' do not belong in the same sentence."

She rolled her eyes. "It raises money for the school — the school where you teach. The school the children you claim to love attend. They're raising money to buy new playground equipment. Don't you want your kids to have a nice, safe playground?"

"Really, Jess? You're going to play that card?"

"I was just kidding. I know you love your kids. But I don't see why this is such a big deal to you."

"I don't run. I never have," I said. "Even as a kid, I avoided running. I'm slow, and I look weird when I do it. So I don't run, especially not in front of people."

"But the money goes to the school."

"I'll write a check."

"You're a single mom. You don't have any money. The only way you can help is if you run in the race."

"Can I walk?"

Jess shrugged. "Sure. You'll probably be the only one, but that's fine."

I sighed. "Great. That wouldn't be embarrassing or anything. I'd only finish the race two hours after everyone else."

"Diane, it's not a race. It's just a Fun Run."

"Running is not fun for me." I said the words slowly and clearly so she would understand.

"You'll be the only teacher not participating."

"That couldn't be true. Mrs. Jones is running? The same Mrs. Jones who has needed to retire for at least the last decade?"

Jess nodded, triumph in her eyes. "Mrs. Jones is running."

She had me, and she knew it. If my septuagenarian co-worker could do it, I'd better at least try. "Sign me up," I said, already regretting it.

On my way home from work that day, I calculated how many days until the race... I mean, the Fun Run. As if calling it that made it any less torturous.

The race was scheduled for the second Saturday in May. The hope was that we would raise tons of money, and the new playground equipment could be installed over summer vacation.

I fully supported the idea of the new playground. I just didn't think the end justified the means. Why couldn't we hold a bake sale or sell T-shirts? Neither of those things is embarrassing in the least.

Many years ago, I discovered something about myself: I'm motivated by the avoidance of embarrassment. Some people will work hard to get something good. I'm more motivated by the idea of avoiding something bad — like losing the race to someone who graduated high school with my grandmother.

I only had two months to prepare.

Fortunately, spring had come early to my Midwestern town, and going outside wasn't completely unbearable. I asked my kids if they wanted to ride bikes. This usually meant that they would ride their bikes up and down the sidewalk in front of our house, and I would watch from a lawn chair in our yard.

Imagine their surprise when I began to jog alongside them,

determined to keep up. Yes, I was determined to keep pace with a four-year-old who was riding a Dora the Explorer bike with pink training wheels.

Less than ten minutes later, I was sitting in the lawn chair, my face red from the exertion.

It was beyond embarrassing, but I knew I couldn't give up. The Not-So-Fun Run was looming.

The kids and I developed a daily habit of them bike riding and me jogging beside them. Okay, I was behind them, and it was more like a hobble. As I huffed and puffed through each session, I hoped none of my neighbors happened to peek out their windows and see me. They're good people; they'd probably call an ambulance for me.

It wasn't pretty, but ten days in, I stayed on my feet until the kids were tired of riding. The lawn chair had beckoned, but I stayed strong.

The kids and I went out for ice cream to celebrate.

One day, about three weeks into our riding/jogging/hobbling routine, my son announced that he was done riding for the day. I was shocked to realize that I wasn't completely exhausted yet. The kids sat in the lawn chairs and watched me jog up and down the sidewalk a few more times.

There might have been ice cream that night, too.

Finally, the day of the Not-So-Fun Run arrived. The kids and I went to the park where they were holding the event. I got in line to get my number and timing chip.

"Are you a runner or a walker?" the volunteer asked.

My eyebrows shot up. "Are a lot of people walking?"

"Yeah, like way more than half of them."

My hopes soared. Walking wasn't at all embarrassing. I could walk the race without even breaking a sweat.

But then I remembered all the training I'd done. I looked at my kids, who'd been so proud of my progress. I had to do it.

"I'm a runner," I told the volunteer.

It wasn't pretty, but I finished that Not-So-Fun Run with the second-slowest time of all the runners. I think a few of the walkers beat me. Maybe I should have been embarrassed by my time, but all

I felt was pride at having finished.

Mrs. Jones came in sixth place. After that, people stopped asking her when she was going to retire.

The race raised a few thousand dollars, and new playground equipment was installed that summer. That next year, every time I had recess duty, I remembered that my triumphant run had helped put it there.

— Diane Stark —

From Screen Time to Race Time

There is something magical about running; after a certain distance, it transcends the body. Then a bit farther, it transcends the mind.
~Kristin Armstrong

They did it! Hunter and Palmer ran their first 30K. It was not easy for them, but they did it. Nine months earlier, neither of them was in any condition to run five miles, let alone 18.6 miles (the distance of a 30K). But they had just accomplished something that neither of them had ever done before, and now they were on track to complete their first marathon, too.

Months earlier, my wife Lisa had woken up at 4:45 a.m. to go to her Camp Gladiator class. She heard voices coming from the upstairs game room and decided to investigate. She discovered that our older son, Hunter, had been playing the video game Fortnite since he got home from school the previous day. What she found angered both of us.

We were sick and tired of the amount of time Hunter spent playing video games. He would often sleep until 1:00 or 2:00 p.m. on Saturdays because he stayed up playing games until 2:00 or 3:00 in the morning.

Driven to break this habit, we tried several different approaches, like limiting the amount of time he was allowed to play each day, but we couldn't find anything that worked consistently. He always seemed to gravitate back to the game, especially when we were not there to monitor him.

I'm not a big fan of video games. Yes, I played my fair share of Pac-Man, Space Invaders, and Frogger in the 1980s, but times were different. In the summer, my parents would lock the door behind us in the morning as we left to play sandlot baseball, street football or driveway hoops. We were okay with that. If we got thirsty, we drank out of the hose. After all, we didn't know any different.

In the early 1990s, I was a summer camp counselor at our local church and responsible for the field sports program. My job consisted of organizing games like kickball and capture the flag. Quickly, it became apparent to me that this new generation of kids was entirely different from mine.

"Mr. Andrew, Mr. Andrew, can we go inside now?" asked one of the campers.

"No, we've only been out here 10 minutes. This session lasts an hour," I replied.

"It's so hot! We need air conditioning," he pleaded.

"You'll be fine," I promised.

I couldn't figure out why kids had changed so much in just one decade. Then it hit me. I noticed many of the campers playing video games on little portable devices. It seemed to be all they talked about, and it was hard getting their attention. Nintendo had created legal crack for preteens, and it was called Game Boy. I began referring to kids who spent more time playing video games than playing sports as the Nintendo Generation.

It's not that I'm against video games; I am just against playing them every waking moment at the expense of exercise. In an attempt to ensure that our kids did not become members of the Nintendo Generation, I came up with an idea and pitched it to Lisa.

Effective immediately, video-game time in our house would have to be earned, just like money. I set the exchange rate: Each mile run equals 30 minutes of video-game play. I put no limit on the number of miles our son could run in a day, so technically the only limit to the amount of time he played was based on how far he decided to run.

The first couple of days didn't go very well. Hunter got frustrated and refused to run at all. He started experiencing heavy withdrawal symptoms that included anxiety, sweating, vomiting, depression, hallucinations, and a nasty attitude. Okay, so maybe I made up some of those symptoms — but he definitely had a bad attitude.

Instead of choosing to run so he could play games, he decided to boycott the new program and instead chose to spend that time sleeping. Although that wasn't what I wanted, it was still better than playing video games.

Eventually, Hunter came around, and the temptation of playing games was just too much. He decided he would give running a shot. A born negotiator, his first question for me was how much credit he would get for his soccer practices and games.

Since the overall goal of the new program was to get him exercising, I thought about his concern and decided it was valid. I gave him a one-hour credit each day that he had a practice or a game. I also added another incentive that on Fridays, weekends or holidays, he would earn double time (one hour) for each mile he ran.

It wasn't too long after we started this program that we decided to enroll Hunter's younger brother, Palmer, as well. Although he didn't binge on Fortnite as much as his older brother, he would watch hours of basketball videos on YouTube.

Although I'll never be excited about our sons playing 10 hours of video games or watching YouTube, you can rest assured that I am super happy about them running the 10 miles it took them to earn that screen time.

Hunter was even excited when he finished second in his age group in his first 10K, finished third in his first 10-mile race, and finished second in his first half marathon. Recently, he took first place in his age group in the 25K in downtown Houston. Palmer finished second in the same run.

Hunter's goal now is to have the fastest marathon time in our family, and Palmer's goal is to become the youngest family member to complete one. Their older sister, Allyssa, ran her first marathon at age 16.

Why did I choose to make them run instead of any other activity? I decided on running because I am an avid runner and ran in high school. I was a member of our cross-country team and ran my first marathon when I was 17 years old. I am still very proud of that accomplishment and want my kids to share a similar experience. I want to give them something they can be proud of doing.

It is my hope that running teaches my sons to invest their time in worthwhile endeavors, to do hard things, and then to enjoy a reward. I never want them to stop challenging themselves.

—Andrew Todd Smith—

A Tenth of a Mile

Rock bottom became the solid foundation
on which I rebuilt my life.
~J.K. Rowling

All my life, I have been overweight. Many factors have played into that simple fact. Poor eating habits and a picky appetite left me eating bulk amounts of the least nutritious foods. A larger interest in video games than sports left little desire for participating in school activities. Mostly, it was the lack of desire to better myself.

Losing my job made matters worse than they ever were as a kid. With plenty of money in my bank account, I decided to coast for a while. Why not enjoy the break? Naturally, my car decided to spring an oil leak a week later. Though still operable, it was in my best interest not to drive here and there.

This resulted in my already-deep depression getting even worse. I lounged around my apartment, barely moving. Having my own money meant I could have whatever I wanted for dinner. Often, I ended up ordering pizza. The calories racked up fast. Since I had no scale, I can only guess what the overall damage was.

The turning point came from an odd place. One night, scrolling through Facebook, I found a picture of an old school friend. Obesity was no stranger to him back in the day. Weighing well more than me, I imagined he would never change.

So imagine my surprise when I saw that he had shrunk to half the size I remembered.

I started my process of bettering myself the next day. Getting groceries from the store was step one. Thanks to my girlfriend, my food palate had expanded ever so slightly. A $30 bill for somewhat healthier meals that lasted a week bested $20 deliveries every day. The next step — which I dreaded most — was exercise.

I started slow. Running was not on my agenda for a while. I began with walks around the neighborhood, circling the shortest block I could find. Even that was taxing at first. Don't get me started on the proper regimen I went through next. Push-ups, lunges and squats, oh my!

My body ached, and nothing excited me more than the prospect of quitting. My girlfriend's encouragement was my only deterrent.

Then, it happened. My walks eventually expanded to several blocks' worth. On the fifth day of my fitness binge, I stared far down the road, probably a tenth of a mile in length. That might sound short to some, but back then it might as well have been an ocean wide.

"Way too far to run," I told myself. The rare bursts beyond simple walking had lasted mere seconds. But, in the back of my mind, another voice spoke.

It said, "I can do this."

My feet took off without a second thought. Right away, familiar burning pulsed through them, all the way up my legs. Passing parked cars and houses alike, a similar pain throbbed in my lungs. I was desperate for air. Silly me had forgotten my water at home. Nothing was going to help me but stopping. It would have been so simple to stop.

"I can do this," I croaked aloud, sounding like a dying man.

My body disagreed. Less than halfway to the end of the street, I started wavering. Running turned to jogging, which turned to a halfhearted trot. It must have been quite a sight for the neighbors. I bet they thought the same thing I did: I should quit.

"I can do this," I said instead.

Embellishment might sell this story a little sweeter, but I won't lie. By the end, I came up a little short. Thirty feet or so divided me from my goal. I thought myself a fool. Clearly, I was never going to make it. But when I looked back, I couldn't believe my eyes. The distance seemed farther then, after almost crossing it all. After months of doing nothing but sitting and eating, I had almost achieved my desire in less than a week.

I'd call it breathtaking, but you can blame the running on that.

Ignoring the agony, I walked home and performed my workout. I must have lain down for hours after my shower. Yet, throughout it all, my smile never faded. By morning, I was ready to take on the challenge again. And, to my surprise, I surpassed it. I blazed through the stop sign and rounded the corner, not halting until I returned to my apartment.

My physical and mental health improved hand-in-hand. The farther I pushed myself, the better I felt. It's been a month now. While I haven't completely escaped thoughts of giving up, they're quieter now. Quieter than the voice that urged me forward, a voice I scarcely recognized as my own.

"I can do this."

— A.J. Martin —

A Real Runner

I am a runner because I run. Not because I run fast. Not because I run far. I am a runner because I say I am. And no one can tell me I'm not.

~John Bingham

I was never any good at running. Running seemed out of bounds, something for the lithe and athletic. Being neither, I stayed away. I saw runners in my neighbourhood jogging down the street in the early morning, getting a jump on their day. Or at the high-school track, long legs flashing, ponytails swinging rhythmically, gliding effortlessly through their workouts. I watched them the way one watches fish in an aquarium: entranced, impressed, but in no way relating. Overweight and ungainly, I was closer to catfish than runner.

Then, in grade nine, our maddeningly enthusiastic physical-education teacher announced that we would be running a mile before each class—as a warm-up. The idea that we would be capable of doing anything after such an extraordinary feat was mindboggling. We rolled our eyes and shuffled off grudgingly, devoting more energy to getting out of the exercise than to actually doing it.

"I have flat feet."

"My dog ate my running shoes."

"But I'll sweat!" Surely, this was to be avoided at all costs. After all, girls were supposed to be pretty and sleek, not sweaty and out of breath.

But we ran, and we panted. After a while, it became, if not actually enjoyable, at least more or less possible and sort of okay. The chasm between the world of skinny, fit runners and myself narrowed ever so slightly. I still felt like I was waddling along, puffing and awkward, but at least I could do so for a sustained period.

I ran with my friend Karen, and we talked as we went along, discussing school, boys, books, and whatever was on our minds. Karen was naturally slim and leggy, but I let her be my friend anyway as she was nice and funny, and we had been friends since first grade. Chatting as we ran, I gradually forgot about the effort and discomfort, focusing on who she thought was better-looking, Kevin or Matt, or why Michael J. Fox was such a great actor.

We explored essay topics, planned trips, complained about teachers—and ran. We did all our runs together, the miles slowly accumulating as we talked. Although I wouldn't have dared try out for the track team, I was gradually becoming, if not a runner, at least a semi-jogger. I preferred to run with others so I didn't attract attention and could distract myself. My jeans got a little looser, my stomach flatter.

Fast-forward to university. As a journalism major, I had a full course load and little spare time. I found the best way to clear my head and organize my thoughts was to go for a run. Although I would not have presumed to call myself a runner, still reserving that designation for those leaner, faster people, I nonetheless ran fairly consistently. I found myself looking forward to heading out on a crisp winter day, enjoying the beauty of the glittering world of white and the steady crunch of my feet in the snow.

I no longer required the distraction of company to keep me going, but rather relished the time alone in my head. Writing assignments took shape, thesis arguments crystallized, and I returned from each run with renewed energy and a stream of ideas. While many of my friends gained the dreaded Freshman 15, I lost more weight.

I continued running as I entered the workforce, although I still hesitated to call myself a runner. There were runners at the PR firm where I worked, mostly men, and they were all fit and fast. They discussed split times and personal bests. They ran marathons and talked about runs in terms of hours. *Like anyone could run for four hours*, I thought disbelievingly. They were clearly some sort of super-human freaks.

Reluctant to compare myself with them, I described what I did as "just jogging," petrified they would invite me out for a run and I would either a) be revealed as a fraud or b) expire. But the idea of long-distance running was intriguing, and I gradually began to increase my mileage. After a while, I was running 10Ks regularly and wondering if I could go farther. In order to do so, I realized that I would have to fuel my body better, and I began eating healthier meals. I dropped more pounds and a few dress sizes.

I was not particularly fast, nor especially lithe, and I reveled in my solitary runs where I didn't have to worry about keeping up or how I looked in running shorts. Still convinced that most people did it better than me, I preferred to go it alone. I continued to increase my distance, and eventually set my sights on the half marathon. This sounded like something only serious runners did, but I thought, just maybe, I might be able to do it.

I trained by myself, logging long, hot runs on the trails and quiet roads. I discovered, the hard way, the necessity of hydrating properly and why I needed to grease my toes with petroleum jelly before heading out in the heat. I ran a half marathon, felt terrible, and then ran a few more.

Then I tentatively considered the marathon. Deciding I needed professional help, I signed up for a marathon course at a local running store. Although I felt comfortable at shorter distances, this was the domain of the hard-core. I almost backed out, convinced I was out of my league. Therefore, as we headed out for our first group run, I was surprised to find people of all shapes and sizes, not to mention speeds.

I struck up a conversation with the runner next to me, a 30-something woman also training for her first marathon. She was no faster nor more toned than me. In fact, she looked, well, normal. Glancing around, I realized that I actually fit in. There was no magical quality that set these runners apart from mere mortals. There was no minimum speed or mileage requirement, no uniform body type. We came from varied backgrounds, had different abilities and histories. All that united us was the running.

I have since run numerous marathons and several ultra marathons. I am a solid middle-of-the-pack runner and content to remain so. I like being surrounded by a multitude of people, united in our love of running. We are teachers, lawyers, and stay-at-home mothers. Some of us have been running all our lives, some less than a year. None of us will win the Olympics, but as long as we continue to put one foot in front of the other, we are all runners. After a long time spent trying to become a "real" runner, I now realize I was chasing a mirage. A real runner is anyone who runs.

— Karyn Curtis —

Hey, 60!

It's never too late in life to have a genuine adventure.
~Robert Kurson

When I turned 60, I made it my goal to run a 5K. I hired a coach from my gym. Pam was several years older than me, had run marathons and still competed in triathlons. She had a petite frame and a cropped, highlighted pixie. Her energy was infectious.

She started me off with strength-training and core workouts once a week. We did leg presses and side planks, chest flies and Russian twists. We also ran. We worked on my cadence and speed, running on the track or treadmill on cold days, and outdoors as weather permitted. We did fartleks and hill repeats, tempo runs and shuttle sprints. I ran on my own, logging miles in parks and cemeteries, back roads and beaches.

Pam taught me about more than running. We discussed nutrition and hydration, too. Once, when I confided in her that I was anxious every time I went out for a run, she gave me meditation tapes and led me in visualization exercises.

For my first race, I chose a 5K in March called the Guinness Celtic. When the weather predictions turned dire with wind-chill factors in the single digits, I kept Pam's visualization techniques in mind, picturing myself wrapped in layers, warm and cozy, as I crossed the finish line. My goal for that race was simply to complete it. But when I crossed the finish line in 37 minutes, I realized that not only had I achieved my goal, I had surpassed it. Three months of hard work had finally paid off.

When I met with Pam that week for our regular training session, I thanked her for helping me achieve my goal.

"I couldn't have done it without you," I told her.

"So are you ready to sign up for your first triathlon?" she responded.

I let that idea sink in for a couple of weeks. I didn't sign up for a triathlon right away, and Pam didn't push me. We continued to work on the running and strength. I began taking swim lessons with her. She taught me how to breathe, keeping the top of my head even with the water line. I worked on my stroke, reaching for the far edges of the pool to avoid crossing my arms above my head. I developed my kick, keeping my knees straight and my movements small.

I bought a pull buoy and hand paddles. I practiced drills: negative splits, catch and rolls, and single arm flies. When spring arrived, I bought a wetsuit, and our early-morning workouts moved to Lake Gardner. There I met an entire community of athletes, all training for various events, from local sprint triathlons to Ironman races across the United States. I found them inspiring. Finally, I decided on my own event: a charity race called Tri for the Y, which benefited various programs at a local YMCA. Having a definite date and a concrete event to train for made training fun… and real. My goal remained the same as it had for my first 5K: to complete the course. To not give up.

The day of the triathlon finally came. I got up at dawn, pumped air into my tires and mounted my bike onto my car. I packed my wetsuit and goggles, protein bars and water bottles, and drove to the race site in the gathering dawn. I set up my transition station the way Pam had taught me. I was such a newbie that I had to ask one of the younger athletes to help me rack my bike. I didn't even know how to attach my number to my crossbar.

Music blared from giant speakers, the bass reverberating in my chest. I paced nervously over the wet grass in the transition area, watching lean, muscular athletes stretch in the rising sun. They were all so fit and at ease. They were also decades younger than me. What was I doing?

I got in line to be marked. A young volunteer held my upper arm in one hand and wrote my race number on it with the other. Then he drew my age on my calf before wrapping a Velcro band with my timing chip around my ankle. I wondered how this teenage boy felt about marking my older body after drawing on so many young, athletic limbs.

Pam wasn't racing that day, but she came to support me.

"What if I come in dead last?" I asked.

"You won't," she assured me.

"I'm so nervous," I complained.

"Just breathe," she advised.

As the announcer called on the athletes to assemble at the beach for The Star-Spangled Banner, I said my goodbyes to Pam.

"Just remember, you're prepared," she told me. "This is what you've trained for."

I joined the others on the sandy shore. I donned my bright green swim cap, the color of my age group. We faced the flag and sang the national anthem. We lined up in waves, each age group with a different colored cap. My group was the last to be called. I stepped over the timing mat and into the calm, cold water. As soon as I started to swim, my fears slid away like so much seaweed. I had swum much farther than this course in my daily drills with my friends. The crowded water with motoring arms and legs kicking up froth was a new challenge, but I had this. I stroked easily around the buoys — one, two, three — and then onto the shore and up the black rubber mat to transition.

"Hey, Carolyn!" I heard from the crowd. I saw Pam using her cell phone as a camera, so I lifted my hands over my head in a victory sign. I peeled off my wet suit, clamped my helmet onto my wet head and hopped onto my bike. I passed a couple of younger athletes on a downhill.

"Go, 60!" one called after me. I waved back, confused.

I pedaled on. Most of the other athletes had fast bikes with aero bars and skinny racing tires. I was one of the few with old-fashioned, fat hybrid tires and upright handlebars. They whizzed by me.

As I hopped off my bike and ran to rack it, Pam called, "Your bike time was faster than I thought it would be!" This gave me a much-needed boost of confidence as I headed out on the run course.

"Hey, 60!" one young runner called from behind me as she approached. She slowed down and jogged alongside me long enough to say, "I hope I'm doing what you're doing when I'm your age!" before she sped ahead of me.

It was then that I realized they were reading the number on my calf and calling me by my age. And as much as those younger athletes inspired me with their lean bodies and conditioned muscles, I realized that I was inspiring them, too.

As I crossed the finish line, I fell into Pam's arms and cried.

"You came in first in your age group!" she told me. "Congratulations."

Now the tears really poured out — another goal achieved.

— Carolyn Roy-Bornstein —

Chapter 2

We're All Crazy Here

Badwater 135: "The World's Toughest Foot Race"

I don't think anyone, until their soul leaves their body, is past the point of no return.
~Tom Hiddleston

It was late afternoon in mid-July, and I had been on the move for 30 hours already in the middle of Death Valley National Park. It had hit a record high of 128 degrees Fahrenheit. I was at mile 96 of a 135-mile race. Not just any race, this was known as "The World's Toughest Foot Race."

I had been running on the white line of the pavement since 10:00 the previous morning. I was barely averaging one mile per hour now as I hobbled downhill. My feet and ankles were a complete wreck—with enormous blisters. The ankle blister was so big that I gave it a name: Bubbles. Each step was overwhelmingly painful. It took the race's foot-care doctor 45 minutes to patch my feet. My feet swelled so much that I had to borrow my friend's shoes, which normally would have been two sizes too big for me.

My crew was pulling out all the stops to help me. They knew I loved Starbucks, so they secretly purchased Starbucks gift cards as a bribe for me to run faster. I sprinted until I reached my crew and the Starbucks card. It was a genius plan until I started feeling bad again. Then they switched to a new strategy. My main pacer pulled out pictures of my daughter Sierra and a drawing she made that said, "Go Mommy Go!"

It helped in the moment, but I was still in agonizing pain. I had 39 more miles to go, and according to my original plan, I should have been approaching the finish line by then. My dad was on his way there already.

Sub 35 hours had seemed like a reasonable time to cover the 135-mile distance.

***

Rewind to the previous year at Badwater. I was invited to pace and crew my friend, Dean "Karno" Karnazes. I was thrilled to be part of Dean's crew. Dean is a legend at Badwater and in many races in the ultrarunning world. Karno had run Badwater seven times at that point. He won the race outright in 2004 in 27:22:48.

At Badwater, it is customary to choose a charity or foundation to run for, and Dean's foundation is called Karno Kids. This foundation provides support to organizations that focus on improving the health and wellness of our youth, as well as preserving and restoring the environment. I was honored to be part of that effort.

Having a crew is a necessity at Badwater. Usually, a crew consists of four people who help take care of their runner by providing ice, water, and food, and spraying them down to cool their core temperature. There are no aid stations at Badwater, so runners have to rely 100 percent on their crew for food, changes of shoes, socks and supplies.

Runners are allowed to have a pacer run behind them from mile 17 to the finish. I knew I would learn a lot about strategy for this punishing race by being Dean's pacer. And this year was especially tough because just days before Dean's father had been hospitalized unexpectedly and ended up having open-heart surgery. Dean did not want to run the race with his father in the hospital, but his father urged him to do it anyway. I know it was very emotional and stressful for Dean to put one foot in front of the other for 135 miles in the searing, unforgiving heat of Death Valley.

I joined Dean at mile 17. The crew meets the runner every one to two miles, but water and ice don't last long in 128-degree heat. We were running solid and steady, making good time. Dean did not stop to sleep. One time, he rested in a chair on the side of the road for ten minutes and that refreshed him enough to continue.

When you're running Badwater everything cold tastes amazing. A photographer gave Dean a blue Slurpee (usually, he would never drink that) and a hamburger with extra ketchup. At Badwater, runners crave things they would not normally eat, and they crave anything cold because it will cool down their body temperature.

At mile 122, we reached a town called Lone Pine. We went inside McDonald's, got a milkshake and continued up the final climb—the final 12 miles to the finish. At mile 133, Dean opened some salty snacks called Boston Baked Beans. As we power hiked, he paused and turned to me, looked me in the eyes and asked, "Do you really want to run this race?"

There was no doubt in my mind. I said, "Yes, Karno, I do want to run it."

He laughed and said, "You're crazy." Ultrarunners use the term "crazy" as a compliment. Karno and I continued the final climb to the last curve, and the entire crew joined us as we crossed the finish line hand in hand. I ended up running 96 of the 135 miles with Dean. He finished in 34:51:20.

There is no better way to learn about Badwater than to crew and pace a runner. Crewing Karno was a gift. I saw firsthand the mental toughness, raw determination, and sheer grit it takes to complete this race.

***

Back to mile 96 of my own race. I am still hobbling downhill at one mile per hour. My dad and his friend had driven back to find me on the course and jumped out of the car to see how I was doing. I didn't want my dad to see me like that. He didn't stay long because

I was upset, and there was nothing he could do to help except give me a hug. He was almost sure I would have to drop out of the race considering the shape I was in. He and his friend drove back home to Irvine, California.

Things were getting worse. I had prepared well for the heat, training every day for seven weeks in the 180-degree sauna. I took heat training seriously. But all of a sudden, my upper body felt boiling and my lower body felt frozen. I was getting the chills. My crew knew I needed to regroup, so we "staked out" at mile 96 and drove to our hotel in Lone Pine.

At Badwater, when runners check into the race, they are given a bib number and a wooden stake with their bib number written on it. They are allowed to place the stake into the ground during the race and leave the course. The rule is that after they take a rest, they have to go back to the stake they left on the side of the road, pull it out of the ground and continue running from that exact point. My crew "staked me out" and we drove to the hotel in Lone Pine. I couldn't walk up the stairs to the hotel room, so one of my crewmembers carried me. As I lay in bed I could hear my crew talking about what to do for me. I couldn't sleep and I wanted a shower badly, but the doctor who bandaged my feet would not allow that.

After four hours, my temperature was better. I got out of bed, took a sponge bath, and brushed my teeth. I started regaining my energy. I brushed all the knots out of my hair and put on lip gloss. I was ready to go back to mile 96 and finish.

As I walked out of the hotel room, a woman from New Zealand who had just finished the race showed me her shiny, silver belt buckle and told me I could do it. I still had time, too. I would be able to finish within the 60-hour limit.

We drove back to my stake and I started running again. I was loving life. My crew was blasting music from the van. They even got me a couple of ice-cream sandwiches, which I had been craving the entire race. All I had left to run was a marathon and then a half marathon. I felt renewed.

The temperature got down to a lovely 108 degrees that night.

It felt much cooler; I was running and making good time. I ran the marathon from mile 96 to mile 122 in five hours. We got back to Lone Pine, and as I ran past the hotel where I had rested I was so happy. I still had blisters, but the pain was not as bad. All I had left was a half marathon to reach the finish. It was all uphill but I was having fun. My crew was blasting the Michael Jackson song "Beat It," and I was trying to run and do Michael Jackson dance moves at the same.

Halfway up the 2,000-foot climb, I saw a good friend, Ben Jones, aka "The Mayor of Badwater." He had run the race numerous times. He gave me a hug, and I made it up the final climb to Mount Whitney Portal, alternating between hiking and running. I reached mile 133—the spot where Dean Karnazes had turned to me and asked if I wanted to run Badwater. I smiled and asked my crew to take a photo of me with the view of Lone Pine below in the distance.

We were all smiling now. It was a very happy vibe, much different from what it had been at mile 96. I could hear the cheers; we were almost there. My crew parked the van and ran over to me. We joined hands to finish together. When I saw the tape, I started sprinting. (I'm sure it was a slow jog, but it felt like a sprint.) When I crossed the finish line, the race director, Chris Kostman, said, "I knew you would make it, Michelle."

I replied, "How did you know I would make it when I didn't even know?"

He said, "I just knew."

We took photos. Chris Kostman handed me my shiny, silver buckle and my finisher's medal and shirt. I thought of Dean and couldn't imagine running this beast of a race eight times. (As of this writing, Karno has completed ten finishes.)

In 15 years of running ultramarathons, I won 80 races. I did not win Badwater, but that was okay with me. I ended up 10th woman, and that was good enough. It took me 45:54:20—10 hours slower than Dean's finishing time—but that didn't matter. I was happy. I had run for Karno Kids and made memories to last a lifetime. Even my ankle blister, Bubbles, lasted three whole weeks before it popped.

My dad had driven home after seeing me in a mess at mile 96.

He was walking home from the gym the following day when a neighbor started jumping up and down and shouting from the balcony, "Michelle finished!" My dad couldn't believe I had turned around my race. He was so happy.

Badwater is magical. It is tough and throws curve balls when we least expect them, but since I completed Badwater, I know I can do anything I set my mind to.

— Michelle Barton —

One Tough Mudder

You will enrich your life immeasurably if you approach it with a sense of wonder and discovery, and always challenge yourself to try new things.
~Nate Berkus

When I first started running, I often had thoughts like, *Sure, I made it through this race, but I could never do that one.* I felt like I wasn't fast enough, thin enough, or dedicated enough to be a "real" runner—one who could finish a full marathon or be wanted by a team for a relay race. But with each new race I attempted, my confidence increased, which propelled me into seeking out more challenges. Soon, I began doing things I said I could never do.

One of the races I originally thought I could never do was a 13-mile obstacle course race (OCR) called a Tough Mudder. OCRs are essentially the marriage of a race course and an elementary-school jungle gym. Racers interrupt their pace to do things like swing across monkey bars or climb up a cargo net. Many of these races are marketed as being "created by Special Forces" or "only for the toughest humans to complete." That can be a tad intimidating for someone like me who started doing short races simply because my friends were doing them—and there were free bagels at the end.

Despite my hesitation at attempting a Tough Mudder, I considered it when my friend Gina asked me to do one with her. I had met Gina years before while training together for the marathon I said I'd never do. On our longest training run—a 20-miler—she witnessed me splitting my pants open and attempting to tape them back together in the aisle of a mini mart seven miles from my car. One tends to stay friends with someone after sharing such intimacy.

Gina and I had similar approaches to exercise (inconsistent and bagel-driven). So when she invited me to run a Tough Mudder with her, I agreed. I always like to find someone similar to me who has completed something and not died. Gina had already finished one Tough Mudder the year before, so that was enough for me to believe I could do it, too.

I joined Gina's training team, which included a couple of personal trainers and a few former Marines. I assumed a crew like that might either whip me into shape or wash me out in a hazing event if they felt I couldn't hack it. Either way, I trusted their judgment.

The team's plan was to run together on the weekends while simulating scenarios we might encounter in the Tough Mudder. According to race reviews, that could involve mud (obviously), water, jumping off high platforms, and even electrocution (mild shocks just to add a little excitement). To paraphrase one race reviewer: "The worst thing those electric wires will do is shut down your body and make you lose control of your bowels. Otherwise, you're all good." Hmm. Hopefully, we wouldn't be training for every scenario.

When we finally got to the start line, we were told to sign "death waivers," which was nice and reassuring. Soon, the announcer signaled the start, and we ran toward our first obstacle—submerging ourselves in icy water. *Why did we pay to do this again?*

Then we proceeded through about 24 more obstacles. We jumped over ditches of mud, only to land on more mud, which immediately made us fall into—you guessed it—mud. These Tough Mudder people really knew how to hammer home a point!

We carried logs. We climbed hay bales. We low-crawled under barbed wire, resembling a pack of uncoordinated lizards. I had a head cold and was reduced to wiping my nose with a banana peel at one point at a refreshment stop because there was nothing else non-muddy to use as a tissue. This race is where vanity goes to die.

One obstacle involved squeezing into what resembled human-sized bendy straws. I inched myself through one, my face following some stranger's rear end ahead of me, and my mind filling with questions like, *Am I claustrophobic? Why didn't I ask myself this before I got here?* One of my teammates got wedged into his straw and had to be helped out by his girlfriend. We would all lose little pieces of our pride before the day was done.

At one point, we leapt off a high platform into murky waters below. The website said it was "15+ feet high." *Fifteen plus what? Ten more feet?* I thought, viewing the world from the ledge. But I leapt dutifully anyway.

Then I realized immediately what a long pause it was.

Just me. Hanging out in the air. Falling… still… falling… *What did I just do?*

That's the thought I distinctly remember having right as I let out a strangled scream halfway down. Later, I told people that, in retrospect, it's the thought we all should've had right after agreeing to do this race in the first place if we'd had any sense. But, eh. You live and learn. Or you hope you live anyway.

At one point, I was separated from my teammates and found myself planting both my hands on the backside of a perfect stranger in front of me to help her up a muddy mound. That moment illustrated one of the best gifts of that race: Everyone helped each other. Yes, we were gross. Yes, we were tired. Yes, we all questioned our sanity. But we were in it together. We all chose to push ourselves and take on a challenge. We all chose to do something out of our comfort zone in order to feel more alive.

Four-and-a-half hours and several scratches and bruises later, my team finally ran together across the finish line. Besides being grateful that none of us perished, I was deeply grateful for the experience all around. I had finished another race I thought I wasn't tough enough to do. Now I had amazing memories of an adventure I was proud of.

And I had earned more confidence and willingness to take on future challenges — in running, and in life.

Perhaps, most importantly, I had earned the right to eat multiple bagels.

— Dana Ayers —

Don't Run in Your Pajamas

Life is either a daring adventure or nothing.
~Helen Keller

It's mid-July and I'm checking into a hotel in Boston at 10:30 a.m., early enough to get in a run before the conference begins. It's Friday, and I haven't met my mileage goal for the week. But free from family and job responsibilities, I am determined to get back on track.

I open my suitcase on the bed and pull out my running shoes, socks, singlet, and painter's hat. I dig deeper. I try not to panic, but I find myself yanking out articles of clothing and flinging them across the bed until the suitcase is empty. I raise my hands to my head. Where are my running shorts?

I enter attack mode. I unzip zippers and shove my hands deep into secret compartments. I check inside my running shoes, dress shoes, and even my sports jacket pockets. All empty. I stop. I have to face reality; I failed to pack my running shorts.

I check my watch. The conference starts in an hour, no time to shop for new shorts. I survey the clothing scattered across the bed. My eyes fall on my green paisley, short pajamas. I pick them up by the ribbed, elastic waistband. The length works, but when I insert a hand inside the thin material, light from the hotel window silhouettes my fingers.

I undress and pull the pajamas over my briefs. According to the mirror, I should be going to bed, not for a run. But as I put on my singlet and socks and tie my running shoes, I remind myself that this is Boston, a large, diverse city. Once outside, I'll blend into the cityscape of pedestrians, joggers, dog walkers, and street people. I will become invisible. I grab my plastic room key. Drat! No pocket in my "running shorts." I slip the key under my cap. Problem solved, or so I think.

I enter the hall outside my room. I am relieved to find no one in sight. I head for the exit door and jog six floors down the concrete staircase. At the bottom, I pause with my hand against the lobby doorknob, waiting for my confidence to catch up with me. *Do I really dare to do this?*

I crack open the door an inch. A gaggle of hotel guests crowds around a bank of elevators watching the floor indicator lights overhead. I take a deep breath and push open my door. A few heads turn toward me and then back as I head for the lobby, where I cruise by the check-in line without drawing a glance. I push through the revolving glass door and step out into the sunshine. A cacophony of street sounds beckons me with the promise of anonymity.

I stretch against the side of the hotel building before setting out on a scenic route suggested by the concierge at check-in. The heat and humidity are already stifling. This run will be more challenging than I thought.

I jog through parks shaded by impressive oaks and around ponds festooned with flowers and shrubbery. I join the parade of pedestrians pushing strollers, sipping drinks, and chatting with friends. I even spot an occasional jogger. I have become part of the cityscape, pajamas notwithstanding.

My run takes me through upscale neighborhoods of red-brick rowhouses accented with window boxes and enclosed by black wrought-iron fences. After 40 minutes, the heat, humidity, and hills take their toll. My head feels like a radiator, and my breathing is labored. I regret not hydrating properly before my run. An unattended hose lies on the red-brick sidewalk with water running from it. I grab it and remove my hat. I let the cool water stream over my head and shoulders and down my front and back. So refreshing! I don't care that I am drenching my clothing.

When I reenter the hotel, I am still soaking wet. Inside the lobby, I lift my hat and feel for the plastic room key I had cleverly placed there. No key. It must have fallen out when I cooled off with the hose. The only hotel employees I see are the receptionists processing check-ins. Luckily, only a lady and her daughter are waiting in line. I get behind them, but when I spot my reflection in a gigantic wall mirror, I nip over to the tourist information rack and grab the biggest brochure I can find. I return to the line.

The little girl, about eight, turns to stare at me. My wet pajamas cling to my body. I hold the tourist information booklet strategically.

"Mommy," she says, "why is that man wearing pajamas?" Her voice is loud and clear.

"What man?"

"That man standing behind us." She points at me as though I am an inanimate object.

Her mother throws me a glance and shushes her daughter immediately.

I look down at my watch, pretending to check the time.

"He stinks, too," says the girl. "Maybe he's homeless."

Her mother grasps her daughter's hand and pulls her toward a receptionist without being called. I remain standing and holding my brochure—wet, apparently smelly, and definitely visible. I hear someone shout my name from a distance.

"Hi, Dave! Been out running?" I cringe.

A conference colleague from the Midwest waves at me from across the lobby.

"Hi, Jean!" I say. I lock my eyes onto hers as though I can prevent hers from drifting. "Yeah. Time for a shower."

I wave and walk toward the reception counter as if I had been called. "Catch you later."

When a receptionist becomes available, I explain my plight to a pleasant lady. I ask for a replacement key.

"No problem," she says. "I just need to see your ID."

"My ID is locked in my room."

"Sorry, sir. I can't issue a new room key without an ID."

"And I can't get my ID without a room key."

"One moment, please." She disappears through a door behind the reception counter and returns with a manager.

"I will be happy to accompany you to your room, sir. You can retrieve your ID, and I will give you a new key."

As we proceed to the elevator bank, I remain close to him so that he is less likely to notice my attire. But I had forgotten about my smell.

"This way, sir," says the manager. He bypasses the elevators and waiting guests and takes me around the corner to a small elevator. He scans his card.

"This is the staff elevator," he says. "It will be more convenient for you."

When we arrive at my room, he opens the door, and I show him my ID. He gives me a new room key. I check my watch. The conference has started. I will miss the information presented in the first session. But I am not too disappointed for I have already learned a valuable lesson, albeit the hard way: Don't run in your pajamas!

—D.E. Brigham—

Running the Crazy Miles

All who have accomplished great things have had a great aim, have fixed their gaze on a goal which was high, one which sometimes seemed impossible.
~Orison Swett Marden

My lower back is tighter than a square knot. A small demon is using a jackhammer on my right hamstring. A war is being waged in my stomach.

My mind is running out of bad metaphors. And I still have 35 miles to go.

I'm attempting to complete my first 100K ultra run, and now I'm running what I like to call the "Crazy Miles." The Crazy Miles are any distance farther than a marathon. I call them this because anytime I tell someone that I'm running farther than a marathon, they always say the same thing: "You're crazy!" (often with an expletive thrown in).

I don't know if it's something I ate, or the 85-degree temperature, but as I reach the aid station, I feel like I've hit the wall. With another 31 miles to go, the wall is the last thing I want to be hitting. I lie down on the ground to stretch for a couple of minutes and regain my composure. A couple of minutes turn to five, and five become ten. My girlfriend, Katelin, shows up. "What are you doing?" she asks.

"Stretching," I mutter.

"Are you here to stretch, or are you here to run?"

She's right. I climb up to my feet, put some food in my stomach and fluids in my system, and hit the trail. Suddenly, I have a second wind. It could be due to the nutrients I've ingested, but I'm guessing it's Katelin's words. Sometimes, a loved one calling you out is the best motivation.

The trail serpentines through a dense forest, hard-packed dirt rising and falling with the terrain. It's only mid-afternoon, but the sun has already fallen behind the hills. I begin tripping on exposed roots. My toes grab, and I stumble forward, fighting gravity to find my balance before my body falls to the forest floor.

At mile 40, I insert my ear buds, but music isn't enough to mask the aches and pains that have engulfed my entire body. This is the part of the run where I'll have to dig deep into my psyche because, from here on out, it will all be new to me. I've never run this far before.

So, I become lost in my thoughts. I think about my life as a runner. I think about the woods behind my parents' house, and the trails I would run down as a child, pretending I was a cowboy, soldier, or escaped convict, always one step ahead of my imaginary pursuers.

I think about my time on the cross-country team at school, and those hills our coach would make us run—hills that seemed so big, so impossible back then, and how they now seem to be mere stepping stones in my life as a runner.

I think about the years I didn't run, when I replaced the euphoric feeling of physical exertion with substances made by man in factories, laboratories and greenhouses. Looking back, those were the most miserable years of my life.

I think about how it only makes sense that running would return to my life after moving to Oregon. After all, this is the home of Prefontaine, Hayward Field and Nike. I think about how I've always been envious of the long-distance runners and how, until recently, I'd always considered their exploits so far out of my reach.

I think about the simplistic idea of powering one's body with nothing more than willpower. No gears, no cranks, no chains, no wheels, no paddles—just 100 percent dedication to the concept of forward motion. In my opinion, there is no movement more pure.

Before I know it, I stumble upon the last aid station. Mile 58—only four more to go. At this point, I don't want to stop for too long. I only want to finish. I down a couple of slices of watermelon, hand Katelin my hydration pack, and ask her to meet me at the finish line.

The last four miles are some of the easiest because I know the end is near. I see visual hallucinations. Shadows on the ground look like millions of spiders. I swear I see a man standing in the woods, staring high into the branches, sketching something into a journal. As I get closer, I realize that he's only a tree stump. I climb the last hill and cross the finish line before the day falls to total darkness, which was my one goal from the beginning. Katelin is waiting for me with a cooler full of beer, but I don't want or need one. I haven't had a drop to drink, but I'm as drunk as I've ever been.

Six months ago, I set a goal to complete a 100K, and today I've accomplished that feat. For the next three days, I will walk around like Frankenstein's monster. For the next three weeks, I will hardly run at all. But before I know it, I will be planning more big runs, always looking forward to my next Crazy Miles.

—Jon Penfold—

Who Me?

Mothers are the only ones that think nothing is beyond their control when it comes to their children.
~Ali Fazal

The letter from the principal couldn't have been clearer: The bus will pick up your new kindergartner at the designated bus stop. Parents are not to ride with children on the bus, and under no circumstances are parents to come to the school, whether to drop off their children or to take pictures. Parking is tight, even for teachers, staff, and buses, and additional cars are strictly forbidden at the beginning or end of the school day.

That was all understandable but they didn't know my five-year-old twins. Shy and sensitive, they hid whenever the doorbell rang. They couldn't be coaxed out of their hiding places with ice cream, candy, or new toys. Their paternal grandparents didn't get a good look at them until they were about seven. They clung to me whenever we ventured out in public — one girl per leg. And while my Frankenstein-monster walk was not graceful or elegant, it did have the advantage of providing a combination of resistance training and aerobics for a busy mom.

My fear on that first day of school was that my girls would hide under a bus seat, or somehow get lost or stolen. The first day of school wouldn't be easy for them (me).

The day came, and it was sunny and beautiful. The girls were adorable in their new dresses and light-up sneakers. Each wore a nametag on a construction-paper cutout of a school bus around her neck.

The bus was late, and they were nervous, but they smiled for the camera. I sat on the front lawn under a shady tree for a minute, and their father finally took his eye off the camera lens and took in what I was wearing.

"Oh, no, you're not," he said.

I had on my running gear and favorite long-distance running shoes. The school was a few miles away.

"I am not going to run after the bus, if that's what you're thinking," I said, insulted.

Our conversation was cut short when the bus approached. I watched Morgan and Chloe get on (how could human beings be so impossibly cute?), turn and wave on the top step, and then…

Okay, then I ran like hell. But I ran *before* the bus, not *after* the bus, so I wasn't lying to the husband. Can't a woman go for a run? I ran faster than I ever ran before.

The bus finally overtook me a few hundred yards before the school building. Panting, I made my way to the front entrance by sprinting from behind one car to another until, hidden safely behind a large SUV, I had a bird's-eye view of every child that climbed down the bus steps and walked into the school doors. As each bus emptied, it would pull away, and the next bus in the row would pull up to the spot directly in front of the school entrance. I willed my breath to quiet down, the blood in my temples to slow its pulse. My legs felt like jelly, and I concentrated hard on just being still because getting caught would be beyond embarrassing, even for me. Sweat dripped down my forehead and mixed with the sunblock I had thoughtfully applied hours before, stinging my eyes and making them tear up.

A few minutes went by. Two more buses emptied and left, and then there they were! Chloe smiled shyly as the principal gave her a big smile and "Welcome!" Morgan stayed tightly behind, chin down, but she was smiling and holding her sister's hand.

I said it was the sweat and the sunblock that made me tear up. I was lying about that part.

— Erika Tremper —

Chased by Zombies

Run. Because zombies will eat the untrained ones first!
~Heather Dakota,
Zombie Apocalypse Survival Guide

Three times a week, my husband forces me to meet him in town after work and pretend to be chased by zombies. Or maybe it was my idea. The details are fuzzy.

We are actually preparing for a community 5K held every year in our town to raise money for those battling cancer. As 45-year-olds who are overweight and incredibly out of shape, with me recovering from two major surgeries last year, I'm not really sure why we don't just write a check and help hand out water bottles or something. That seems like the practical, logical thing to do. But then I suppose we wouldn't get the T-shirt.

This all started when we flew to the West Coast and spent a week with our two-year-old grandson. When we returned, we realized that if we didn't do something soon, we would never be able to keep up with that child. There's a reason we had our children in our twenties, but we're still young enough that following a toddler around the playground should not be so exhausting. So we returned to the East Coast, took a nap, and started a 5K training program.

We are using an app for couch-to-5K training. The idea is that anyone can run if they work into it slowly. This particular app has a story line involving zombies to help make the training a bit more interesting.

Because, let's face it, running is hard and boring. The really nice—or really horrible, depending on the day—thing about this app is that it incorporates additional exercises such as knee lifts or heel lifts to strengthen our legs. So not only can our muscles scream in pain from running, but they can be stretched out to feel pain in different ways!

Advil is now a staple on my grocery list. After the first week, my husband, suffering from horrible shin-splint pain, bought special "shin-splint socks." These are a real thing. He realized a week later that he should have read the instructions when he found out that he was wearing them backwards. When I pictured our empty-nest years, this was not quite what I had envisioned.

Then around week four, something amazing happened. I jogged five minutes straight without stopping. For most people, that won't sound like much. I'm not even comfortable calling it running at this point. But I was definitely jogging.

For me, it was a major accomplishment considering my past history. For the past few years, my iron was so low that I could barely walk across a room without being out of breath. Even after surgery to fix my iron issues, walking was still difficult. Then I tore the meniscus in my knee. The surgery to repair the tear was not, as I had hoped, an instantaneous fix. The recovery took months, not the three days I had allotted it on my calendar. I had thought the doctor was just being super cautious, but he actually meant it when he said it would take six months to a year to stop swelling and hurting so much. Mid-forties bodies, especially those not well taken care of, do not recover like 20-year-old bodies.

But, eight months after the first surgery and six months after the second, I'm jogging. Five minutes is not going to get me through a 5K, and I don't see how three more weeks will get me to a point of running for 40 minutes straight, but right now I'm just happy to jog five minutes straight. For a woman who could hardly walk across a room last year, that's a big step.

So, to recap, three times a week, a very overweight, out-of-shape, middle-aged couple meets in town to pretend to be chased by zombies along a historic canal path so they can pay $25 for a “free” T-shirt later this summer. And one of them has his socks on backwards.

— Heather Truckenmiller —

Barefoot Rebel

You learn a lot when you're barefoot. The first thing is every step you take is different.
~Michael Franti

It's fun to walk through a water puddle. Just put your feet in the water, look straight ahead and trek through—no big deal. So what if your feet get wet?

Watch as those with footwear walk carefully through the water lest their shoes get too wet. See how much longer that takes!

Look! You are making distinctive barefoot prints. Embrace them. Those are your markers, showing the world that you walk unrestrained and free. Smile at the shoe walkers and their now soggy shoes. Isn't it too bad that they will have to get out of those wet shoes or deal with painful, irritated feet for the rest of the day? Shoes squeak, smell, and are uncomfortable. But your feet are quiet, odorless and soon comfortably dry.

I know that you are feeling anxious and self-aware, worrying that others will notice. What if they comment about your lack of footwear? What are you going to do?

Relax. Everything will be all right. Some may stare because you are breaking the norms. You will be noticed. Just embrace your inner rebel and try having fun. Remember, you are doing nothing illegal. You are just taking a walk without shoes. It's been done before.

Once you begin walking barefoot outdoors, you will wonder what the fuss was all about. You will discover, as I did, that the world comes alive with tactile sensations. It is as if you can see through your soles. The softness of freshly mown grass resembles plush carpeting. Some small blades of grass will inevitably wiggle their way through your toes, while others will rub against the sides and heels, leaving a slight tickle, making you feel happy and alive.

That cannot happen with shoes; not even sandals can tickle your toes. There are other sensations waiting for your soles to notice: the ooziness of mud, the warmth of a sidewalk, and even the roughness of a rock-strewn path. All of these offer myriad textures and experiences, and add another dimension to your walk.

Like me, you went barefoot outside as a child, only to be told to put on your shoes. I had that drummed into my head. I was told that it was inappropriate — and reminded the world is dangerous for bare feet, even in nature.

And if that were not enough, we also learned that going barefoot came with a social stigma. It brought embarrassment and shame, especially to parents or close friends. We were supposed to look our best to blend in. Yet, as you have noticed, walking barefoot can be enjoyable. Once again, that inner rebel comes out, as we trade style for comfort and personal choice. By going barefoot, you are breaking rules. It feels kind of scary, doesn't it?

I do not remember when I began walking barefoot outdoors. It probably began when I hiked into the woods behind my house. Away from others, I felt alive amid the trees. It was peaceful and invigorating. There in woods, at one with nature, it made sense to remove my shoes and socks. They felt heavy anyway. Digging toes in the soft dirt became the next logical step. Soon, the tips were caked with dirt, but they felt free. I liked that sensation. At first, it was as if I was doing something naughty, and I needed to make sure that no one knew. It felt satisfying to be rebellious and break the norms.

Look. Other people are on the path. It is one thing to walk barefoot in nature where no one can see you. And even though you have been brave and have enjoyed the trek up to this point, there is something about seeing others that causes your palms to sweat and heart to race. I know what you are thinking for I have been there — your feet are muddy. How are you going to explain this? That is why you are anxious. Relax and embrace that inner rebel. Remember that walking barefoot is natural and fun.

I used to be shy and introverted, but I have embraced my rebellious side by walking barefoot. Usually, I like being quirky and different; it brings me pleasure. In accepting my own eccentricities, I am more accepting of others, for we are all eccentric in our own way. So continue walking barefoot on grass, through puddles, and in mud. You will discover that it is enjoyable and a little rebellious. Embrace that, as we are all rebels in different ways.

— S. Scott Sanderson —

Never Too Late

We all have dreams. But in order to make dreams come into reality, it takes an awful lot of determination, dedication, self-discipline, and effort.
~Jesse Owens

I came to the sport of triathlon late in life. I spent years accompanying my super-fit husband to triathlons and waiting for him on the hot sidelines while he swam, biked, and ran for hours. Then a light bulb turned on in my brain. I could be out there physically torturing myself, too, instead of suffering intense boredom. It was twisted logic, but to be a triathlete, it's imperative to possess some of that.

Three questions plagued me as I began training: Could I successfully transform myself into a triathlete? Was the saying, "It's never too late, you're never too old," actually true? And how in the world was I ever going to squeeze this body into the skimpy triathlon outfits?

Starting with what I knew best, I began swimming. Attempting to channel my former competitive swimmer self, I swam up and down the YMCA pool, somehow convincing my slightly chubby, 54-year-old sedentary body that my inner mermaid was merely dormant, not dead. Swimming is heavily reliant on technique. Thankfully, muscle memory kicked in, leaving me feeling fairly confident that I would at least survive the first leg of the triathlon.

For the bike segment, I pulled out my trusty, old ten-speed, a clunky metal apparatus, but it fit the bill for a beginner triathlete. I should have known from watching my husband, but I guess I wasn't paying close attention: becoming a biker involves lots of "stuff." I needed a helmet, water bottles, a computer, clip-in shoes and, worst of all, tight, padded biking shorts that revealed every middle-aged lump and roll. Preparing for the bike leg of a triathlon wasn't nearly as much fun as I remembered from my childhood days of cruising the neighborhood on my purple Stingray. But with coaching from my patient husband, I persevered. I was as slow as could be. Small children with streamers and baskets on their bikes often passed me on the trail, but all I cared about was finishing the ride upright.

I joined a couch-to-5K running group at my neighborhood running store to train for the run. In the beginning, I could only run 30 seconds without taking a walk break, but I kept moving forward. In a couple of months, I was ready for a 5K run. Evenings that were once filled with making dinner and helping with homework were now filled with meeting friends to go on training runs. Running was a great way to transition to the empty-nester phase of life!

Then came the true test—putting it all together for my first triathlon! To avoid any hometown embarrassment, I traveled to a neighboring state for my first attempt. Knowing I would never have to face the other racers again helped to ease my anxiety. But there was still an ugly little voice whispering in my ear: "Why do you think you can do this? You're 54 years old, overweight and not good at any of this. Just give it up!"

Fortunately, there was an encouraging voice in my other ear saying, "You can do this. You've done the training. You are about to become a triathlete!" I chose to listen to *that* voice. I managed to finish, not first but also not last. It didn't matter. I was a triathlete! But it wasn't enough.

My plan for "one and done" disappeared as I felt compelled to continue and do longer distance triathlons. Eventually, the thought of completing a half Ironman distance started nagging at me. I was afraid to mention it to anyone, too scared to even write it on my bucket list. On a good day, I was a mediocre athlete, hanging mostly toward the back of the pack. How was I ever going to swim 1.2 miles, bike 56 and then run 13.1 miles—all in the same day? The lure of the 70.3-mile race haunted my thoughts. When I tentatively admitted my crazy idea to my husband, he jumped on board immediately. He said he would do it with me. The training was arduous, taxing my physical endurance to the limit. Biking miles through the heat of the summer didn't make me love biking any better; it was still my least favorite leg of the triathlon. Swimming didn't worry me; that was my strength. As for the run, I was sure I could manage to at least walk my way through the 13.1 miles after the bike.

After months of training, the day of the event finally arrived. The swim was a bit rough, but I came out of the water a few minutes ahead of my husband. I savored that small victory, knowing my husband was the much better athlete in the other two legs. I wish I could have held on to the feeling of mastery as I struggled through the 56-mile bike ride. At about the 22-mile mark, I stopped, got off my bike and whined to my husband, "I think I'm going to quit. This is too hard. I can't make it."

My husband replied calmly, "You can quit. But you know if you quit, you will want to come back and try it again next year." He knows me too well. I got back on the bike and slowly pedaled my way to the end of the ride. The run was more like a walk; the old engine (me) didn't have enough gas to manage a run after the grueling bike ride. My athletic husband could have run easily, but he chose to stay with me. The sun was beating down on us. We were sweltering hot in the 93-degree weather, and our feet quickly became blistered. But we knew the end was in sight. We talked, laughed, stopped at every water station, and waved to friends along the way. We were going to finish this beast of a triathlon! We crossed the finish line together, a sweet moment of relationship solidarity and a dream come true for me.

I'm now in my sixties. I'm still squeezing myself into triathlon suits and showing up at the start line. Sometimes, I'm the only one in my age group, which fits into my winning strategy. I'm not fast enough to get on the podium often, but my plan is to keep competing after everyone else quits. I'm going to outlast the competition!

Triathlons have taught me it's never too late to pursue a dream. I'm not the fastest or the best athlete, but I can possess the best attitude of gratitude for the good health that enables me to finish a race. It may be too late, and I may be too old for a few things in life, but I plan to squeeze every drop of happiness out of life and stay active as long as I can, no matter what the pace may be.

—Diane Morrow-Kondos—

Head, Body, Heart

I've learned that finishing a marathon isn't just an athletic achievement. It's a state of mind; a state of mind that says anything is possible.
~John Hanc

There's a certain magic in the misery of running. Throughout the majority of any given race, you're in pain. Your lungs feel like they're being squeezed by an unseen hand, your muscles as though tendrils of fire are curled around them. But it is in this very same fire that a great runner is forged.

My first cross-country coach told me that every race is run in three parts. The first part is with the head. This is where strategy and patience are factors. The second part is with the body, to run the race using experience and training. Lastly, the race is to be finished with the heart. I've carried this advice with me for hundreds of miles, but I'll never forget the 5K where this gem of wisdom was the only thing that carried me across that finish line.

It was a course I'd run many times before. In fact, I'd thrown up for the first time in my running career there. I carried extremely fond memories of those trails. This particular race carried with it the burden of a season coming to an end. All of my teammates were eager to bring the season to a close with massive time drops off their personal records.

Before every race, it's tradition to walk the course and reacquaint yourself with its twists and turns. A few fellow runners and I embarked on a mini-quest to do just that. The conversation remained fixated on our goals and different ways the team could run as a pack, knocking off both time and points. I always liked to imagine an invisible rope was tied to me and whoever was in front of me. If they moved up, I had to move up as well—whatever it took to keep that invisible rope from snapping.

The weather was cloudy, and a chill embraced us. On any given day, this was good weather, but on race day, it could not possibly be more perfect. Once we completed our course walk, we gathered at the starting line to do some last-minute stretches. Runners are terribly superstitious. Lucky ribbons were woven into our ponytails to ensure success, socks were worn inside out, and chants were uttered in a ritualistic manner. It was crucial that the pre-race regimen remained exactly the same so as not to tempt fate. Routine demanded that we belt out the chorus of John Denver's "Take Me Home, Country Roads" before the gun fired.

After we properly butchered every single note, we lined up ready to start. The brief moments of silence before the gun are what I live for. Bodies are quivering in anticipation, and adrenaline is at an all-time high. Last-minute prayers are said, and we stand poised, ready to start our watches. The tension in the air is tangible. Hundreds of hearts hammer in unison as the starter raises his pistol. Then the floodgates of ecstasy are opened as the trigger is pulled. We're off.

Instantly, the wheels in my mind were turning. I started running with my head. Weaving between runners, I managed to work my way up in the first 400 meters. Falling in with a cluster of my teammates, we began to climb together, flanking other racers on both sides. In an ode to good sportsmanship, we each huffed out a "good job" or "keep it up" to every person we passed. Despite being competitors, running was a connection we all shared, and for better or worse, that put us all in the same boat. If David and Goliath were both runners, they probably would have bonded over it and shared tips instead of facing off.

The initial thundering of feet gradually lulled as the packs of the race solidified. Front, middle, back, and all the stragglers in between. The first mile always passes quickly in a blur of excitement and zeal, so when the second mile began, it was time to cash in all the training

I'd been putting in the bank. It was time to focus on my body. I consciously checked that I was doing everything right, breathing in through my nose, keeping my hands unclenched and pumping my arms. The shadow of fatigue danced in my peripheral, but I pushed it out of my mind.

All around me, excellence was coming out of the woodwork. Allegiances were formed between rival teams in unspoken agreements to keep each other going. I felt empathetic pats on my back as I was passed, and I returned the favor to those I passed. If one person tripped on a root, six hands would reach out to steady him or her. It was in those moments that we were ethereal; nothing in the world could touch us.

Inevitably, however, reality cast its line and reeled me back to earth. My old friend fatigue had taken residence in my muscles as I neared the third and final mile. Sweat trickled down my temple, threatening to make a detour into my eyes. It was time to finish the race with my heart.

"This is it," I said to myself. "This is where you give everything you've got left."

The bubble of euphoria I had been in earlier was well and truly popped. The same girls I had run with for the majority of the race had either pulled ahead or fallen behind, heaving into the trees. I refused to be among those who fell behind. Instead, I chose to pump my legs a little faster and push myself a little harder. As the half-mile mark loomed ahead, the crowd of spectators grew denser, and their cheering became louder.

"Good job!"

"Push it!"

And my personal favorite: "Only a half-mile left!"

Around the next corner, I could see my coach bouncing on his toes in excitement. Focusing on him, the noises softened, and faces blurred. When we locked eyes, it was only his voice that cut through the veil of exhaustion.

"You've gotta run like you want it!"

This was all the prompting I needed. For the next 800 meters, not a single girl was permitted to pass me. Honestly, I couldn't say what I was thinking in those final moments of my race. All I know is that I was reduced to my most primal instincts and was likely rendered inarticulate. Sheer desperation pushed me to break out into a sprint for the final 400 meters.

Everything in my body screamed at me to stop, walk, or at least slow down. The tendons in every limb felt taut; my arms flailed; my good form was abandoned. The only thing I was racing against now was the clock. My stomach clenched, threatening to upend itself.

When I finally sailed over that finish line, I nearly cried from relief. My last animalistic glance at the clock told me I had blown my time out of the water. A concerned-looking official handed me a medal and ushered me along in case my stomach made good on its threats. Instantly, I was encircled by my team. I fell into their arms, grateful for the support.

I live for those last moments of a race; it's why I run. It's ecstasy and insanity. It's freedom. For a few minutes, I can fly.

—Olivia O'Toole—

Milestones

The miracle isn't that I finished. The miracle
is that I had the courage to start.
~John Bingham

First marathon. Portland, Oregon. October 9, 2015.

26.2 miles is a long way. A LONG WAY. Way longer than our 15-mile practice run, infinitely longer than my 10-mile run from work to home.

26.2 miles is an odyssey of conflicting thoughts and emotions. It's joy at the miles behind you, despair at the ones still ahead.

Miles 1–5 are euphoria. It's the crowd jostling for position, the starting gun and the cheer of 13,000 people roaring down a sky-scrapered canyon and washing over you in the semi-darkness. It's the one-man rally squad at the first turn that I wish would come to my office every morning and cheer me from my car to the door.

"You look great, man. You're doing awesome! I'm proud of you!"

It's passing through the line of cheerleaders, each of them posing for the camera. (I've waited 20 years to hear a dozen high-school cheerleaders screaming my name from the sidelines; it was worth every step!)

Miles 5–10, it's tossing your sweatshirt aside to join 1,000 (10,000?) jackets strewn along the sidewalk like dead leaves fallen from a forest of Walmart trees.

It's trying not to look ashamed that you're losing ground; from then on, it's just hoping you can keep running to the end. I mean, it's just running, right? Good Lord, how hard can it be to just keep putting one foot in front of the other?

Mile 11 is re-taping your feet as the first blisters start to appear. It's joking with your friends about whose stupid idea was this anyway? It's cheering the sweaty, oblivious runners passing you from the back of the pack, and when you hit the long double-back it's your heart breaking for the woman struggling at the very end of the walkers, a police escort car and a long line of traffic following her at a crawl.

Mile 13 is just unfair. After that gut-busting climb up to the bridge you discover that it's the slow jog down the other side that really hurts. It is unjust.

Mile 15 is the memory of nasty tasting power bars, stomach turning glucose drinks, and some horribly sweet honey sludge, suddenly being erased by angels from Heaven bearing tubs of gummy worms and bowls filled with tootsie rolls. It's reminding yourself to post a warning in your blog: if you ever decide to slurp down a packet of Stinger honey, don't ever wash it down with two Red Bull energy drinks. Not ever.

Mile 18 is the best rendition of Free Bird you have ever heard, or maybe you're just low on glucose again. You don't care.

Mile 20 is realizing that the cheering seemed nice at first, even a little embarrassing, but now it has gone from cute, to appreciated, to producing eye-watering gratefulness.

Mile 22 is abandoning your friends to fate and pushing through in a heavy-metal cocoon oblivious to cheerleaders and traffic lights. It's dodging crowds in Saturday market and vaulting sleeping old men down skid row. You let nothing slow you down now.

Mile 26 is finishing up between two larger groups and running the center line down the last two blocks completely alone. It's your wife screaming, "That's my husband!" just loud enough to be heard over the music. It's knowing that nothing is better than that.

The finish line. It's forgetting to check your time. (Who cares? You finished!)

It's a bag of bananas and peanut-butter cookies, a rose and a gold medal, and strangers patting your back. It's suddenly realizing that next year's marathon will be much easier just knowing how the finish line is — what the finish line is.

It's realizing suddenly that there will be a marathon next year.

You cross the finish line totally spent, physically and emotionally exhausted, which was just how you wanted to end it. It is a long, hard walk, but the last 60 seconds made it all worth it. Crossing the line is like a shot of speed — suddenly you no longer register the pain in your feet, the grinding of your hips. You feel great.

You are a gladiator walking into the Colosseum, and all the crowds of Rome are lining the fence, chanting your name and cheering.

It's the post-marathon rush of endorphins lasting about 15 minutes. Then, as your friends (whom you now feel like a dog for abandoning) cross the line, you cheer with the rest, and your feet wake back up and the glory of the finish line is overwhelmed by visions of beer, pizza and a soft couch.

It's your post marathon party: crashed at your friends' house, the three of you semi-comatose on a combination of Guinness, Advil and pepperoni with extra cheese, while your wife (who is a gift from God, wonderful beyond words) plays Florence Nightingale, running more beer and pizza between foot massages.

It's limping proudly through the office the following morning wearing your bright-blue finisher's shirt and trying not to grin.

Or maybe it's none of that for you. Maybe it's something completely different and just as completely wonderful. Maybe it's not wonderful at all.

Maybe it's just me.

— Perry P. Perkins —

Camaraderie & Community

Running by My Side

Find a group of people who challenge and inspire you;
spend a lot of time with them, and it will
change your life.
~Amy Poehler

When I relocated from the warmth of the South back to the Northeast in 2010, I worried that I wouldn't enjoy running without the gravel paths and early-morning ripples on the water of the Tennessee River to nudge me along. The bike trail in Knoxville was directly outside my front door. The gravel path was dotted with beautiful oak trees and benches for relaxing. Experiencing spring on that path, passing those blooming dogwoods, running under the blue skies and explosions of pink, "was a godly experience," as our pastor in Tennessee liked to say.

My first few runs back in Delaware brought the visions and scents of my childhood rushing back. I couldn't resist stopping to pick up pinecones to smell their sticky-scented rough edges. But running didn't fill me with joy the way it had in Tennessee. Gone was the tree-lined gravel path, replaced by the main road. And the honking horns of SUVs replaced the quiet of the river and dogwoods.

I trained for a half marathon with my husband, hoping that training for a race would reignite my passion for running. After completing the half marathon, I found I still mourned the long runs and warm winters of the South. One day, a mom from my children's school approached me. "I see you running in the morning. A few of the moms have a running group if you are interested."

I perked up. Running solo had always been who I was, but lately I was finding the solitude, well, a little too solo. "That sounds great. When do you run?"

"At 5:30 a.m., so we can get home and get the kids up and ready for school." I spit out my drink as I grappled with the notion of waking up pre-dawn to run.

She looked at me. "There are actually two groups of us, though. One group goes before drop-off, and one goes after drop-off at 8:30. You should call Deb. She runs after the morning drop-off."

I contacted Debbie and she welcomed me into her group with open arms. "We meet at my house after drop-off on Monday," she said. I arrived in her kitchen and met Jennifer, Liz, and Michelle. I became excited to run again, having found camaraderie in these amazing women.

Over time, members of the early-morning run suffered losses: spouses and children ailed, and some lost loved ones. At this point, the "before-drop-off group," and "after-drop-off group" bonded in spirit. We came together to host birthdays, and one friend hosted a Running Girls Cookie Exchange over the holidays. These gatherings to commemorate our good times were essential in keeping up people's spirits during hard times. And while I knew how important our support was, I couldn't honestly know what the support provided — until I needed it myself.

Our running group always became a bit disjointed in the summer, due to travel schedules and kids' camps. So it was that I found myself in New York City on a sweltering day in July 2017. My son was attending a one-day camp in the city, and my whole family had accompanied him to make a weekend of it. We were sitting at lunch in our hotel when my husband got a phone call. He raised an eyebrow and gestured with his head to the corner and I knew what that meant: "Not in front of the kids."

We walked outside. "What's wrong?" I asked.

"The police are at our house."

My husband spoke into the phone. "Roanoke County?" My mother lived in Roanoke County.

I looked at my husband standing against the door to the hotel, the sun glistening on his tan nose.

"My mother's dead?" I asked.

He nodded. My memory is spotty after that, the way one's hearing works only intermittently after a loud blast. A kind concierge helped walk me into the security office in the front to give me privacy. I remember calling my brother and making sure he wasn't driving when I delivered the news. "Sudden cardiac arrest," I relayed.

I wandered down to the lobby and started making phone calls away from the kids. One thing I learned is that if you don't keep your iPhone contact list current, and you accidentally send strangers a text saying "I am so sorry to tell you this, but my mom died," you will find kindness still lingers in the hearts of many. I received several text messages telling me that, while I had the wrong number, these strangers were sorry for my loss.

I also sent a group text to my running group. "I am in New York. I am okay. Well, I think I am okay, but my mom died. I don't know where to have the funeral. I don't know how to have a funeral."

Immediately, my husband started fielding calls from my worried running girls asking how I was and what they could do.

When we arrived home the following day, I made arrangements for the funeral to be held in the chapel of my high school, an all-girls' Catholic school that my mother had loved. But as to how to make the other funeral arrangements, I was mystified.

Then a funeral program with several options for readings and psalms arrived in my e-mail inbox. My running friend Michelle had put it together and sent it to me. Once I made the choices, and selected songs and readings for my mother's funeral, my friend Liz picked up the draft and had it printed for the service. When I called my friend Jennifer to ask for help with the menu, she said not to worry about it. Then she proceeded to find a caterer in Maryland, planned the menu, and arranged the food delivery with the school where the funeral was being held.

I was in such a fog those first few days that I didn't even notice Liz picking up a box of photos from my husband. But once I arrived at the funeral, framed pictures of my mother were placed everywhere.

Liz had blown some up and made collages of others. No one had asked her to; she just did it.

I was hosting a dinner for my mother's friends the evening before the funeral, in D.C., two hours away from Delaware where we live. When I asked my friend Carolyn if she would come, completely forgetting that Carolyn is a doctor who had a busy schedule the evening of the dinner and the day of the funeral, she didn't hesitate. "Of course, I will be there." She canceled two days of patient appointments to support me.

Everyone in my running group came to my mother's funeral. They spent four hours in the car to support me that day. And when I returned home, dinner showed up at the house for weeks. My running friend Lisa, a photographer, scanned all of the photos of my mother because I mentioned to her that I didn't have any negatives.

Running was the constant in my life after my mother died. My running girls held my shoulders on the days that I would start crying while I ran, sometimes doubled over with grief on the middle of a gravel path. I miss the beautiful views in Tennessee, but I have learned that it isn't the distance, the view or the pace that makes running great; it is the people running by your side.

— Helen Boulos —

Walking in Another Direction

For you, as well as I, can open fence doors and walk across America in your own special way. Then we can all discover who our neighbors are.
~Robert Sweetgall, Fitness Walking

When I moved into my current home almost 30 years ago, my street was a quiet country road. Most of the houses sat on lots of at least three acres, and several homeowners had horses, cows, or chickens. I rarely saw my neighbors unless I invited them over for a party, or we happened to visit the clustered mailboxes at the same time. As an animal lover, though, I often stopped to talk to the horses and cows and rub their noses during my evening walks. I loved walking after dinner, both for the gentle exercise and the uplifting effect that the animals and nature had on my mood.

Sadly, within five years of my arrival, developers began buying up tracts of land in the area and building huge homes on quarter-acre parcels. The horses and cows disappeared as the small farms became housing developments. Soon, my country road was a dangerous thoroughfare with cars rushing by. Since I could no longer walk safely on the shoulder of my own street, I began taking a route through Crestwood, one of the new developments nearby. At least it had a sidewalk and fewer cars.

One day, during a seminar at a local wellness center, a woman sitting behind me tapped my shoulder. "You look familiar," she said. "Do you live in Crestwood?" I said that I didn't, but that I lived nearby. "That's where I know you from — I see you walking every day. I'm Claudette." She said if I ever wanted a walking partner to knock on her door.

The next time I passed her house and saw her in the yard, we waved hello. She invited me to join her neighborhood "Girls' Night Out," which took place once every other month and rotated between several homes in that community.

At the first Girls' Night that I attended, Claudette introduced me around. It turned out that many of the women there also recognized me from my walks. Apparently, I was a regular fixture in the evenings, even though I had no idea people were watching me. Eventually, these women became my friends.

The women of Crestwood weren't the only friendly ones. Often, I passed Dave as he was doing yard work or playing catch with his sons, and we eventually struck up a conversation. His positive energy brightened my day. I got to know Jeff, a retired schoolteacher, because we walked the same route daily. We chatted frequently and got to know each other well enough that we eventually exchanged phone numbers and e-mail addresses. He encouraged me to call if I ever needed anything that he or his wife could help with, and I did the same. I also became friendly with most of the dogs along my route — from Bruiser, a teacup Chihuahua, to Duke, a Yellow Lab/Akita mix.

A couple of years ago, I retired, and my work-related social activities tapered off. I was a bit concerned I might become one of those reclusive "cat ladies" who have little human interaction, but I needn't have feared — my neighborhood social circle continued to grow. I walked more during the day and got to know other Crestwood residents I hadn't met before: stay-at-home moms and people who worked from home who were outside during daytime hours.

I like having a personal connection with people nearby — ones I can talk to without an Internet or phone line. This came in handy especially during an ice storm last winter that knocked out my power for days, but not Crestwood's. One friend lent me her portable cell-phone charger, and another offered to keep all my frozen food in her huge freezer. When Duke's owner broke her leg shoveling snow, I walked Duke for her until she was well enough to resume that activity, and she fed my cats when I had to go out of town unexpectedly. Periodically, I share travel- and health-related information with Jeff, adding depth to our discussions. And when Claudette's son, Michael, broke his kneecap, I told her I'd drive him home from school every day so she or her husband wouldn't have to leave work early.

Now on my walks, I enjoy my new neighbors' holiday decorations as the seasons change. I see the progress of their landscaping and home-improvement projects, and I watch their children and pets grow. I attend most of Michael's band concerts and school plays, proudly noting how his confidence and maturity are increasing.

Almost two decades since it was built, the once-stark development is now lovely, with tall flowering trees and meticulously kept lawns. My new walking route is just as beautiful as my old one, only in a different way. And walking there every day keeps me in touch with my new friends.

I never thought anything good would come from the developments in my neighborhood, but thanks to walking, I discovered a whole community of supportive new friends. I realized it's not the land and surroundings that make a community, but the people who live there. To my surprise, although I began walking for my mental and physical health, it had the added benefit of widening my social circle. One might even say that when I was run out of my old neighborhood, I walked into a new one!

— Susan Yanguas —

Strangers in Seattle

I want to run every race with a big heart.
~Ryan Hall

In my mid-thirties, I moved to Seattle in search of a better career opportunity. I was working part-time for a friend and living just over a mile from Green Lake Park. In the afternoons, I often jogged at the park in preparation for the Trail's End Marathon in Seaside, Oregon.

On a beautiful mid-week afternoon in April 1982, I planned on doing four laps on the 2.8 miles of paved path that circled the park's lake. Counting the short jog to and from the park, I figured the workout to be 14 miles.

I had nearly reached the park's path when two men suddenly approached me from a nearby bench. The man closest to me reached out his arm, beckoning me to stop. He asked quickly, "Young man, would you be able to assist us?" At first glance, the guy seemed harmless enough. He was probably in his early sixties, heavyset, pleasant-looking and dressed in a sweater, slacks and street shoes. His partner, maybe 50ish, had an athletic build and was wearing jogging attire.

My defensive mechanisms turned from warm to red alert. There was never a day when "helping strangers" appeared on my to-do list. In fact, I was adept at avoiding situations where a stranger might ask for my help. I had no desire to be put in a precarious position.

"What is it?" I snapped while taking a break.

"Are you going to jog around the lake?" he asked.

"Yes," I responded in as gruff a tone as I could muster.

Then he quickly took hold of his partner's arm and brought him closer to me. "Would you mind if my friend here jogs along with you?" This encounter had taken about 10 seconds. Why then did this rather harmless request not only intimidate me, but put me in full-flight mode? I couldn't help thinking of the disdain my friends and I held for singles who wanted to join our group on the golf course. There was usually a reason they were by themselves, and we were not about to find out what that reason was. "What do you mean, jog with me?" I asked cautiously.

He replied, "Jerry likes to jog around the lake but needs someone's help."

"Why is that?" I shot back.

"He's blind."

You've got to be kidding me. While jogging, they wanted me to guide him all around that lake? It was a gorgeous day. The path was teeming with people, many with leashed dogs, some with baby carriages, all with no concern for my predicament.

On second thought, I figured it wouldn't kill me to delve a little deeper into this request. Turning my attention to Jerry, I inquired, "You want to go jogging?"

Jerry replied, "I do. Will you help me?"

"I guess so, but I don't know how this can work."

He smiled and said, "Oh, it's quite simple really. I have a cord that attaches to our wrists." With that, he showed me a rubber cord he was carrying. The cord was about 3/8 of an inch in diameter with loops at both ends. Each loop was big enough to just put a hand through. The cord's length, including the two loops, couldn't have been 16 inches.

After a brief introduction, Jerry asked which of my wrists I preferred his cord be attached. Giving his question a moment's thought, I felt, since I was right-handed, it might be better to have the cord on my right wrist. I took one end of the cord and slipped the loop over my hand onto my wrist. He attached the other loop over his left hand and onto his wrist. We were tethered.

Jerry was ready to hit the path, but I was not. Before that moment,

I could not recall speaking to a blind person, let alone jogging three miles fastened to one. Stalling, I asked Jerry, "What pace would you like to go?"

He said quickly, "Doesn't matter. Whatever pace you choose will be fine." After a couple more of my foolish questions, I figured we might as well get this herky-jerky show on the road.

The first few slow strides went well enough. I figured I might have to give him a play by play of what was happening, but he didn't seem concerned about anything. Whereas I was uptight about our precarious venture, he appeared confident and relaxed. After 100 yards, I was surprised to discover we were jogging along smoothly. Gradually, I picked up the pace, and again we were stride for stride. If I hadn't been so self-conscious, I may have forgotten we were tethered. Within a half-mile, I realized this was not Jerry's first rodeo. This man was an extraordinarily gifted athlete. Not once had the short cord tightened as he stayed about eight inches from my right wrist and three to four inches behind me.

Five minutes into our jog, I lost any ambivalence I had about guiding Jerry. He was fearless, and judging from his demeanor, he was enjoying himself. We began to chat freely. I wish I could remember specifics of his life, but I cannot. I do remember he said he came to Green Lake almost daily during the spring and summer. He said that someone they knew was often available to jog with him. Days like today when they asked for assistance were infrequent.

We cruised around the lake. My only concern was keeping three feet of space open on my right. The 25-minute jog through and around the maze of people went without a hitch. While dropping Jerry off with his friend, I commented on what a terrific experience the jog was for me. They seemed to appreciate my having said that. They thanked me for helping and, with that, we bid adieu. Then I turned back to the path, three laps to go.

That jog with Jerry was over 36 years ago. Now, I'm five years retired from a 31-year career in the newspaper industry. In retirement, I run nearly daily. Within my age group, I compete in anything from 5Ks to marathons. Sometimes, during an arduous training run,

I remember Jerry. The man displayed courage, enthusiasm and a zest for life I have rarely encountered. Little did I know that during one lap around the lake, a man with a disability would show me life as it should be lived. I am a better person having briefly met Jerry. The rhythm of his footsteps will linger forever in my mind.

— Kenneth Heckard —

A Runner's Hi

We are at our best when we cheer each other on and build each other up.
~Taylor Swift

I've often seen you running
In the early morning dawn.
Your pace is very steady
And you very soon are gone.
Sometimes, I've also seen you
In the fading evening light.
You nod your head to say hello
And then are gone from sight.
It's always good to see you
On my solitary run.
Your presence has a lot to do
With just how far I've come.
Perhaps you might remember this—
The day was very hot.
You were running very well.
But, sadly, I was not!
We were running up a hill
One I'd never tried.
You started way behind me
But we soon were side by side.
You nodded your familiar nod

And said, "Go on, don't stop!"
You slowed your pace and ran with me
Until I reached the top.
I don't know much about you
And we don't have much to say,
But I think that you should know
You share the best part of my day!

— Kathy Lynn Miller —

I Don't Walk Alone

If time was measured in footsteps, walking together
with my friend could go for days on end.
~Author Unknown

Two good friends, talking about everything and nothing on our morning walks. It might start off like this: "Did you see the moon?"

"No, where is it?"

"Just above the bridge."

"Wow! Hey, I saw a great movie last night."

"Oh, yeah? Who was in it?"

"That English guy, you know—dark hair, tall—he used to be married to what's-her-name."

"Well, if I had another hint, maybe…"

For 15 years, give or take, Chris and I met around dawn in front of her house and walked the hills in our Oakland neighborhood. During the school year, when she taught middle-school science and I did college counseling with high-school seniors, we hit the street at 5:45 a.m.—every day, rain or shine. With her dog Eddie in tow, we walked and talked as the stars faded and the sun came up.

Our daily up-and-downhill chats covered years of drama, trauma, joys and triumphs. Our kids were a frequent topic as they navigated their way through school, driving, romance, college and young adulthood. Although we proudly shared their moments of glory, we unabashedly shared all the boneheaded things they did, too: lost keys and jackets, missed curfews and airplanes, blown deadlines, dents in the car, and so forth.

We spoke in the kind of shorthand that good friends develop, and often finished each other's sentences in a way that is never considered rude or obnoxious, as it might be if, say, our husbands did it. After all those years, we knew each other's cast of characters and their back stories. I knew her students, colleagues and family—and she knew mine. Sometimes, a storyline ran for weeks, while some episodes were one-shot "can you believe what happened?" vignettes. There was the time I attempted a home-repair job that nearly caused my garage door to fall down. And then there was the day her classroom's pet mouse escaped from its cage. Chris took this as a "teachable moment" and had the kids brainstorm the best way to lure little Ralph back into captivity.

"You should write about this," I said to her.

"You write it," she shot back. "You're the writer."

Our friendship has a unique twist: We were born on the exact same November day in the city of San Francisco. Minor details aside (her large Catholic family as opposed to my small Jewish one), we are the same height, have blue-green eyes, and our curly hair has more salt than pepper in it these days. We are like twins, without the baggage of having grown up together. Other people find it amusing when one of us asks the other, "How old are we?" or "How tall are we?" But that's just the way it is with us.

During our walks, we listened patiently to each other, huffing up hills while we worked out thorny family problems and talked ourselves into leaving jobs when it was time to move on. We kept each other grounded; we relied on each other to start each new day with a few laughs, some good advice and a willing ear. Perhaps Chris's mind sometimes wandered to lesson plans or field trips during one of my rambling stories, but she would always be right there with an appropriate response when I came up for air. One day, I asked Chris to tell me to shut up if she was tired of hearing me vent on a particularly vexing subject. She waited a beat, and then said, "Okay. Shut up." It was just the right thing to say. Of course, she asked me to do the same for her, but I never felt the need.

We could always interrupt each other to point out signs of the changing seasons: the shifting position of the constellations, the ripening of persimmons or blackberries, the first blossoms on the tulip magnolias. At the highest point of our walk, we would often pause and take in the vista that included the Bay, the bridges, Lake Merritt and Mount Tamalpais. "Aren't we lucky to live here?" we would ask each other. We would literally stop and smell the roses. At the walk's end, I would head up the block to my house, saying "See you tomorrow!" over my shoulder as she climbed up her stairs.

Even though I'd known for months that Chris was leaving the neighborhood, leaving the state, leaving me without a walking partner—the day the big orange-and-white moving van pulled up in front of her house, I felt a wave of sadness.

Chris moved on to challenge herself personally and professionally in graduate school—a dream come true. I had encouraged her to search for an educational opportunity that would allow her to broaden her skills and share her gifts with others. Now she'd gone and done it. What was I thinking?

Since she left, my whole rhythm is off. As I told her through my tears that morning in front of the damn moving van, I'm only sorry for myself—though I suspect she will miss our routine and me, too.

During the everyday-ness of our walks, I didn't really think about what our friendship meant to me. I think about it a lot now. It isn't just the ridiculous souvenir tea towels we gave each other, or the things we borrowed (everything from the standard eggs and garlic to a vacuum cleaner and long black gloves). It isn't the mornings we got soaked to the skin by a sudden downpour, the disagreements about whether we were walking south or southwest, the sampled blackberries at the end of our walk—or not being able to wait until 6:00 a.m. to share a piece of good news. It isn't just about having suffered losses and surviving them together.

We are not sappy and sentimental, either of us. We're just a pair of tough cookies with a secret gooey center. But with our lifeline thinned to e-mail and an occasional phone call, I feel the loss of contact deeply, and I know Chris does, too. Maybe a friendship like ours becomes like its central characters — living and growing and gaining strength when its limits are stretched and tested the most.

There's one thing I know for sure, though: I miss those morning walks.

— Risa Nye —

Street Greetings

We cannot live only for ourselves. A thousand fibers connect us with our fellow men.
~Herman Melville

There he was, turning the corner of Hawley and Main Street like clockwork. His red hair seemed to catch the sunlight, giving his head a soft candle-flame glow. He caught my eye, and up went his arm in its usual wave. It wasn't a fast flash of a wave or a flickering of the fingers. It was the kind of wave you see when children know the answer to the teacher's question. It was the wave I give my husband when he's at the opposite end of the grocery aisle. As usual, I waved back and gave him a warm smile.

"Do you know that guy, Mom?" asked my son from the back seat. "He seems to know everybody."

I shook my head. "I don't know his name, but he's very friendly. I see him walking almost every day." It was true. No matter the weather, the man was out. He kept a good pace, considering his advanced age, and covered a lot of territory. At this time of day, we often passed each other at the intersection near the school.

We were relatively new to this town. Having moved from a larger city, I wasn't used to waves from strangers. Actually, where we were from, people hardly acknowledged each other. We simply bustled by each other, heads down, minding our own business.

Perhaps that's why I enjoyed these daily waves. It felt good to be noticed and receive that message of "Hello!" On days when we didn't happen to pass each other, I missed him and wondered if he was all right. The next day, I'd find myself driving with only one eye on the road. It was a happy reunion when I'd spot him, and I'd wave first in my eagerness.

I, too, enjoyed walking. I often went out in the evenings after the dinner dishes were done. I'd stroll along, enjoying the twilight call of the robins perched high on rooftops. I treasured the solitude, but one night my thoughts traveled to "The Waver," as my children called him. I wondered if I could be bold enough to wave at people I didn't know. I wanted to give it a try, but I hesitated. *I'll feel silly,* I thought to myself. I continued walking, faster now, as though arriving home would put an end to the temptation. I stared at the sidewalk and watched my shoes take step after step. I heard a car approaching.

I felt like my head was attached to a string, and a puppeteer was giving me a yank. I made eye contact with the person in the passenger seat. The puppeteer gave my right arm a tug. I smiled and waved.

The woman's face softened, and she waved back. I was a little stunned. *They do this here!* I reminded myself. *It's okay. It's actually kind of cool!* I waved to everyone I saw the rest of the way home.

That was the day I became a "waver." Walking really is nicer when combined with waving. My favorite return waves come from little ones in car seats. I don't do the full-arm wave, though; being on the shy side, I give a more casual greeting. But it's sincere, and that's what counts.

I'm sure everyone at some point in their lives wonders if they've made any impact on the world. If the original "waver" is out there wondering, I can answer that for him. "You have, sir. You don't know it, but you have." We don't have to change the world drastically to improve it. It's enough to help sweeten it a little.

—Marianne Fosnow—

Running for Your Pads

The strength of the team is each individual member.
The strength of each member is the team.
~Phil Jackson

In the summer of 1974, I was a sophomore trying out for the high-school football team—standing five feet, four inches tall and weighing all of 110 pounds. This was at Logan Elm High School, a rural, single-A bastion of secondary education located 30 miles south of Columbus, Ohio.

That summer, the Logan Elm Braves had a new head football coach, Mr. Perry Griffith. He was a graduate of Worthington High School, a triple-A powerhouse located in a wealthy Columbus suburb. There, he had been a football star and state champion wrestler.

Now he had been tasked with turning country bumpkins into not only winners on the football field, but also winners in life.

The sports page of the local newspaper, the *Circleville Herald*, always printed when the first day of football practice would be held for the four high schools in the county. Logan Elm was to start on August 1st, which I learned by reading a tiny byline beneath a huge article about the Cincinnati Reds' current home stand.

So, 60 kids showed up at 6:00 on the evening of Thursday, August 1st, not sure what to expect. To start, we were all herded to the 50-yard line and told to take a knee.

There, with the new assistant coaches standing in a row behind him, Mr. Griffith introduced himself. With the bill of a baseball cap pulled down low over his eyes, he glared at his young tutelages. The short sleeves of his polo shirt strained to contain his biceps, and the whistle around his neck hung in a valley between his pectorals. Sporting classic black polyester coaching shorts, white knee socks, and 1960s football cleats, he reminded me of Vince Lombardi.

With a clipboard in one hand and a stopwatch in the other, he stated that we were about to be timed in a one-mile run. That mile would consist of four laps around the school's cinder track in shorts, shirt, socks, and football cleats.

I mumbled, "What?"

Was a timed mile Mr. Griffith's way of taking stock of what he had to work with?

Then Mr. Griffith continued, explaining that we would be timed again on Friday the 9th. At that time, backs and ends would have to complete the mile in six minutes, and linemen would have to finish in six minutes, thirty seconds. Those who failed wouldn't get their pads. It was that simple.

My eyebrows went up.

In my head, I called his policy "running for your pads." Did other high-school football teams do that? Or was that just a big-city-like-Columbus thing?

But at the same time, I didn't object to Mr. Griffith's policy. Young, pubescent males needed to learn the valuable lesson of overcoming obstacles to achieve their goals.

"Okay, get up and follow me," Mr. Griffith commanded. He spun about and began walking toward the Logan Elm sideline.

"GENTLEMEN, TONIGHT IS AN OPPORTUNITY TO EXCEL!"

In the gaggle that followed him, my head was spinning. Run a timed mile? Sheeesh! I guess that Mr. Griffith expected us to show up with at least a bare minimum level of physical fitness. And I would be okay. But there were boys who had held summer jobs while other boys worked on farms. They hadn't been running. Some boys had gone on long vacations, and others had spent the summer with their girlfriends. They hadn't been running either.

Meanwhile, I overheard older juniors and seniors grumbling that they didn't like the policy.

"Man, we didn't have to run for our pads last year."

"Yeah, I liked it better under Coach Stant."

"You don't run a mile in a game, so why should you run a mile to get your pads?"

Mr. Griffith halted in the grass behind the Logan Elm bench. With the clipboard and stopwatch in hand, he jumped upon the bench to a more domineering position.

Then he dispatched his new assistant coaches to the four inside corners of the track — to simultaneously provide encouragement and prevent cutting corners.

Then 60 country bumpkins crowded the starting line on Logan Elm's track.

From atop the bench, Mr. Griffith simply commanded, "ON YOUR MARK… GET SET… GO!" *Tweeeeet!*

Eight minutes later, my shins hurt from running in cleats on the track's cinders. But that was small potatoes. I remember boys doubled over in pain and gasping for air. Some boys begged for water. Some puked on the track. Some boys even got in their cars and never returned.

The very next evening was our first real practice. However, before starting, we were all corralled together again, but this time it was at the 50-yard line of our parched practice field.

"Take a knee," Mr. Griffith instructed again.

A smaller horde knelt down in front of their new head coach. The five-minute speech that followed would best be summarized with the following three sentences:

"Getting out of shape is a natural thing."

"Don't worry about it."

"I'll get you where you need to be."

Then Mr. Griffith called us all in to huddle around him, and he commanded, "READYYYYYY… BREAK! GENTLEMEN, TONIGHT IS ANOTHER OPPORTUNITY TO EXCEL!" *Tweeeeet!*

What followed that night and for the next week were basic conditioning drills like we had never seen. Even the "warm-ups" involved more running than the prior year's entire daily practices.

Nine days later, there was an excitement in the air at practice. Forty aspiring football players — 20 had quit — didn't have to be herded out to the track. Instead, we all walked there on our own... to Mr. Griffith's surprise.

With clipboard and stopwatch in hand, Mr. Griffith returned to his perch atop the bench.

"GENTLEMEN, THIS EVENING IS ANOTHER OPPORTUNITY TO EXCEL!"

I merely nodded my head.

"BACKS AND ENDS TO THE STARTING LINE." *Tweeeeet!*

About 15 boys crowded the track at the 50-yard line.

Mr. Griffith instructed, "Get off the track and run on the grass around the inside. That will prevent shin splints."

My jaw dropped to the track. No complaints here!

And a hodgepodge of clothing and cleats instantly jumped over onto the grass.

Meanwhile, the linemen lined both sides of the track to root for their teammates.

From atop the bench, Mr. Griffith smiled — his first in nine days — and then commanded, "ON YOUR MARK... GET SET... GO!"

What a difference a week made. After completing the mile, instead of doubling over or begging for water or puking, each back or end stayed at the finish line to cheer for his teammates. When the last runner crossed the finish line, everyone celebrated.

Every back and end had finished in less than six minutes.

Clap. Clap. Clap. Clap. Clap.

"LINEMEN TO THE STARTING LINE." *Tweeeeet!*

I inhaled and joined the gaggle on the track at the 50-yard line.

Then Mr. Griffith repeated, "It's the same policy, gentlemen. Get off the track and run on the grass around the inside."

Twenty-five linemen scrunched together on the grass at the bench.

"ON YOUR MARK... GET SET... GO!"

Wow! Running on grass made all the difference in the world. I crossed the finish line just as Coach Griffith yelled, "5:10!" Then I walked back over to the edge of the track to hail my fellow linemen who had yet to finish.

Enter a junior named Seth. He wasn't a fat junior—he just had "big bones." He would be the starting left offensive tackle… that is, if he could complete the mile under 6:30. And there he was, dead last on the other side of the playing field with an eighth of a mile to go. Seth was huffing and puffing, barely moving his tree-trunk legs.

Mr. Griffith began to yell the time: "5:40."

And 39 country bumpkins began screaming, "GO, SETH, GO!"

"5:58."

"YOU CAN DO IT, SETH!"

"6:12."

"C'MON, SETH!"

The big boy crossed the finish line.

Mr. Griffith yelled, "6:27!"

"ALRIIIIIIGHT!"

"WAY TO GO, SETH!"

"NICE JOB!"

Seth doubled over with his hands on his knees.

Every lineman had finished under 6:30.

Clap. Clap. Clap. Clap. Clap.

Mr. Griffith commanded, "CONGRATULATIONS, GENTLEMEN! READYYYYYY… BREAK!"

That was it for our mile test.

And Seth had learned a valuable lesson in life.

Come to think of it… so had I.

The next morning was equipment-issue day, when all of the football equipment was laid out on the basketball court. The line extended out the double doors and around the corner from the fastest senior to the slowest senior, the fastest junior to the slowest junior, the fastest sophomore to the slowest sophomore, and the fastest freshman to the slowest freshman.

Four hours later, the forty of us felt as if our pads had not just been handed to us—our pads had been earned.

That was a year of growth for the Logan Elm Braves, but we finished the 1975 fall campaign with an 8–2 record, as co-champions of the Mid-State League. Coach was right. Running helped.

—John M. Scanlan—

Hey, Can I Walk with You?

Be genuinely interested in everyone you meet, and
everyone you meet will be genuinely interested in you.
~Rasheed Ogunlaru

When our treadmill broke a few days before Christmas, my husband and I didn't bother to buy a new one. Instead, I told him I would continue my walking routine outdoors. Although it was December and cold outside, I bundled up and hit the asphalt. On one of my first days of getting in a mile and some change through our subdivision, I spotted a dark-haired little boy watching me from his front yard.

I walked through the neighborhood again the next day, and there stood the little boy, staring up at me as I rounded the corner near his driveway. He called out, "Are you that lady from yesterday?"

"Yes," I said, surprised by his boldness.

With a hopeful smile on his face, he asked, "Hey, can I walk with you?"

His question threw me. A little boy wanted to walk with me? I never had children of my own, although I inherited some wonderful adult children, and then delightful grandchildren, when I married later in life. I was also close to my nieces and nephew, but they hadn't been little in years. Aside from hosting a few tea parties for my friends' little girls, I hadn't been around young children in quite a while.

I looked around and spotted no parents I could ask for permission to walk with the boy. "Are your mom and dad around?" I asked.

"No, just my brother and sister."

A tween-age boy and girl were nearby, so I approached the girl and said, "I don't mind if he walks with me, but do you think it'd be okay with your parents? I'm only walking to the end of this road." I pointed up the hill. "You'll be able to see us the entire time."

She shrugged and said, "That's fine."

Even as a middle-aged woman, I was cautious about walking with a child I didn't know, but he was chatty and seemed eager to make a new friend. And that was what the little boy named Ethan became that day—my friend.

His family, new to the neighborhood, had previously lived out in the country. He missed the country, and he missed his grandparents, he said. Before I knew it, he was telling me his parents' names, his siblings' names, his phone number, and how he felt about school. (Not good.) He was a refreshingly honest child.

While I hadn't been too excited about walking outdoors in cold weather, I found myself wrapping up in a heavy coat and gloves for my daily walk, not wanting to disappoint Ethan, who was usually looking for me.

After a few days, he apparently got bored with walking since he said, "Let's run."

"Oh, Ethan," I said. "These knees can't run."

"Come on," he said. "Just try it."

So I did. I thought I'd have a heart attack before I made it home, but I ran—up the hill, I might add. I told my husband later that I suspected someone had secretly hired Ethan to serve as my personal trainer.

As an introvert and someone who works from home, I hadn't yet made a habit of getting to know my neighbors, but Ethan changed all that. "Do you know Mrs. Carol?" he asked.

"No," I replied. "Who's that?"

"She lives in the gray house. Let's go see her."

I was forever telling Ethan that we couldn't just barge in on the neighbors to say "hello." He would look at me as if to ask, "Why not?"

One day as Ethan and I were walking, "Mrs. Carol" was standing outside, and Ethan ran ahead of me to say "hello" to her. Quickly, I realized I wasn't Ethan's only new friend in the neighborhood. Thanks to Ethan, I soon got to know not only "Mrs. Carol," but "Mrs. Amanda" and her children, too.

My friendship with Ethan was not without its challenges. He was a nosy child, for one thing. When he learned I had a husband, he wanted to meet him, so I had to make the introduction so Ethan could check him out.

Late one Friday afternoon, I had skipped my walk, and as I pulled into the garage and parked, I saw two small bicycles pulling up behind me — Ethan and a friend.

"Where have you been?" Ethan demanded.

"The bookstore."

"Who were you with?"

"One of my girlfriends."

"What were y'all doing?"

"Talking."

"Can I meet her?"

I had to remind myself which of us was the middle-aged grown-up and which of us was the child.

By the time Halloween rolled around, I had grown quite fond of Ethan and his siblings, and I dropped off Halloween treat bags for them since I wasn't going to be home that night to greet trick-or-treaters. The next day on my walk, I was happy to see Ethan and hoped to learn he had enjoyed the treats. But he didn't mention them. No "I got them," no "thank you," no nothing. So, I prodded.

"Did you have a nice Halloween, Ethan?"

"Yes."

"Did you get to go trick-or-treating?"

"Uh-huh."

"Get some good candy?"

"Yes."

Still, not a word about my oh-so-cute treat bags. Finally, I broke down and asked, "Did you get the treats I left for you and your brother and sister yesterday?"

"Uh-huh," he said.

Well? I thought.

After a momentary pause, he said, "I don't like Butterfingers."

It was all I could do not to laugh.

"But don't worry, my dad ate 'em."

When I shared the story with "Mrs. Carol," she told me that Ethan had already informed her which candy was his favorite, so she'd made sure to have it for him. I would know better next time.

As often happens in a neighborhood, people come and go, and Ethan mentioned that his family might be moving. I'd gotten to know his mom by then and thought they wanted to move back to the country where there was more room for the kids — and the family's dogs — to roam and play. I couldn't argue with that.

Before I knew it, Ethan and his family had disappeared. I never saw a moving truck, and there were no goodbyes, which I actually didn't mind. I hate goodbyes.

And yet Ethan's influence remains. My new friends Carol and Amanda came to my home for tea last Christmas, and I often have the pleasure of walking with them — sometimes individually and sometimes together.

My husband and I have long since replaced our broken treadmill, but only he uses it as I prefer walking outdoors. I've also managed to lose 30 pounds. In a sense, I have Ethan to thank for getting me out of the house and onto the road.

So when I'm out walking and it's a particularly quiet afternoon, I wistfully approach the two-story white house around the corner, wondering whether, one day, I might see a dark-haired little boy there again, one who pipes up and asks, "Hey, can I walk with you?"

— Angela McRae —

Wonder Women

Don't be afraid. Be focused. Be determined. Be hopeful. Be empowered.
~Michelle Obama

Arriving at the stadium, we check our weekend gear and listen to the opening ceremonies. My teammates and I are dressed in Wonder Woman attire — 10 of us in red or blue capes, yellow armbands and a Wonder Woman headband, like Lynda Carter's in the 1970s TV show. The primary colors stand out in the throng of pink boas, tiaras, and tutus. Scanning the crowd, my eyes tear when reading the "in memory of" T-shirts with pictures of spouses, mothers, grandmothers, and children. For a split second, I imagine my kids and husband wearing cotton T-shirts adorned with my face, and my heart pounds in my chest.

Three thousand walkers surround us, each affected by cancer. Our nametags hang from colored lanyards. Those of us with pink lanyards are survivors. The remaining walkers wear blue. For most of my life, I have associated pink with ballerinas and Barbie; today, I embrace this pale pink lanyard. My fingers run the length of it, reminding me I belong to a sisterhood that has faced their own mortality and endured.

I motion to my 10 friends to gather for a group picture. Team Wonder Women is oddly quiet. I realize they are all feeling contemplative and excited at the same time, like I am. My smile feels forced, my eyes watery. I swallow hard, my voice faltering as I thank each of them for what we are about to do. I am one blink away from an ugly cry. Observing the teary faces of these women I love, I realize I have known some of them for more than 30 years.

We are here to make a difference. Families, friends, colleagues and even strangers sponsored Team Wonder Women. One hundred percent of our donations will benefit The Princess Margaret Cancer Foundation. We are here to give back, to celebrate life after cancer — my life after cancer treatment. Inside my scarred chest are tissue expanders, wonky in shape, stretching my skin. My third and final surgery is weeks away; I will have the tissue expanders removed and breast implants inserted. I notice other women survivors in all shapes, sizes and ages. I take in the compression sleeves, bald heads, and wigs. One woman is on oxygen, another in a wheelchair. All are about to walk 60 kilometers over two days. We are Wonder Women: walkers and warriors.

My friends are apprehensive; a few doubt their physical ability to walk the distance over the weekend ahead. Some of us have trained extensively, and others not at all. We are equipped with gently broken-in running shoes, sweat-resistant socks, bandages, extra socks, and sunscreen tucked in fanny packs. We are as ready as we are ever going to be.

I stifle a yawn. Last night, I lay in bed watching the lightning light up my room, listening to the heavens open up. I prayed that the rain would end before we began our walk this morning. The idea of soggy feet weighed on me. I had participated in this charity event 10 years ago. My sister and I walked to honor our grandmothers, who had battled lung cancer. One won; the other lost. I was out of shape, a new mom with a one- and three-year-old. Somehow, my feet managed to stay intact. The first-aid stations were jammed with people needing foot care. Nasty blisters, cuts, chafing — the memory was painful. I was fortunate.

Exiting the stadium, we spill out onto the wet streets of Toronto. We begin our walk. It has stopped raining!

As we walk through the distinct neighborhoods of Toronto, we meet Indian dancers on Gerard, Chinese dragon dancers in Chinatown, steel-drum players, bands, singers, belly dancers — all cultural representations of our great city. We are welcomed by community lemonade stands and kids handing out treats and water. A smiling woman sprays us with sunscreen in High Park. Then there is the "weekend crew," who make every traffic light memorable. Paul, in particular, a passionate volunteer, quotes Nelson Mandela and other inspirational speakers as we stretch our legs. Listening to his words, we feel a surge of pride as he reminds us that we are indeed making a difference. The light turns green, and off we go.

As Team Wonder Women passes pedestrians or people driving cars, we see faces light up. We hear cheers. "Go Super Girls!" "Go Wonder Women!" "Great costumes!" It pumps us up, and we feel like superheroes knowing we are helping women to avoid chemo, radiation or an invasive surgery. We put one step in front of the other.

Blisters form. Someone complains of a rash. There are a couple of bug bites, sore joints, and fatigued feet, but the team keeps going. Walking to raise money for cancer research, we are reminded that these minor irritants are insignificant. Onwards!

On Day 2, we reminisce as we walk through the east end of the city where some of us had apartments and our first homes, where a few got married, where we all danced and drank too much, where we mended broken hearts, and where we had our babies. This meandering through Toronto represents my life, my history, my youth, motherhood, and marriages. Today, it reminds me of my diagnosis, treatment and success. I am here, seeing this city through a new lens.

I smell the ripe aroma emanating from the sewage treatment plant at Ashbridge's Bay close to where I used to take the kids for walks along the boardwalk when they were little. I would never have imagined then that, in the future, I would be on the same path dressed like Wonder Woman (without the breasts), walking toward a goal that I desperately needed to accomplish. This charity walk was something I had planned while undergoing chemo. It kept me hopeful and allowed me to fixate on health, moving toward physical and mental renewal.

I hear a bumblebee and the honking of a distant car. Someone yells that the end is near. We are close to the stadium. The CN Tower shoots up into the sky, beckoning.

We lock arms, trying to awkwardly coordinate our gait in unison. It is hot, and the sun is beating down on our exhausted bodies.

Sweat-drenched and parched, I am weary, yet giddy. I am ready to walk across the finish line with my beautiful friends who have shared this time with me. I admire them all.

The loudspeaker announces, "TEAM WONDER WOMEN!" One more step, and we cross the finish line together. I see my family waiting. Flowers and love ahead.

I break down and cry.

—Kristen Knott—

A Silver Braid

You have a choice. You can throw in the towel,
or you can use it to wipe the sweat off your face.
~Gatorade ad

What a mistake. Starting in the back of a large race with the walkers and joggers left me in a mile-long human traffic jam. Running through a wide green valley in the Ogden Half Marathon in Utah, I already felt a sense of loss. And it was still only mile 1.

I started at the back of the pack to keep my nieces company. I thought I could work my way up to the two-hour pacer who was holding a bright orange sign. But at the end of the first mile, I was still stuck between joggers and walkers, trying to work my way through the crowd. The pacer had left me far behind.

The two-hour half marathon had been a goal I'd chased for years. Between giving birth to five children, I'd done lots of half marathons and gotten decent times: 2:05, 2:08, 2:02. But the elusive sub-two-hour evaded me.

This was my year to blow away that goal. I'd been training hard for that distance and that time. I'd done the speed work and gone overboard on long distance by training for the full marathon. My goal time was within my grasp. This was my race. But in the back of my mind, I knew my time in the first few miles was critical. And that first mile wasn't nearly fast enough.

To make up for the lost time, I would need to go faster than I had trained for the remaining 12 miles of the race—a rookie mistake I had learned not to repeat long ago. It's a recipe for burnout and failure. Today, of all days, I did not want to fail.

During the second mile, I finally worked my way out of the joggers in the back. I found a clear lane and plodded forward, determined to finish strong. Self-doubt gnawed at me as I saw the two-hour pacer dip over a distant snow-capped hill. I wondered if I would ever see the pace group again.

That's when a silvery braid bounced by me. Going a little faster than my current pace, a woman about my height and build strode away. Her tanned skin showed the flaws and wrinkles that years of endurance training bring. She was probably 20 years my senior. And there she was, stepping away from me in my race.

I wondered how long she had prepared for this event. Months? Years? This was clearly not her first half marathon. I felt it also wouldn't be her last. I found myself accelerating to match her even strides. I imagined reaching out to hold that braid like a guide rope. If I could hang on with her, I would finish strong.

Near the fourth mile, what felt like a miracle occurred. My silver-braided companion and I caught up to the two-hour pace group. I relaxed, happy to be with the right crowd. But she did not. She passed through the two-hour group, surging steadily ahead of them.

Something in my heart was still attached to her flowing braid. I followed her, knowing even if I slowed near the race's end, the pacer was behind me and I could still make my goal. Coming down a craggy, rock-lined canyon, she ran even faster. I followed, drafting in her wake.

Miles blurred together, and the canyon leveled out to a broad river path winding toward the finish. Around mile 10, the increase in crowd support inspired me to pick up my pace. The disco music at the water stop really got me going. I caught a second wind. Silver Braid was slowing. I passed her as the music filled the air around us.

Mile 11, with the music behind me, I felt the sadness in my poor, tired legs. Glancing at my watch, I was thrilled to be far ahead of my projected training time. But I also felt the strain of the additional speed. I had outpaced my training. I was getting to the end of my endurance.

My body hit a wall.

Silver Braid passed me again. She gave me a thumbs-up and said something encouraging my exhausted mind didn't process. Praising her steadiness, I fell in behind her. My focus was still on the end of her braid.

Mile 12 was the hardest mile. Knowing the finish line was close, but feeling the aching strain of prolonged effort, I was tempted to walk. But just then, new inspiration found me. A college-age girl from the crowd started shouting and running ahead of us.

"Go, Ann! That's my mom!" the girl shouted. "Keep it up, Ann!"

Silver Braid had a daughter and a name. If Ann could keep going, so could I.

The thought crossed my mind that maybe someone behind me was watching my brown braid, needing my strength. A chain of runners stretched ahead of me and behind me. We pulled each other along.

I crossed the finish line a full 10 minutes faster than my old personal record and eight minutes faster than my goal. 1:52! Looking at my watch, I could barely believe it. It was more than I had hoped for. But I couldn't take credit for it. I ran the race borrowing strength from Ann.

Ann finished a few seconds ahead of me. She hugged her cheering daughter and then turned to embrace me. She said my persistence had inspired her. I know her steadiness carried me.

That day, Ann gave me something that she didn't know she was handing out. She gave me an example of fortitude. Hard days and slow miles come to all of us, but we keep running. If we draw on the people around us, we can all finish strong.

— Kate E. Anderson —

Runners' High

Running together makes friendships
stronger and stronger.
~Chrisje Taesendonck

I've run a lot of miles — 10,000 at least. But not alone. I ran them with Nelle, Anita, Vicki, Jan, Irma, Smoz and Margaret. Eight of us, counting me, ran through the streets of Westacres every weekday morning for 13 years, give or take a sick day, vacation or sleep-in-late day. That's a lot of miles. And a lot of conversations.

I think it was Nelle, my around-the-corner neighbor, who started running with Anita way back then.

"Ink, you want to run with us?" she asked me. I had never even run around the block.

"Sure," I said.

Pretty soon, Vicki and Smoz joined us. We ran a few blocks and then turned around and walked home. After a couple of months, we picked up Irma. By then, we were up to a mile, and we had a route. At 7:00 a.m., Nelle started out on Winterberry and turned down Lilac to pick me up. Down Arrowood we ran to where Anita and Irma lived and then down Buckthorn to get Vicki. Finally, we ran down Oakleaf to get Smoz. By then, it was time to turn around and go back.

We dropped off in the order we started: goodbye Nelle, goodbye Ink, goodbye Anita and Irma, and goodbye Smoz (who was all by herself by then, of course). We went back to our lives, jobs and families feeling good about this invigorating start to our day. I went back to my little writing room upstairs, ready to put pen to paper, to work on my short story, poem, or novel. Not that I was ever published—except for opinion pieces in the *Westacres Weekly*.

We were all about the same age—late thirties. Our kids were all in school, and so were some of us. I was an aspiring writer, always taking an adult-education writing class somewhere. Nelle and Vicki were working on a teaching degree and a business degree respectively. Only Smoz had a regular job as a grade-school teacher. Irma and Anita were faithful volunteers—chairing rummage sales, art shows, church suppers, and the Westacres Fourth of July Parade. We talked as we ran, of course. Truthfully, we ran so we could talk. Though we didn't quite realize this in the beginning, it became ever more apparent as we hashed out the issues in our lives.

For instance, Vicki had to pass Spanish to get her degree. So, as soon as we got to Buckthorn, she would hand one of us the vocabulary card, and we would start quizzing her. "How do you say, 'It's going to rain tomorrow'?" Irma, who could actually speak some Spanish, might ask Vicki something more complex, something about tenses or conjunctions. When Vicki passed Spanish, we all cheered and clapped loudly for her in the middle of Buckthorn at 7:15 in the morning. At that hour, many of the neighbors were probably still trying to sleep, but this was cause for celebration.

By the time that Margaret, a new woman on my street, and Janet, a new runner also on my street, joined us, we were up to three miles. Margaret had a job that required her to be there at 8:00 a.m. Same with Jan. And it was looking like Nelle was going to be hired at the elementary school, so she would also have an early start time. So the runners had to start earlier, too. Now, Nelle left at 6:15 to pick me up. During the winter in Michigan, it was dark and slippery. Did we let that stop us? Certainly not. We ran through the dark, and we ran through ice and snow. When we fell, we picked each other up. We ran through the swirls of red and yellow maple leaves in October. We ran through our laughter, and we ran through our tears.

One spring evening, Nelle's beloved nephew, celebrating his high-school graduation with drinking and driving, was killed. Nelle was devastated, and so were we. Anita's brother, who had been sick for several years, died from AIDS. Anita was heartbroken, and so were we. Several of us lost our mothers and fathers. We brought hams and baked cakes for the funeral lunches. And, of course, we cheered when Anita got the office manager's job in a pediatric office where we had taken our babies. When Nelle, who had moved here from Canada, became a U.S. citizen, the runners sneaked over and planted 50 red, white and blue helium balloons in her yard while she was being sworn in at the immigration office.

As I mentioned, my aspirations to be a writer had not met with much success. At least weekly, the mailman brought rejection letters from the many publications I submitted to. So when the letter came that spring day from *Woman's Day*, I put it aside to open later. When I finally opened it, I learned that they wanted to publish a Christmas story I had written for a local contest (and not won). Furthermore, they wanted to pay me — not in copies of the magazine, but in hard cash — $1,000! I couldn't wait until the next morning.

Nelle, Jan and Margaret showed up at my door at the usual time, as the sun was rising over the stop sign at the corner just as the school bus passed by. "What's with the diaper bag?" Nelle said.

"You'll see," I said, as we took off for Anita's.

Anita pointed. "Is that for us? Doughnuts and coffee?"

"Maybe." We took off for Irma's, then Vicki's. Of course, they all asked about the bag. And, of course, I waited for the right moment. When we got to Smoz's, she came bounding out, chattering as usual.

"Hey, girls — great morning, isn't it? Hey, Ink! What's that in the diaper bag? Are you pregnant?"

"No, I'm not pregnant." I set the bag down at the end of her driveway. "I am..." I unzipped the diaper bag and pulled out a bottle of chilled Moët & Chandon champagne, "an author!"

"*Woman's Day* magazine," I added, "is going to publish my Christmas story. And pay me $1,000!"

They were all over me, high-fiving, slapping me on the back and shrieking with delight at this unbelievable news. Of course, many of the neighbors were still trying to sleep. But if there was ever cause for celebration, this was it!

I popped the cork, and Anita pulled the glasses out of the diaper bag. We sat down on Smoz's lawn, and I poured. Then, as the school bus rounded the corner, we lifted our glasses—a sight the teenagers of Westacres had never seen and would likely never see again. Eight middle-aged women stretched out on the grass just past dawn, laughing and drinking champagne, celebrating success, friendship, sunshine and the sweet life.

—Ingrid Tomey—

Doing It for Myself

Always There for Me

It's never too late to go out and get that feeling back.
~Loretta Swit

Dear Running,

We've been together for 20-plus years, and like any lasting relationship, we've had some speed bumps.

You: Accessible. Welcoming. Reliable. Available at every hour, on every surface, tempting me with pavement-ribbons of hills, trails through dense forests, and paths that always lead me to wonder, *Where does that go and when can I find out*?

You're not high-maintenance, which I appreciate in a partner. You require so little to get started: shoes, a sports bra, an alarm clock, and a smidgeon of cardiovascular endurance.

I start to jog, and, you envelop me in warmth. I sigh and settle in.

Why wouldn't I? You lift my mood. You infuse me with confidence, strength, and patience. You allow me to justify spending ridiculous amounts of money on shoes. You tone my butt and give my calves definition. You accept my girlfriends, never complaining that I spend too much time with them. You give me a legitimate reason to live in my capris.

And you pretty much saved my life. I know you've heard this story too many times already, but postpartum depression knocked me over after I popped out kid number one. As I swung between insomnia, hysterics, and doubt over why I wasn't feeling the motherly warmth I imagined I would, I realized the depression wasn't likely just postpartum.

Chronic low-grade depression and anxiety had clouded my spirit for at least a decade, but you, always the supportive partner, kept them in check. The soothing rhythm of moving forward, the satisfaction of soaking through a sports bra, the consistent structure to my day, and the inner strength you delivered were enough, most days, to keep my mental skies only partly cloudy, if not downright sunny.

I didn't run for most of my pregnancy—it just didn't feel right—so it took me about three months postpartum before I could string together a whole mile. At that point, I had lived pretty much a year without you.

I didn't feel your absence acutely until I huffed and puffed through a mile on Santa Fe's uneven sidewalks, in 13 minutes. As I walked the half-mile home, my mind's hovering clouds became a bit less menacing. That night, I slept better than I had in months.

So I hope you realize I'm beyond grateful for our partnership. But let's be honest here: You're not as simple as you seem.

You pretend you're all *Hey, just get out your front door and let me love you*, but we both know it's much, much more complicated than that.

You lure me with visions of gazelle-like splits that feel effortless (never happens) and post-run glows where the perfect selfie simply materializes (ditto). Your Instagram-worthy clichés are endless—all it takes is all you got; if it doesn't challenge you, it doesn't change you—and endlessly frustrating when I'm clomping along out there. Your simplicity can feel passive-aggressive at times: How can it be so difficult to just put one foot in front of the other?

Yes, you give me miles, experiences, endorphins, and friendships I'd never have otherwise, but to be sure: This relationship is definitely a two-way street.

I self-inflict serious pain (foam rolling and physical therapy exercises) so I can hang with you. I spend gobs of money on shoes, dry needling, and race entries so we can be a couple. I give up other things—normal things that normal people do, like staying in PJs on a Saturday morning with the newspaper and a latte—so I can join you.

The emotions? Don't get me started. I get jealous of your other girlfriends trotting along, making running look easy. I get angry when you're not available to me because it's icy outside or I forgot to pack my shoes or I'm injured. And even when things are going well, heaven knows, you're on my mind way more than is healthy: *When can I run? Where should I run? How long should I run? What should I wear on the run? What will the temps be on my run?* Repeat, repeat, repeat.

Worse, when passion kicks in, you smother me. When we become inseparable, you head right for my vulnerable feet and leave your version of a hickey: a stress fracture or some other mark that makes me limp around and shows the world you've had your way with me.

That happens, and I have to spend weeks or months away from you. Cheating on you in the pool, on the bike, or—yes, I said it—on the elliptical. Remembering why I love you, and reminding myself why I want to rekindle our fire.

Recently, you've zinged me with some nervy glute thing that you can't even define clearly. "I don't want to talk about it," you say, not explaining why you started it or how it will end. Instead, you just poke and poke all day long, acting juvenile and reminding me not to forget you.

Twenty-plus years, and obviously something is going well. So I leave you alone, and keep doing clamshells and glute bridges so we can be reunited. But I do them silently while cursing your name, wondering if I should finally just call it quits. Cut the cord, break up, splitsville. Twenty-something years is long enough.

Then we met again. Just 15 fleeting minutes—slightly over a mile—yesterday. Our first contact in months.

A cloudy, cool afternoon on a suburban route dotted with minivans.

My nerve-thing was talking, but you were louder. And damn, you're *sooooo* good.

I put my feet in motion, and you knew exactly what to say.

You were whispering sweet-nothings, filling me with visions of half-marathon personal records and trail outings; mornings with sunrises that feel like they were created just for me; elation-laced moods that come only after double-digit runs; runs so spectacular, I'll be reviewing them on Strava for days and weeks to come.

A little over a mile, and I'm completely smitten. Again.

Whether we hang for 15 minutes or 15 miles, you'll always win me back. And I couldn't be more grateful.

—Dimity McDowell—

You've Been Geezered

I have a plan...
To live forever...
So far... It's workin'.
~Steven Wright

I'm Geezer Doug and my story begins in January 1997. As I read the sports section of *The Orange County Register*, I found a big picture of Baz Hawley, a design engineer from Australia whom I hired back in 1973. The picture showed Baz hugging a young lady just as she crossed the finish line at his trail race. It really was the Baz Hawley I knew. The article stated that Baz was the Race Director for something called the Winter Trail Run Series held in the mountains of the Cleveland National Forest.

I wondered what a trail race was. I couldn't imagine people running in the mountains. I had backpacked in the Sierra Nevadas on multiple weeklong trips and had even made it to the top of Mount Whitney in 1995. However, I never saw a single person running in the mountains. Could people actually run in that thin air?

Fortunately, the newspaper article had Baz's contact information. I called him and we ended up getting together several times. He always invited me to try his races and I always responded, "No way." I could never run up hills, let alone in thin air. I had the road runner's mentality that if I ever had to stop and walk, I wouldn't be a *real* runner. I also thought Baz was lying to me when he told me that many of the runners walked the steep sections. Besides, the last time I did a serious run was the Los Angeles Marathon in 1993, four years earlier. I remembered that my back bothered me the next morning.

It took a year of prodding, but Baz finally coerced me into attempting his 12K, the shortest race of his series. I had to get up pretty early to drive the long way out along the twisty Ortega Highway to get to the Cleveland National Forest and the Blue Jay Campground where his trail races were held. This was January 1998, and I was already 58 years old. I really thought I was too old; however, I soon found out a man older than me, Lee Francis, was running. He was 65.

Although I planned to run the entire course, I failed. I had to walk some of the steeper sections. I observed quite a few other racers walking them, too. Perhaps Baz wasn't lying to me after all.

The next morning, my back felt great—as if I had had a magical massage. A week later, I decided to sign up for Baz's 15K. Later, I joined the 18K and eventually his 21K (half marathon), which had 3,700 feet of climbing.

I started to love trail running, but it took a while for me to figure out why. Eventually, I realized that since the early 1980s, this new-to-California boy from flat and gray Chicago had loved backpacking in the Sierras. I had been taking annual, week-long hikes with my neighbor, retired U.S. Marine Major Bob Johnson, and that was with 45-pound packs. With these races, I got to run through that same gorgeous, remote, uncrowded scenery with less than a three-pound pack!

I also found that the up-and-down of the trails was surprisingly easier on my body than the hours on end I spent running on constant, near-level paved roads. Of course, I was initially concerned about all the rocks and roots one encounters on trails. I felt it would be almost insane to try to run through those sections. I did learn to slow down a bit and be careful. I am absolutely sure this has helped me keep my balance skills in good shape as I age.

My daughter, Michelle Barton, started joining me in my trail-running training about a year after my granddaughter Sierra was born in January 2000. Three years later, Michelle did her first trail race. Yes, it was a Baz Winter Trail Run Series race. Michelle has since evolved into a now-famous ultrarunner with numerous 50K and 50-mile course records to her credit, including some she set while beating all of the men. I am very proud of her. These adventures together in the scenic mountains evolved into a special, long-term bond.

In 2007, things changed for me once again because Michelle entered something new called TransRockies. It was the inaugural year for the race. TransRockies is held in Colorado in August and involves trail running above 8,000-feet elevation with the high point being Hope Pass at 12,600-feet elevation. It is 120 miles in total distance, but spread over six days. The new term I learned was "stage race." Back then, it was strictly teams of two racing together. Michelle and Adam Chase from Boulder, Colorado won the Mixed Team category that year.

After seeing all of her scenic pictures and asking her endless questions about this multi-day stage concept, I became convinced I could enjoy that race, too. Imagine all new mountain scenery in Colorado to toodle through and no 45-pound pack to carry! Just a three-pound hydration pack with a few lightweight emergency supplies. Aid stations, too.

I did my first TransRockies in August 2008. At age 68, I was the oldest runner. Steve Harvey and I were Team "California Old Goats." I have done it six times now and have *always* been the oldest runner. I am currently signed up to run it again in 2019—at age 80. This will be my third time teamed with Gordy Ainsleigh (age 72). If we pass you on the trails there, we hope you enjoy receiving one of our "California Old Goats" semi-famous "U Bin GEEZERed" cards.

Trail running, even at my easy pace, has kept me healthy, especially for my age. No one likes the thought of getting old and useless, so why allow that to happen? I hope my story gives all "young" people under 60 an awareness that if they keep walking and running, they can continue to do the same. If Geezer Doug (me) can do it and still have fun at 80, so can everyone. I'm proof that there is no reason to retire from physical activities and the health they bring.

—Doug Malewicki—

Olympic Dreams

The Olympics remain the most compelling search for excellence that exists in sport, and maybe in life itself.
~Dawn Fraser

The announcer's voice boomed over the PA system at the finish of the Senior Olympics triathlon. "And in first place overall…" I heard my name and ran up to the stage to collect my gold medal. As I stood on the stage, I choked back tears, overwhelmed by how far I'd come — from the devastating diagnosis of breast cancer to the winner in the Senior Olympics triathlon!

What a contrast from another day when I heard my name called; only this time it was in a doctor's office to receive the results of a biopsy. I was positive it couldn't be cancer because I was the fittest, healthiest person I knew. I was 47, running marathons, and I had been a daily runner for 14 years. I'd given up red meat, eating what I thought was a healthy diet.

When I heard the words, "infiltrating ductal carcinoma," a wild panic seized me. I wanted to scream, "No, wait a minute. Wait just a darn minute — I can't have cancer! I'm a marathoner, for Pete's sake!" The doctor showed me the pathology report. A sinking feeling overwhelmed me, my knees went weak, and my head swam. I barely heard the doctor's words, something about more surgery, chemo, radiation, and then more tests.

Then I thought back even further — to high-school days back in the 1950s when I took up swimming as my sport. Since I was the only female on the team, I was, by definition, the "best," which I needed to hear because I was usually last in racing with the boys. From there I entered the State Championships, winning a gold medal. My dreams went soaring! I would enter the Olympics and be an Olympic champion!

After graduating from high school and starting college, I found that between classes and the full-time job required to pay my way through college, there was little time to train. I decided that all kids have dreams of being a champion athlete, movie star or President, but day-to-day working and studying are usually the stark reality. My dream faded over the years.

In 1968, I saw the book, *Aerobics*, by Kenneth Cooper, MD. I wondered what that word meant since I'd never seen it before—not surprising since Dr. Cooper had just coined the word. Thumbing through the book, I learned about running's many benefits. In fact, for every ailment I had, it seemed that running was the answer, from head to toe, insomnia to flat feet!

I bought the book and devoured it in one sitting. I finished about 2:00 a.m., falling asleep but determined to start a running program. I woke up at 5:00 a.m., an hour earlier than usual. Jumping out of bed, I scrambled through my closet and found my old tennis shoes, some shorts, and an old T-shirt.

It felt really weird when I started running. I was thankful that nobody in the neighborhood was yet awake because I certainly would have been embarrassed!

I continued to the end of my street, a half-mile away. I was feeling pretty smug, thinking that if I ran all the way home, I would have run a whole mile! I felt so energized, fit and strong that I decided to do this routine every morning. As I got stronger, I extended the turnaround point.

One day, someone mentioned a race coming up, a three-mile Turkey Trot. I thought it might be fun; plus, I wondered how I'd do after nearly five years of running.

As I toed the start line, I looked around and saw nothing but guys. "Wow, I'm the only female here—just like the high-school swim team," I told myself.

This was 1973, when road racing was just getting started with very few men and even fewer women. Since all I had to do was finish, I came home with a gold medal, an automatic first place. I was excited about my new road-racing career, training to go farther and faster. As women started to enter, there were age divisions. As I got older, I was still winning and racking up gold medals.

The diagnosis of breast cancer didn't fit, and yet there it was. Then I learned two things that turned my life around. First, foods made from animal products increase the risk for cancer. Second, cancer cells thrive in an anaerobic (no-oxygen) environment. Running is aerobic, so it had to have been my diet. I changed to a low-fat, vegan diet.

Then I saw the 1982 Ironman Triathlon on TV. I decided that just in case running wasn't aerobic enough, I would start swimming again and add cycling to be really sure. To give me a goal, I sent in my application to do the Ironman. Never mind that no woman my age had ever completed one; never mind that I was now a cancer patient. I trained and got stronger. My goal of becoming an Ironman became a reality. I'd never been this fit in my whole life, and I was in my fifties!

One day, someone said, "Why don't you enter the Senior Olympics?" My Olympics dream came rushing to the forefront. That old surge of excitement and challenge was almost palpable. The next Senior Olympics was in Las Vegas. I sent in my application, got plane reservations, and doubled my training.

Once in Vegas, I checked the venue of the triathlon course. The street names meant nothing, but thinking I didn't need to worry about the course, I figured I would just follow the person in front. But, to my great surprise and shock, I was first out of the water and first on the course. I had no one to follow!

Here I was in first place, and I was going to blow it by getting lost. I steadied myself, coming up with a strategy: "When in doubt, go straight." My heart settled down, but the anxiety was almost unbearable as I pedaled as fast as I could. I kept waiting for the sign, fearing that someone would overtake me, and I'd lose first place. I also thought it would be a tremendous coup to beat all the men, so I wasn't about to slow down.

Finally! There was the sign pointing to a right turn. What a relief! The relief, however, was short-lived. *Where do I go from here?* "Settle down, lady. Remember, when in doubt, go straight." That strategy got me through both the bike and run, and I crossed the finish line first overall!

Standing on that stage, I thought how far-fetched the whole drama was. Here I was 61 years old, and I'd just won an Olympic gold medal. This taught me to never give up on our dreams, even if they are Olympic dreams — Senior Olympic dreams!

— Ruth Heidrich, Ph.D. —

The Trail to Myself

You can't change who you are, but you can change what you have in your head, you can refresh what you're thinking about, you can put some fresh air in your brain.
~Ernesto Bertarelli

On the morning of my 45th birthday, I stood at the bathroom mirror and stared at a reflection that startled me. "You have a problem," I said to the woman glaring back at me. Resentment and fear showed in her eyes. She was angry with me. And I was disappointed in her.

The past decade had been a whirlwind of work, travel and staggering stress. I had evolved into someone I didn't like very much and allowed myself to veer off-track; it felt like I was living someone else's life. The power to my creative outlets had been shut off and I had stopped writing.

Privately, I was fighting a battle against brain fog and depression. And I feared I'd never be able to end my love/hate relationship with alcohol.

Physically, I was just as broken. An unhealthy lifestyle had padded my body with excess pounds. My knees ached, my back hurt, and I was plagued with insomnia. Mornings were like a bad dream and required large doses of coffee and ibuprofen, an attempt to take the edge off the pulsing headache that resulted from the glasses of wine I'd consumed the night before.

I didn't know myself anymore. Oh, how I missed that adventurous, creative girl who had a passion for words and art and loved the outdoors. I longed to get in touch with her again.

That encounter in the mirror, followed by an argument with my husband, were the push I needed to reclaim control of my life. My husband told me I'd probably feel better if I'd "just get out of the damn house once in a while." So, I did. The argument ended when I grabbed my coat and walked out the front door.

Outside, I stared into the gray January sky. Then, without thinking, I put one foot in front of the other and followed the pavement. I was a mile from home when I realized I hadn't even thought about the argument. The world around me came into focus, and a tiny spark of hope fired in my brain. As I turned toward home, I considered the possibility of making a new start — where pursuing creativity seemed the most logical solution to my troubles.

That first mile began a chain reaction of events that would reshape me — literally — and give me renewed purpose. I enrolled in a program to help me stop drinking, and then purchased a fitness tracker and a new pair of sneakers. It was the beginning of a journey that would eventually lead me to someone I'd been dying to meet — me.

By March, there was a noticeable difference in my outward appearance, but the real changes were happening on the inside. As the weeks passed, I transitioned from sidewalks to walking paths to narrow, winding mountain trails. And by summer, my new addiction was fresh air and altitude.

Something powerful happened on those rocky forest trails. There was shift. My brain started functioning at a higher frequency — as if someone had flipped a switch and turned on the creative energy. The inner critic fell silent, as I let my thoughts wander and explore, the same way I let my eyes explore the landscape. Not only did those steps and miles help me decompress, but they invited a world of new stories and ideas to unfold.

My senses came to life as I learned how to use meditation and mindfulness. As I hiked, I focused on the rhythmic *crunch, crunch, crunch* of the trail under my shoes and the whisper of wind through the pines. I noticed everything. Tiny ants clung to blades of grass, and chattering birds scolded me from the branches overhead. I breathed in the rich scent of loamy earth on north-facing hillsides, where the sun warmed my face, and cool, damp air caressed my arms. I stopped often to take it all in — to breathe, whisper a few words of gratitude, and capture the experience with my camera.

All this led to a physical transformation that resulted in more than 30 pounds of weight loss and eliminated a long list of aches and pains. It also led to a spiritual transformation, where I gave myself permission to stop ignoring my calling. That small, creative voice that used to hide behind excuses was now running down the trail in front of me, waving and shouting, "Come on, follow me!"

The trail saved my life. It made me sane. Made me strong. And helped me find myself again.

What started as a simple "time out" on a cold, winter afternoon led me to the place I was meant to be — which, most days, is spent in front of a computer screen, crafting stories and editing images I hope someone, somewhere will enjoy. But I'm always within calling distance of a trail — that place I go to often to rediscover my joy and reconnect with a world of age-old miracles and new ideas.

— Ann Morrow —

Learning to Listen

Every day is a good day when you run.
~Kevin Nelson

When you run, you learn to listen
to your body: the tiny bones
of your feet as your shoes
tap the pavement — from sidewalk
to street you pad along
on tree-lined paths
accompanied by birdsong.

You grow to expect your quads
to respond, your calves
to urge you on, your wind
to answer the call
as you pass your mile markers.

On moist days, your knees
creak, cranky beneath
thin skin, scar tissue,
tendons that strain
under your weight.

Only when you stop
can you hear your heart,
blood pulsing in
your neck, wrist, chest,
repeating, "This is what
we were meant to do."

—Ed Meek—

Chemotivation

Motivation remains key to the marathon:
the motivation to begin; the motivation to continue;
the motivation never to quit.
~Hal Higdon

One of the first things I learned after hearing the words "you have cancer" was that my body no longer belonged to me. The following days become a whirlwind of scans, blood work, bone-density tests, poking, prodding, and doing what I was told.

When I was diagnosed with non-Hodgkin's follicular lymphoma, I was a 43-year-old, salad-eating, three-mile-a-day running, full-time working, all around healthy woman. I didn't feel sick. When my doctor called with the news, I told him politely that he was wrong. He assured me he was not. Then the tests began, and I, like so many before me, surrendered my body to the process.

I decided early on that I would never be identified by this disease. Instead, I transformed myself into "The Happy Patient," always smiling and cracking jokes with the office staff. When the receptionist brought my liquid contrast, which I was to drink before my CT scans, I would quip, "Wow! You brought refreshments! How lovely!" The phlebotomist at my oncologist's office nicknamed me "Sunshine." I was fantastic at hiding my fear. Cancer schmancer!

Then my chemo started. The treatment for follicular lymphoma is much milder than other cancers. They said my hair would thin, not completely fall out. (For the record, it all stayed, but my curly locks went straight. Weird!) I wouldn't suffer the harsh nausea and vomiting side effects, but lesser ones like anemia, fatigue, and neutropenia were likely. I was given a large binder filled with all the information I'd need concerning the drug and its side effects, along with deep detail concerning my plan of treatment. I never read it. I tried a few times, but it scared me, so I put it down. I figured I'd consult it on a "need to know" basis, which seemed much less daunting.

I figured my chemo would last the normal three to six months, give or take a few weeks. At the conclusion of the first month, my husband Alan and I began to plan how we'd celebrate after my last treatment. Take a trip? Throw a party? The possibilities were exciting! Alan suggested the fantastic idea of running the Chicago Marathon. What better way to prove I was back, strong and healthy as ever?

We signed up in February while sitting in the infusion room, my chemo IV delivering its life-saving medicine into my veins. We figured I'd have just another month or two of this, with plenty of time left to train for the race in October.

But the chemo appointments kept coming. And coming. Finally, I broke down and asked the research nurse how much longer it was going to take. She hauled out my big, fat chart and began thumbing through papers. Then she paused, looked up at Alan and me, and murmured quietly, "It says here your treatment will conclude in 30 months." Thirty months. That's two-and-a-half years, if you're attempting the math.

I'm not going to lie; that was a hard day. But we recovered quickly. I said to Alan, "I think we should run it anyway." Granted, I wasn't going to break any speed records, but I still felt like I could do it. I had to. We asked my oncologist for permission. I could have kissed him when he said, "Hey, if you feel like you're up to it, knock yourself out." What a peach!

Alan downloaded a training program, and we began our schedule in mid-July. We found a park with several shady trails and immediately designated it our spot for long runs. On the days when I wasn't feeling great, we'd just take it slow and easy. But we always finished. After every run, I'd cross that day off the schedule, another workout in the books, another step closer to race day.

Early on, I started noticing something profound happening. I was taking back control of my body. I wasn't sitting in a chair, trying to act positive and smile while the poor new girl tried for the twelfth time to hit my vein before asking her superior for help. I was running. I wasn't sitting in the waiting room at the oncologist's, staring at the bald heads and skinny bodies, wondering if this was my future. I wasn't lying on a conveyor belt, dutifully holding my breath while being inserted in and out of a CT scan machine. I wasn't terrified. I was running. My body was all mine, all to myself, and the fresh air, singing birds, darting chipmunks, and my sweet husband yelling encouragement. Cancer couldn't have me during those runs; I was taken.

It didn't stop there. When race day arrived, I realized my task had become something greater. I was running for all of those who couldn't. I was running for that young, frail, bald man in the chemo chair next to mine and his twenty-something wife sitting quietly next to him, holding his hand and hiding her tears. I was running for all those weary people I sat with in that radiology waiting room, preparing to be scanned, praying for positive results. I was running for everyone who ever heard the words "you have cancer." I wore a T-shirt that read, "I Have Cancer. I'm on Chemo… SO?" Spectators on the route high-fived me and yelled, "Really? That's amazing!" I felt like a rock star.

Over five-and-a-half hours later, Alan and I crossed the finish line holding hands, our arms raised above our heads in exhausted victory. Take that, cancer!

The following Tuesday, I showed up for chemo, still sore and achy. But I wore a medal around my neck. I flashed it to everyone — the receptionists, the phlebotomist ("Sunshine! That's fantastic!"), the nurses (even the one who missed my vein 17 times again), the doctor, and every single patient sitting in those chairs hooked up to a bag of poison. We did it!

My cancer journey is not over. Although my current scans are clear, lymphoma is still in my blood. There is a high chance that the disease will flare up again one day, and chemo will be required once more. When I find myself fretting over these facts, I just remember that race. I run my fingers over my medal and recall that day I laced up my running shoes and stomped on follicular lymphoma for 26.2 miles. Cancer schmancer!

These days, I get calls occasionally from friends or family who have just been diagnosed themselves. They're shocked, nervous, and terrified. The first thing I say to them is, "You will get through this. If I can, anyone can. Actually, did I ever tell you about the time I ran a marathon?"

—Joan Donnelly-Emery—

Not a Typical Runner

Our running shoes have magic in them. The power to transform a bad day into a good day; frustration into speed; self-doubt into confidence; chocolate cake into muscle.
~Mina Samuels, Run Like a Girl

"You know, you don't have the body of a typical runner." I heard those words a few days ago from an acquaintance I bumped into at a grocery store. There was no preamble — no previous talk of running or anything of that nature. He's just someone on Facebook who sees my running posts, and I guess it was fresh on his mind so he decided to let me know his thoughts.

Alrighty then.

So... I don't have the body of a typical runner. Got it.

Later, when I mentioned this to my husband, he insisted that the guy couldn't have meant it "that way." You know: *that* way. As in, the way *I* took it. And how did I take it? He was saying that I was too fat to fit the stereotypical mold of a runner.

And as hard as I try, I can't think of anything else he could've meant. But you know what? That's okay.

Because he's right.

Let's just go ahead and get this out there: I'm a fat runner.

Now, I'm not obese by any means. I'm not even considered "overweight" on some charts. I'm five feet, six inches tall and weigh 152 pounds. But as far as runners go? Yep, I'm a chubster.

If you're not a runner, you may not be familiar with the fact that some races have what they call a "Clydesdale division." Yes, you read that right. Clydesdale. As in a big, fat horse. One local race I run annually has this very division. And guess what? I qualify. Yep. A five-feet-six-inch, 152-pound woman falls into the big and fat category. I've always been terrified to sign up for it, though. I don't know why. It's almost a guaranteed trophy because no one else signs up for it either. Last year, I watched the "winning" (only) woman in the category walk up to get her award, and she looked even smaller than me. I couldn't help but wonder how she felt walking up there. "And the chubby runner award goes to...!"

But you know what? After this random comment in the grocery store from this guy, I've given this a lot of thought. And I wonder if maybe I've been looking at this the wrong way.

Let me tell you what it's like to not be a tiny runner.

First, my legs are strong as crap. No joke. These things have to lug 152 pounds around — not 110. They have had to work hard these past five running years and, therefore, I have massive muscles. One day last week, I had to put down a new rug that needed to be scooted under a couch. Rather than waiting for help, I put out the footrests on the recliner end of the sofa, lay down on the floor, positioned my feet under the footrests, and used the strength in my legs to lift the couch while I scooted the rug underneath.

How about that?

I'm sure it wasn't pretty, but I got it done.

Also, fitness does not come naturally to me. I've never been an especially "active" person. In fact, I was pretty sick my senior year of high school, which left me weak and lazy for years. Before my lymphoma diagnosis, I weighed over 200 pounds. Of course, I lost some weight during the treatments, but it didn't stay away after I started improving. I've always been a "bigger" girl. After I started running five years ago, I dropped a bit of weight, but not a ton. And the funny thing about it?

I didn't even care.

I had attempted running so many times in the past for that very purpose — I just had to lose weight. But it never worked because I didn't stick with it. And I didn't stick with it because my heart was not in it. Once I made the decision to run to strengthen myself — body and mind — that's when I started noticing changes.

Another thing about being a not-so-small runner? I'm pretty slow. Now, I know — "slow" is relative. To some people, my 11/12:00ish-mile pace might seem fast. But trust me, in the racing community (especially the smaller races I do locally), that's not fast. In fact, I finished last in a local race once. Dead last. (It kind of sucked at the time, but now it's just a funny memory. And now that it's happened, I'm not scared of it happening again. I finished last. So what?)

So, yeah, I'm a chubby runner. But should I have been offended by what that guy said to me in the grocery store?

Heck no.

You know why? Because I still do it. Some days, I'd rather sit on the couch and drink Coke and eat ice cream instead of running; I still get my chubby butt up and do it. I know my "stats" will show up on Facebook when I post my runs, and they could be laughable to the more fit runners who see them, I just go on and post them anyway. I have fat rolls that show up in running pictures from races; I post the heck out of them anyway.

I am not trying to be skinny. I'm not trying to be perfect. I'm trying to be strong. I'm trying to be a motivator, both to others and to myself. I'm trying to show others that finding something you love as much as I love running can change you. And you don't have to fit a certain mold or look a certain way or be a certain speed to get out there and do it anyway.

This morning, I lost a running friend. She was the brightest ray of sunshine you'd ever meet in your life. In February of this year, Tammy was still running half marathons and signing up for full marathons later in the year. And then today, August 14th, six short months later, she's gone. Just like that. She lost her battle to a cancer she hadn't even known she had until recently.

I keep thinking about her. I think about her spunk. Her smile. Her laugh. I keep thinking about how much she adored running. I keep thinking about the last race we ran together. It was an unseasonably hot half marathon at the end of October. She was well ahead of me for most of the race, as usual. But with only about two miles to go, I couldn't run a step farther. I stopped and started walking. And, to my surprise, I saw Tammy just ahead of me as I rounded a corner. She was walking, too. Once she saw that I was behind her, she stopped dead still in the road, not caring about her time, and waited for me to catch up. We walked the last two miles together. She smiled, laughed and chatted the whole way, knowing that neither of us would have any kind of finishing time to brag about, yet not letting it bother her a bit. We were going to finish, and that's all that mattered to her.

That is what I'm going to carry forward with me—that determination, strength and knowledge that I may not be the best, but I am there. I am moving forward. Every step is taking me closer to the person I want to be. Like Tammy, I am learning to be happy just to be there. To just be a part of the process. To be a participant in this game of life and to enjoy every single second of it so that I leave behind a legacy like she did.

Am I going to let a snarky comment from some guy in a grocery store change that? No, sir, I am not. I won't let someone else determine who or what I should be.

Now, if you'll excuse me, I'm training for my ninth half marathon and second full marathon.

—Melissa Edmondson—

Bolo

Remember that it's never too late and you're never too old to get the body you were born to have.
~David Kirsch

My daughter is a runner. When she was a baby, she didn't just learn to walk; her first steps sent her running. I ran with her, or rather *after* her, to guide her past obstacles, but I was never built for running. It was obvious by the time she was eight that she could run circles around me and nearly everyone else. I used to call her my "deer." Not dear, but "deer"—she was that fast.

She was on the track team in school and never walked anywhere if she could run there instead. Of course, she was lean and sleek. Even in college, she had time for her morning run. If she was the family Greyhound, I was the family Pug.

She lived with her intended, a very nice fellow she met in college. The wedding was nearly a year away, but they could not wait to begin their life together and got a little apartment off campus while he finished his master's degree.

Since I'm a widow, Jenny and I used to have dinner together once or twice a week when her beau had a late class or a paper to research. But college and our separate to-do lists left her little time for leisurely eating. And she had races to prepare for. She asked if I wanted to go running with her, which made me laugh.

"Run?" I chuckled. "I haven't run since I used to chase you all over the neighborhood. I'm 20 pounds overweight and out of shape."

So, she didn't ask me again. She was training daily for a fall marathon.

One Saturday, she called and said she was going on a run with friends, who were also training for the marathon. "Lonny will be studying for an upcoming exam, and there's no one I can get to take out Bolo. Could you?" She was referring to her dog.

Bolo was her fiancé's dog. He was part Boxer, part something else, probably more "something else" judging from the haphazard way he was put together.

"When I come home, I'll bring Chinese," she said, bribing me.

It worked.

"Be sure to get his leash on him before you open the door," she warned. "Bolo means 'Be-On-the-Lookout-For.'"

Yeah, yeah.

I got to her place, re-met Bolo, and then my daughter was off on her run.

Bolo slept on the sofa while I cleaned up the breakfast dishes. Then it was time to take out the dog.

"Come, boy, want to go for walkies?"

He sure did. He was dancing, prancing and slinging drool from his floppy jaws. I got out his leash, glad it was a sturdy one, and prepared to clasp the hook onto his collar. He was wiggly, but I thought I had managed to clip the leash onto his collar. I opened the back door at the same instant that I saw the leash had only snagged a bit of his neck hair, not the collar. Before I could do a thing about it, he was out.

"Bolo!" I yelled, but he was gone like a flash. That huge pony of a dog was galloping down the walk. I yelled again, but I could just as well yell the sun out of the sky as stop that racing dog.

There was no way I could catch him. He was at the corner of the block and across the street into the small park before I had gone 100 feet.

"Bolo out again?" a boy on a bike asked.

"Yeah," I gasped back, running faster than a 40-something, overweight woman should ever run.

"I'll help," he said, grabbing the leash and pedaling toward the park.

I was gasping by the end of the block. *I'm going to die right here,* I thought.

"Bolo on the run again?" a man, mowing, shouted. I nodded. I was too winded to speak.

"Try down by the lake," he said. He shut off his mower and took off after me, passing me as we crossed the street. "Sometimes, he likes to play in the water," he called back as he raced ahead at a pretty good pace for a guy who looked to be in his fifties.

The boy on his bike, the able 50-year-old man and the puffing woman strung out across the park, chasing after the dog.

"Bolo!" the boy called.

"Bolo!" the man repeated.

"Puff-puff," I gasped as we neared the lakeshore.

Sure enough, Bolo was splashing happily in the shallows of the lake.

The man caught up to him and held him as the boy brought forth the leash and clipped it on his collar.

I thanked the boy, who nodded and whizzed away on his bike without so much as one hard breath.

"I've run my first and last marathon," I puffed out between gasps.

The man laughed. "You're about a block from where your daughter lives."

"I was taking Bolo out for his walk. My daughter is training for a marathon."

"And he slipped away. Yes, he does that now and then. Are you Jenny's mom?" he asked.

I said I was, and he told me what a funny, joyous, bright girl my daughter was. He was right. I could have added that I was once like that.

I thought about that as the nice man, David, walked me back to my daughter's place. Bolo behaved nicely once on his leash.

We stopped and continued to chat.

"Jenny said she'd bring Chinese on her way home," I said. "You know how they pack so much food in those little boxes. I'm sure…" I started to say, and then realized what I was doing. I know I blushed. I could feel the heat on my face.

"I'd love to," David replied.

"My daughter said she'd be home around six."

He waved and went on to his mower, and I walked Bolo back to my daughter's apartment. Every bone in my legs, knees, and back ached with that sudden wild dash… yet, there was a new sort of exhilaration, too. Was that what running did?

I doubted it, but for once I felt free of my dirge, the sameness of my life. I would never be a runner, but maybe a nice, brisk walk now and then… Who knows where that could lead?

— Nancy Lee Davis —

A Way of Life

Walking is the best possible exercise.
Habituate yourself to walk very far.
~Thomas Jefferson

"You walk so much," a friend said recently. "I bet you can eat anything you want without gaining weight!"

"You could, too," I pointed out. "Anyone can walk."

"But I don't like to walk," she said.

Don't like to walk? To me, that's like saying, "I don't like to breathe."

I don't just like to walk. I *love* to walk. I walk all the time. I walk everywhere. I walk so much that I have no need for a step tracker.

I scoff at your daily 10,000 steps. Ha! I cover that much ground before lunch.

My lifestyle of incessant walking began 30 years ago when I was diagnosed with endometriosis. I discovered that lots of walking lessened the pain, so I re-tooled my life to include an unusual amount of walking, and I've been walking ever since.

It started as something that was good for me—but it's turned into something I love.

I enjoy being outdoors, moving forward, attuned to the world around me. Breathing in the fresh air. Pausing to chat with my neighbors. Walking always makes me happy.

Unlike many serious walkers, I don't put on walking shoes and head down a trail. Instead, I've incorporated walking into every aspect of my daily life.

If you invite me to lunch, I'll counter with "Can we go for a walk instead?"

If you insist on enjoying a meal instead of a walk, I'll insist on walking to the restaurant... and back.

I walk to work every day. I've made sure that my bank, hairdresser, dentist and pharmacy are all within walking distance. I never get in my car unless I absolutely must.

Last year, my car's battery died because I didn't drive it often enough.

I walk with friends. I walk the dog. When my grandson needs a nap, I stroll him around the block until he falls asleep, and then continue to stroll with a sleeping baby—one of the best walks there is.

And, thanks to my treadmill (and my smart phone), I also enjoy frequent walks with my pal Irene, even though she lives in Seattle and I live in Philadelphia.

Sometimes, you need to be a little creative to get in a walk. When my son was little, he wasn't wild about walking, so I would bribe him to go for a walk with me by paying him a nickel a block.

Once, snowed in at my then mother-in-law's tiny mobile home in the middle of a New Hampshire blizzard, I was so desperate for a walk that I put on my sneakers and circled her dining-room table for an hour. (Yes, she thought I was nuts. But if you want to be a truly devoted walker, you have to be willing to be unconventional.)

I always dress for walking. All of my shoes are comfortable walking shoes. I don't even own a pair of heels. I'll never turn up at your dinner party in the height of fashion. But I can walk to that party... and back.

Bad weather rarely slows me down. Unless there's an actual tornado or lightning storm in progress, I walk instead of driving. Do I occasionally get caught in a downpour? Absolutely! But I'm not scared of getting soaked. That's why there are hot showers. And once you've accepted that you're going to get drenched, it's fun to walk in the rain.

Another plus? One cannot waste the time of an obsessive walker who has a treadmill.

Whenever Comcast puts me on hold, I just hop on and stroll along to the canned music until the person I was speaking with returns. As the minutes go by, I'm not fuming about the fact that my valuable time is being wasted. I'm enjoying an extra walk!

And now that I've joined an online dating service, I conduct all those obligatory getting-to-know-you phone calls at 1.8 miles an hour. "Hey… are you on the treadmill?" a prospective date might ask suspiciously at the faint sound of my treadmilling feet going *thump, thump, thump*.

"Why, no," I'll fib. "Unless, that is, you're interested in strolling into the sunset with somebody who *really* likes to stroll."

I have yet to meet Mr. Right, but when I do, I'll enter into the relationship with excellent muscle tone and plenty of stamina.

As much as I love my treadmill, most of my walking takes place outside in the fresh air. Over time, I've become a beloved neighborhood character — "The Librarian Who Walks Everywhere." As my neighbors drive by, they'll give me a cheerful honk.

"I always see you walking!" they'll tell me later.

"Feel free to join me," I'll respond. I truly wish more of them would.

Walking is good for your health. It gets you out of the house and in touch with the world around you. It makes you happy — you'll be high on endorphins all day! It's good for the planet.

And, of course, you can eat whatever you want without gaining an ounce.

— Roz Warren —

Flock Around the Block

Nothing builds self-esteem and self-confidence like accomplishment.
~Thomas Carlyle

When our two sons were young, I looked for ways our family could volunteer. A friend introduced me to the Interfaith Council on Poverty, a collection of churches that ministered to the needy in our community. We were soon delivering Thanksgiving baskets to elderly residents, filling in at the food pantry, and packing boxes with Christmas gifts for low-income families. Interfaith projects became annual events for us.

But I didn't know what I was getting into when my husband and I joined a different congregation, and I began representing our new church at Interfaith board meetings. Veteran members I'd worked alongside for years welcomed me to the board.

Two months later, they elected me president.

Wait, what? "Well, somebody has to do it," they said, "and you know as much about our projects as anyone. We'll help you."

I sighed and gave in.

Fall neared, and we began discussing Interfaith's only fundraiser, a 5K run called Flock Around the Block. One of our member churches sponsored it. This year, they'd arranged for professional timers so runners could use the race as a qualifier for later marathons, encouraging more entries. They also offered a $100 prize to the top finisher.

The event organizer addressed the board in her no-nonsense

manner. "All the Council members need to sign up."

Me? Run? No way! I was always the nonathletic kid who got a stitch in her side just playing volleyball.

"You don't have to run," she continued. "Plenty of walkers participate."

I walked regularly around the lake in our subdivision. I could make the two miles in an unimpressive 40 minutes. But five kilometers is over three miles. How would it look for the Council president to drag in an hour after the race started? No.

"We've had moms push strollers and even some people participate in wheelchairs."

Yeah, those moms probably had the fancy jogging strollers with three huge wheels designed for runners. Now, wheelchairs—that was more my speed.

"And remember, this is for Interfaith."

I sighed and gave in. Again. After all, how would it look if the Council president didn't participate?

The day of the race dawned cold and clear. Little puffs of vapor rose from the lips of participants as they mingled and warmed up. I had talked my husband, Stan, into joining me, and we filled out application cards complete with gender and birth dates so we could be placed in appropriate categories. I wasn't worried about him. He had played soccer for years and was in great shape. I just hoped to finish the course. On two feet.

"I don't see a lot of people our age here. Maybe we stand a chance at winning a medal," Stan said, eyeing the awards table.

I shot him a look that said he'd lost his mind, and he made no more mention of prizes.

At last, police cars blocked traffic from the race route, and runners, walkers, and potential crawlers lined up. The starting whistle blew, and the crowd surged forward. Soon, serious runners pulled ahead, and the rest broke into little knots, walking at different speeds. I could tell Stan was itching to run, and I told him to go ahead. I would be fine.

"No, we're doing this together," he said. "Let's see if we can pass this group."

I saw mostly older ladies in front of us, chatting together as they walked. That looked doable. I walked a little faster, and we overtook them. After that, my husband encouraged me to pass group after group. It became a challenge as I put on the speed, becoming a power walker — at least for me. We left the 1K and 2K markers behind, and I was still going strong.

As the finish line came within sight, I encouraged Stan to go for it, and he broke into a run, passing several others. Then someone tried to pass me. How dare she! By the final few feet, the race was on. While I wouldn't say I was running, I still made a stoic effort and crossed the finish line just behind my rival to the cheers of my husband and others who had completed the race. I placed the card with my finishing time in the correct age basket and walked around, basking in the race afterglow.

When an announcer presented the prizes, I wasn't surprised that my husband won first place in his age group. But when they called my name as the first-place winner, I thought it must be a mistake. Stan assured me it wasn't. I'd beaten four other women in my category. And I did it without getting a stitch in my side.

Altogether, the race netted more than $2,500 for the food pantry and other projects. As president of the Interfaith Council, I was thrilled. That was the whole purpose of the event, after all. But as a race participant, I felt an unexpected satisfaction in excelling where I thought I might fail. I still have my winning medal, and now I know I can flock around the block with the best of them.

— Tracy Crump —

Sole to Soul

The further you get away from yourself,
the more challenging it is. Not to be in
your comfort zone is great fun.
~Benedict Cumberbatch

As an avid walker, past smoker and middle-aged woman, running was not on my bucket list! But my friend Mary encouraged me to run my first 5K. I decided to learn about running as a sport at the age of 45.

I showed up one early, foggy morning for a 5K, scared, nervous and unsure as to whether I could even attempt that distance and race against others. I won my age group that day, received a medal for my efforts, and was hooked from that moment on.

I ran in the heat, rain, below-freezing temperatures, on city sidewalks, dirt roads, through cotton fields, pine plots, beaches and mostly alone. I learned along the way to find delight in my surroundings, including stunning sunrises, picture-perfect sunsets and the most spectacular scenery that can only be appreciated on foot.

I started looking for races outside of my comfort zone. I also found my tribe! A local group of women who were serious runners asked me to join them in training for the same half marathon I had signed up for. They encouraged, mentored and supported me in every way. My first half marathon was completed in November 2015 in Savannah, Georgia, on a record-breaking hot day.

I became a new person. I was now a distance runner! I set new goals, conquered fears, and overcame doubts… and I signed up for a marathon.

Our group, the Running Girlz — Bonnie, Laura, Tamara, Pam, Vicki, Sheri, Alisha and Mindy — all formed wonderful relationships, spending countless hours training together for common and individual goals. Ice packs, Epsom salt baths, foam rolling, determination and constant encouragement from friends and family got me through the six months of intense training. The Walt Disney World Marathon in January 2017 is now completed and checked off my list!

Not only was I a runner, I was now a marathoner.

I decided that my next challenge would be to "run somewhere breathtaking." The Great Smoky Mountains Half Marathon in September 2017 fit the bill. Because of the distance from home and the timing, this became a solo adventure. I'm from Florida, where it's mostly flat, so it was difficult to train for the mountain elevations.

On race day, it was a beautiful 50 degrees, perfect running weather. The scenery was indeed "breathtaking." Then I met Rita! Along mile 8, I noticed that a woman and I kept passing one another on the course. We introduced ourselves and began to chat. Finally, we were at the same spot at the same time and began walking together. We both felt fatigued from the extreme hills, so we challenged each other to different goals along the course. We finished the race with smiles and thumbs-ups for the event photographer. I treasure our finish-line photo and display it proudly. Rita lives in California, but we have maintained a long-distance friendship via social media since that memorable day in the Smokies.

Putting on a pair of running shoes has been life changing for me. Running has nourished my spirit. It has proved to me that I can do anything I put my mind to. If I had not put on those shoes, I would have missed some of life's most valuable treasures, those sensational natural backdrops, memorable events and fascinating new friendships.

I believe my journey is unlike any other. No one did it for me; I earned every mile. I turned my fear into courage. I have found a deeper strength than I ever imagined. I have been dead last over a finish line. I have been first over a finish line. I have run my way through menopause. I've received big hugs and high-fives! I have found joy, but most of all, I found myself.

— Rene Jordan —

Friends for the Long Run

Most often, it is not the workout that gets us out of bed in the morning. It is the friendships and unspoken bonds of those counting on us to show up.
~Author Unknown

I gave birth to four sons in six years, so our home was chaotic. My days were a haze of diapering, feeding, and napping. I missed many aspects of life before kids and I craved adult interaction. But more than anything, I yearned to slide into my familiar running shoes and jog along the trails. However, finding time to run proved challenging.

Then, I came upon Emily, an acquaintance and mother of four young girls, in the frozen-food section of the grocery store. "I just went for a run," she announced while dropping frozen peas into her grocery cart.

I barely contained my surprise. "How on earth did you run?"

"I woke up early and ran at 5:30," she responded. "There's a whole group that meets in the morning to run. You should run with us."

She had said 5:30 — in the morning. Clearly, we weren't connecting. I gazed at her with a look of concern. Did she really expect this sleep-deprived mama to get up even earlier than usual?

"Just try it," she coaxed. "I promise you'll love it."

With nothing to lose but sleep, I set my alarm clock for 5:10 a.m.

The next morning, the alarm blared too soon. I jolted out of bed and slipped on my running clothes. With bleary eyes, I drove to the trail and pulled into the parking lot. Under a blanket of darkness, I eyed five women huddled together. I tumbled out of the car and lumbered toward the group.

Emily made introductions. Minutes later, the group surged forward and fell into step. The conversation meandered along the trail. We were all young mothers facing similar joys and challenges. Despite being strangers, I immediately sensed a kinship.

"Has anyone tried sleep training a baby?" inquired Marie around the first mile marker.

For the next few miles, the group chatted about nap times and sleep schedules. Gwen shared her recommendations on potty training. At mile 5, Maggie delivered a funny story. The group erupted into laughter. Less than an hour later, we arrived back at the parking lot. In the span of a run, these strangers morphed into friends.

It's been almost a decade since that first run. Most mornings, the group still meets at the same trailhead. Over the years, a few women have left the group due to moves and injuries. Some fresh faces have joined the ranks. Core members arrive faithfully at the trail.

We run in all four seasons. In the winter, we bundle in layers and brave the snow and frigid conditions. In the summer, we battle humidity and heat. It seems friendship makes any sort of running weather bearable.

Our children have grown older. We are now mothers of teenagers. On runs, our conversations center on driver's licenses, college admissions, and prom dates. We bemoan screen time and mouthy teens, while we celebrate scholarships and newfound independence.

"Any recommendations on a hairdresser for prom?" Nicole asked the group recently on a run.

Running friends tossed out a few names while jogging along the trail. The chatter drifted between dresses, tuxedo rentals, and bargain shoes.

Over runs, we've cried alongside women battling family problems, deaths, and discord. We've run wearing birthday tiaras and laughed until our sides ached. We have trodden upon every topic under the sun and still have more words to say.

Suzanne's youngest child just graduated from high school. On a run, she expressed a gamut of emotions. The trail provided a perfect venue to share the sweet sadness of letting go.

In a few more years, we'll all face the inevitable shift of life. Our children will fly the nest. I imagine those runs will become even more precious.

With each step, we cling to the women we have run alongside for years. We don't charge toward a finish line, since none exists for this group. The miles lead us to a better destination: each other.

— Rebecca Wood —

One Step at a Time

The Better Half of a Marathon

There is a moment in every race. A moment where you can either quit, fold, or say to yourself, "I can do this."
~Jerry Lynch

"What do you think about running a half marathon?" my wife asked.

"I try not to think about it," I answered. "Just the thought of it makes me sore and exhausted."

Even though I was an occasional runner, I had never considered a distance of 13.1 miles as something I would want to run. I wasn't sure that 47 was the right age to start doing so. But my age was only my first excuse.

"I've never run that far. I don't know if I can."

"I don't think I have the knees for such a long distance."

"The race isn't for another 12 months. I'm not sure we should register yet, in case I change my mind."

After one of my excuses, my wife said, "I'm going to register, and you're coming with me either way, so you can either watch or run. I've always wanted to do it, but I'm not sure I can train by myself or even finish if I'm not being pushed by someone else. I think we need to do it together."

And that is what nudged me to the starting line of a half marathon with my better half. Her idea to be a team sounded reasonable to me.

At least she wasn't asking me to run a *full* marathon. We would run the first 13.1 miles of a marathon and stop at that. I don't think anyone can argue that the better half of a marathon is the first 13.1 miles. The first half seemed like enough; we could avoid the last half. So we registered for the race and started training.

We were in better running shape than we'd ever been, although race day would be the first time we would run a consecutive 13.1 miles. Just as we had broken down our training into smaller segments, we paid attention to the shorter distances during the race. We had our best three-mile time and our best six-mile time. We seemed to be trucking along at a better pace than ever before, but as we approached the 10-mile marker, my wife's actions made it clear why I was needed. I heard some noises next to me that did not sound like heavy breathing.

"Are you crying?" I asked. She warned me this might happen. Just like anyone, she knew that her emotions could get the better of her when the pain of exercise was too much to bear.

"I don't want to do it anymore," she said. "Everything hurts."

I may have been running for my own health and sense of accomplishment, but this moment was the real reason I was on that racecourse. At that point, I realized something: I may have trained to run 13.1 miles by pounding the pavement, but I had trained through the exact same number of years of marriage to be by my wife's side no matter what. I was there to help her get through this challenge, even if I wasn't too sure she was going to listen to me, so I tried to distract her from the pain.

"Do you know how long we've been married?" I asked.

"Thirteen years," she responded.

"And how far are we running?"

"Thirteen miles."

"That is not a coincidence. We are finishing together. You are not stopping. We've got this. You are not going to leave me here to do this by myself."

I may not be much of a motivator, but it was enough to keep her going. We didn't go fast, but we kept steady. We passed the 10-mile marker, gave each other a high-five, and kept going. As we passed the 12-mile marker, we had been running side by side for two hours and

45 minutes, giving each other a high-five at every mile marker, as if celebrating a yearly anniversary for each mile. I realized that we were definitely going to meet her first goal of finishing. But if she wanted to meet her second goal of crossing the line under three hours, then we would have to pick up the pace for the last mile, which we did. We completed our first half marathon together, clocking the exact same time as we crossed the finish line in unison.

She posted a photo of us crossing the finish line on social media. We had smiles on our faces despite the pain, sweat, and tears. She wrote: "It's been on my bucket list for a long time. Last weekend, I got to check off my first (and perhaps last) half marathon. I could not have done it without my husband by my side every step of the way." I also realized after the race that our most recent anniversary, which had only been a few weeks before the race, was also our champagne anniversary, celebrating 13 years on the May 13th date of our wedding. Thirteen seemed to be our number — in miles and years — so it was inevitable that I finish the better half of a marathon with my better half. It was a challenge I never would have undertaken without her.

— Darin Cook —

The Night Running Saved My Life

The only journey is the journey within.
~Rainer Maria Rilke

I'll never forget the day that running changed my life. On September 18, 2010, I got into a huge fight with my fiancé. Angrily, I got dressed in the only sub-par workout clothes I owned, and I stormed out of the house in the heat of battle. I just had to get away! I took off down the street at a full sprint.

I was 70 pounds overweight and very unhealthy. My body just couldn't keep up with the emotions I was feeling. I was so angry with him, and running it out suddenly felt like the only way to find comfort. After about a half-block, I was out of breath, and it felt like my chest was caving in. Not only was I still angry with him, but I was angry with myself, too. The world felt so small, and I had so much frustration. I couldn't see straight, and I couldn't hear anything except myself gasping for air and my heartbeat pounding in my ears.

In that dark and somewhat embarrassing moment, I felt my spirit sing. I may have been very overweight and completely out of shape, but I could clearly see a way out. I saw a version of the person I knew I could be. I felt for the person who had somehow gotten lost deep beneath the emotional eating, the apathy for life, and turmoil. It was a strange juxtaposition between the life I'd been living and the life I felt I should have been living all along. Capturing my emotions and running with them made me feel freer than I'd ever felt before.

I remember clearly getting to the end of a three-quarter-mile strip from my house and collapsing onto the sidewalk, and then bursting into tears. Finally, I began to grieve. I was grieving for a childhood laden with trauma, and a young adulthood rife with the development of unhealthy coping mechanisms. Then, out of nowhere and clear as day, I saw a vision of who was living underneath all the physical and emotional baggage. I checked in with myself for the first time, maybe ever.

Who was I? Who did I want to be? How was I going to get there? How had things in my life gotten so convoluted? I felt like I'd been playing someone else's role in a play. I never really fit in. Until that run, I'd been slipping further and further into depression and bitterness; I'd been distancing myself from my potential.

After that night, I ran almost every night. Every step helped undo the years of hurt and abuse. After a time, I lost 70 pounds, found the courage to leave my fiancé, found my voice, and finally became the person hiding underneath.

I have grown so much since that time. Every step I've taken has moved me forward. The catharsis of that night still echoes across my life every single day. Nothing offers stark perspective quite like racing down the road as fast as your legs can carry you in the middle of the night. Nothing allows your internal voice to become louder than when there's only the sound of your feet plodding down the pavement. In that moment, I finally heard my inner self crying out for love, help, and acceptance.

My life has been changed indelibly. Now, I've explored most avenues that fitness has to offer. I have run 5Ks, a 10K, a half marathon, and tons of obstacle races. I've lifted weights, cycled, and done HIIT and CrossFit. In all of that, I can't help but reminisce about the night when running saved my life.

Now a personal trainer, I always tell my clients, "If I can do it, so can you." Truer words have never been spoken. Getting out there and taking those first few brave steps into the future became my saving grace. Running will always hold a very sacred place in my heart.

—Elizabeth Calcutt—

Can't Bring Me Down

The reason we race isn't so much to beat each other...
but to be with *each other.*
~Christopher McDougall, Born to Run

A little over three miles into the 2015 Los Angeles Marathon, my first-ever 26.2-mile adventure, I noticed a group of runners wearing Down syndrome awareness T-shirts. My little buddy Brianna, who "rocks an extra chromosome," was my inspiration for running. We'd been paired together in 2013 through I Run 4, an organization that matches runners with people who have special needs, and we've supported one another through the miles and milestones ever since.

I always loved meeting other advocates, so I ran up alongside the group. A young girl turned to me with a big smile. Her familiar facial features caught me off-guard. "You're doing great!" she said. The Brushfield spots in her almond-shaped eyes sparkled as she held out a hand for a high-five.

It was her first marathon, too, but she wasn't worried about it. She and her friends were running as a team in a relay. Some of them had Down syndrome and others didn't, but they were all in it together. I told her about Brianna, and that I hoped one day my little buddy and I could run this race together.

"Tell her she can do it!" she said, and I promised I would.

I'd always heard that the marathon was the great equalizer of races, the one that would test my limits and show me what I was really made of. But it wasn't the distance that made Los Angeles so memorable. It was the other runners I met, and the limits and labels they challenged every step of the way to the finish line.

Everyone runs for a reason. Some of us run toward goals; others run to overcome obstacles. We run to prove others wrong, or to prove ourselves right. At times, I've run to clear my mind and forget; other times, I've run to remember. Some people, though my husband will argue this, run just because it's fun. He runs only when the Air Force tells him he has to.

I've been in the Army National Guard for almost 20 years, and even though running has been a requirement for me for the past two decades, I haven't always loved it. My frustrated podiatrist will agree that I was not born with a body that supports running, but the Army doesn't believe in excuses like that. Luckily, I was born with stubborn pride and ferocious determination, and they were enough to keep me going.

Brianna gave me a renewed sense of purpose and a new way to define myself as a runner. She was just 11 months old when we were first matched. She hadn't stood up or taken her first steps yet. I hadn't run a full marathon yet, either.

But just because we hadn't didn't mean we wouldn't. Children with Down syndrome are too often labeled as limited, simply because of their diagnosis. Brianna may have been born with an extra copy of her 21st chromosome, but she was born to a family that didn't believe in limits or labels as much as they believed in her. Brianna would accomplish her goals in her own time, and I'd cross that marathon finish line in mine.

Runners, by nature, are a very positive and encouraging community. Tim Boyle did a great thing when he started I Run 4. A Facebook post from his buddy, Michael Wasserman, who has Down syndrome, inspired him to help others build similar friendships.

It's absolutely amazing how much stronger and more capable I felt every morning when I woke up and posted photos and messages for Brianna. My days were made when her mom would share a video of my adorable little buddy. Our extended running family cheered together as Bri stood for the first time and spoke her first words. Hundreds of friends sent prayers when she was hospitalized with respiratory issues during a rough winter. Together, we were all stronger.

I mailed her my race medals, sent balloons for every birthday, and had a quilt made from our race T-shirts that she took with her on her very first day of kindergarten. Brianna and I met for the first time at a Down syndrome Buddy Walk in Texas, where she and her family lived. As fate would have it, a couple of years later, I ended up moving there, too. In 2017, she was the flower girl in my wedding.

Brianna just turned six, and she knows more sign language than I do. She can build towers of tiny blocks that end up taller than she is. She can recognize all the words in the children's books I've written for her. She continues to accomplish her own goals on her own timeline. She can only be labeled as limitless. One day, if she wants to, I will happily return to Los Angeles to finish that marathon with her, in any way that works for us.

One of my former military commanders lived by the motto: "Life is a marathon, not a sprint." Those 26.2 miles in Los Angeles brought new meaning to that phrase for me, and so did Brianna. We live in a fast-paced world where it's easy to miss out on those big smiles and high-fives. But at the end of the race, those moments become the memories that make the ache worthwhile.

— Tammi Keen —

Aunt Fanny

We do not stop exercising because we grow old—
we grow old because we stop exercising.
~Kenneth Cooper

I looked up at the steeply pitched knotty-pine ceiling and thought of the danger faced by the workers during its construction. The organist played "To God Be the Glory" as I checked out my nearest unfamiliar neighbors. Directly in front of me, an older lady with perfectly styled gray curls sat at rigid attention. She wore an impeccable baby-blue suit. An older gentleman, whom I surmised to be her husband, sat beside her. His head leaned forward slightly, and I thought he might be dozing.

The music stopped, and Pastor Scarlett rose to his position behind the lectern. Even in preacher attire, he looked as friendly as when he had knocked on our door earlier in the week and invited us to church. We had moved to Florida to be near my husband's brother. Howard and his wife sat beside us on the slippery pew.

The hour-long service passed quickly, and soon we found ourselves in the foyer surrounded by friendly, inquisitive faces. The lady with the gray curls and blue suit was the first to greet us. Appearing to be in her sixties, she was slender like her husband and towered over my five feet, two inches.

"I see you've met Aunt Fanny," Pastor Scarlett said. He extended a warm hand and seemed genuinely happy we had responded to his invitation. "She's our go-to person whenever we need something done.

And if you come to our church suppers, her lemon pound cake and homemade peach ice cream will make you wonder how she stays so trim." He winked and moved on to greet others.

That first day in a new church, many in the congregation encouraged us to come back, and soon we became regulars. I spoke often with Aunt Fanny and found she really was always helping out in some way.

It wasn't long before I discovered how Aunt Fanny kept herself in such good shape. She walked. Every day. And as chance would have it, she always passed by the front of our development. So after a few weeks of getting friendly, it was natural for me to mention how I would enjoy walking with her sometime. She was delighted to hear that, and we arranged to meet out front the next morning at 9:00.

That evening, I confided my big plans for the next day to my husband.

"You're going walking with Aunt Fanny?" He had an astonished look on his face and a twinkle in his eye that soon metamorphosed into an all-knowing grin.

"What? You think I can't keep up with a woman twice my age? I'm no slouch, you know. I walk sometimes, too."

"I didn't say a thing. Go. Have fun."

Well, I'll show him a thing or two, I thought. That night, I laid out my almost brand-new jogging suit and my very brand-new Nikes. I heard a niggling little voice of self-doubt about my questionable athletic ability, but I ignored it. After all, Aunt Fanny was in her late sixties — 69, I heard someone say — and she certainly was not Wonder Woman!

Later that evening, I measured our route in the car. It was one-quarter mile to the front and two-and-one-quarter miles to our destination — a card shop where Aunt Fanny wanted to buy a variety of greeting cards. That would make my round trip a total of five miles. I had never actually walked five miles, but it didn't seem that far in the car.

The next morning, I stepped outside into an unusually warm November day. I was too proud of my jogging outfit to consider changing. I did a couple of stretches and took off at a slight jog toward the front of the development.

When I reached the main road, I could see Aunt Fanny coming

around the bend on the sidewalk. As she neared me, I gave her a big smile and prepared to chat about my morning. She breezed right past me, not missing a beat. With the smile frozen on my face, I ran to catch up. I noticed her flowing cotton shirt and comfortable-looking slacks. An old Braves baseball cap shaded her face, and a water bottle bounced on her hip.

"Wow, you must be in a hurry," I said, trying to catch my breath.

"Just my normal pace. Do you need me to slow down, honey?"

"Oh, no, I'm fine." What could I say? She was twice my age.

For every step she took, I had to take one-and-a-half or two to keep up. Supposedly, Florida is a flat state. That is not true. Several creeks run through our town, and each one has a valley and then a hill. It seemed like all the creeks converged on our route. And going downhill is no easier than going uphill. I began to feel burning pain on the backs of my heels inside those new Nikes, but there was no way I was going to mention it. Aunt Fanny took her walking seriously, and luckily for me, she did not believe in much chitchat. Whenever she did ask me something, I tried to answer in as few syllables as possible to hide my breathless condition.

When we reached the card shop, I thought we would take a break and recoup. Aunt Fanny went through that store like a bat out of you-know-where.

"Have to keep moving. Keep our blood flowing for our walk to do the most good." Those words were thrown back at me as she headed toward the checkout.

The cashier looked at me a little funny as I passed through. "Are you okay?"

I nodded. Aunt Fanny was already out the door and didn't hear.

The walk back was no easier than the first half had been, plus my heels were really stinging now, but I would not give in to my pain. Inside my warm jogging suit, I could feel the sweat trickling down my back. I practiced some slow, deep breathing I had learned from yoga. Finally, I reached the entrance to my development with Aunt Fanny none the wiser. I waved goodbye as she continued walking another mile to her home.

I slowed down but did not stop because I knew if I did, I probably would not be able to get started again. The first order of business when I got home was to remove those brand-new Nikes and peel off my socks. Thin strips of skin hung from the backs of my heels. Some stuck to the socks, and the separation brought tears to my eyes.

Resting, I thought about what had happened and what a ninny I had been to think that age alone could slow down a person. Granted, Aunt Fanny may not have been a normal 69-year-old, but maybe she was. I would not be making those kinds of assumptions ever again, especially about a regular walker.

— Connie Biddle Morrison —

The Thrill of Victory and the Agony of Da'feet

All you need is the courage to believe in yourself and put one foot in front of the other.
~Kathrine Switzer

The athletic world and I were never a good fit. I tried, but my fluffy physique kept me from success. As a child, we had an ice-skating rink in our back yard every winter. To hide my lack of skating ability, I constantly shoveled the ice like a human Zamboni. I would hear, "She can't skate. She's using that shovel just to stay up." Ice skating—off the list.

One summer, we got our first skateboards. My fearless sisters flew down our driveway like professional surfers. I rode that board lying on my stomach all the way down Embarrassment Hill. Skateboards—out!

In eighth grade, our girls' basketball team was short one player for the tournament. The team captain pleaded with the class, "Can anyone play today?" Tentatively, I raised my hand. "Anyone?" Thinking she didn't see me, I waved my arm. She did see me, but was hoping for someone else... anyone else. "If we don't fill that spot, we'll forfeit the tournament." I was the only one in the class offering. "Fine, we'll take Peppiatt, but we might as well forfeit." Sports—no!

With that history, why would I undertake a marathon? Yeah, I said it — a full-on 26.2 miles. Because I had something to prove!

Every Olympic year, I had dreamt of standing on that podium, hearing the National Anthem and experiencing the thrill of victory. But looking in the mirror, I realized that some dreams must be put aside. Olympic gold or even Olympic attendance had to hit the showers.

When the Leukemia Society's Team in Training reps came to my office, I knew that this marathon would be the way to prove my worth. Eagerly, I grabbed the paperwork, but my confidence was shaken slightly when the perky rep gave me the dismissive once-over and offered, "Good luck," with an annoying smirk.

The marathon would be held in Vancouver, my mother's hometown. She had just passed away, so this would be my tribute to her — plus, it was the only city allowing walkers. I had to raise $1,500 to participate, so I sent letters to everyone I knew. The people who donated told me they never thought I would finish, but they were happy to give to a good cause.

The first training began at 6:00 a.m. I was going to prove that this "fat lady ain't over till there's singing at the finish line." It was January in a Chicago snowstorm. Luckily, the wind was howling so loud that it drowned out my screaming.

Every Saturday morning, we trained. Two other ladies, Mary and Katrina, joined me in the same category — slow walkers. We were a team. Through four months of training, the Three Slow Musketeers came in last but together. "All for one and one for all" was the motto of the ladies in peach velour sweatsuits!

The night before the big event, Mary, Katrina and I joined the training groups from across the country. We shared a carb-loading dinner. We picked up our official numbers and computer chips to attach to our shoes to measure our exact time. Then we received the best news of all: Walkers got an hour's head start.

The big day dawned. At 5:30 a.m., the sun was glinting off the gorgeous Vancouver skyline. The walkers lined up anxiously. The official started, "On your mark, get set… walk." Mary, Katrina and I strode out of the gate. Immediately, we got a good pace going, enjoying the crisp morning air. This was not so bad.

Then it happened—the rhythmic thumping of the Kenyan runners. Their strong, regular strides pounded the pavement as they passed us, disappearing in the mist and leaving only the echo of their steps behind.

The lull was broken by the thunder of the remaining runners. It was a stampede, with everyone jockeying for position, knocking the poor walkers every which way. The real runners must have thought we were suburban shoppers who got lost in the big city. I was just starting and was already behind. It felt like the opening of the film, *Chariots of Fire*, but in reverse.

Within hours, I lost Mary and Katrina. I was now alone on the course. It was recommended we bring taxi money in case we couldn't go on. I would not do that as I had something to prove to a lot of people, but mostly to myself.

The hours dragged on. I didn't do fun things for this length of time. The water stations were closed. No more fans cheered on the runners, so I nearly took a wrong turn. Luckily, another marathoner, an 80-year-old woman, got me on the right track and then left me in her dust.

Every step was agonizing. Up ahead, I saw the 20-mile marker—only 6.2 miles to go. Suddenly, all the Team in Training coaches began walking with me.

"You're doing great. But you need to go faster."

"Faster?"

"Yeah, they have to close down the finish line."

"I can barely do what I'm doing now."

"We can help you."

"What does that mean?"

"We can drive you a few miles." I noticed the VW driver waving. All he needed was horns and a pitchfork.

"I am not going to go through all this to say I did a marathon except for six miles," I said.

They jumped into action. They radioed ahead to keep the finish line open. One of the coaches walked ahead of me to get me walking faster. Drunk people on their porches shouted encouragement. "Go for it!" I don't think they knew what I was going for, but it was nice to be noticed.

The finish line was up ahead. The other Team in Training participants had all showered, changed and rested, but came out to cheer me on. Even my slow-walker friends, Mary and Katrina, were there.

The announcer called my name. “Now, dead last, from Chicago, Francesca Peppiatt.” The crowd cheered.

It’s pretty obvious that I was never going to participate in the Olympics. But the moment they looped that medal around my neck, I might as well have been on the Olympic podium. The thrill of victory surpassed the agony of defeat — and these feet.

I would never forget a journey that changed me so much. Nine-and-a-half hours… But I did what no one thought I could do, not even me. I beat the odds, and I would never be the same woman again.

— Francesca Peppiatt —

Going the Distance

You gain strength, courage and confidence
by every experience in which you really
stop to look fear in the face.
~Eleanor Roosevelt

Walk. Sixty miles. Three days. I am not an athlete, and I am likely to circle the parking lot for a space two steps closer to the grocery store. So why, at age 48, would I even consider this?

Something about the ads for the first D.C. Avon Breast Cancer 3-Day Walk in 2000 resonated with me. At the orientation meeting, watching the promotional video, I noted between sniffles that the people in the room were all ages and sizes. Like me, many had never done anything remotely like this before.

I coaxed my best friend Karen into walking with me. She registered immediately, and I… waffled, sucked into the quicksand of all the very practical, fearsome arguments against it. I could let it pass, like so many other things, and my life would continue as it was… not bad, just familiar. I would hear about the Walk and run into people who were doing it, and I would say, "Yeah, I thought about doing that, but…"

I realized I didn't want to do that. I wanted to trust that first exuberant impulse. I mailed my registration. I started walking.

My first official training walk was 7.2 miles on a cold day in January, three times around a beautiful lake. There were many of these walks, organized by other walkers, some of whom had been training since November. I liked the lake because I returned to the bathroom and parking lot every 2.4 miles, so I could choose whether to go around again.

Gradually, I advanced to a weekend routine of five laps (12 miles). At my pace of three miles per hour, it took over four hours with stretching and bathroom breaks.

An early challenge was the instruction to walk without distractions. Could I really spend that much time alone with myself? I began to notice things—a woodpecker, the way the light hit the trees at one especially pretty spot, two men fishing, a father helping his son wobble along on training wheels, a young couple holding hands, a mother with a stroller, several teenagers Rollerblading, a marker in memory of a loved one.

When people passed in the opposite direction, I was privy to their conversations for just a moment. I joined their world very briefly, and then we parted. If we passed again, we smiled as if we knew each other.

My vocabulary changed. I used words like "COOLMAX," "hydrate," "GORE-TEX" and "Thorlo." I ate things called LUNA Bars and shopped in the Rugged Outdoors section of Hudson Trail Outfitters.

I realized I had not been "friends" with my body, never comfortable with its form or confident in its function. I had struggled with my weight most of my life. Now I was learning to listen to my body when it needed to stretch or slow down—because the consequence of not doing so was pain. My body learned to listen to me, too, when I asked it to push its limits. I felt greater energy. I delighted in knowing that, where before I would yell upstairs to the kids to stop fighting, now they knew I could take the steps two at a time.

In March, Karen and I began 14-mile walks together every weekend. The talks, laughter, and shared physical challenges are among my fondest memories. It was often raining or drizzly, and either one of us might call to ask, "Should we cancel today?" The other usually said, "No. Let's go."

At last, Day One of the Walk arrived. After training for months in cold or rainy weather, May 5–7 were three days of 97-plus-degree heat. Fire departments and residents along our route turned on their hoses.

One rest stop had blocks of ice sculptured into a chair for us to sit on. I developed heat rash all over my legs and had to walk in long pants.

Day One's hallmark was a steep, nasty hill. I couldn't see the top from the bottom. I started crying halfway up and crumpled on the side of the road, convinced I would have to be airlifted home. With Karen's encouragement, I dug down and found strength I didn't know I had. I was able to top the hill.

I have driven back to that hill and, though it is steep, it doesn't look as monstrous as it felt that day.

I woke on Day Two in terror of what lay ahead. We had 20 miles to cover in near-100-degree heat. I felt like a soldier preparing for battle, but unlike a soldier, I had a choice.

"This is stupid. I don't want to do this," I said, sobbing. Where is the line between bravery and foolishness? I learned that courage is not the absence of fear but the determination to do something in spite of it.

We set out at 7:30 a.m. and arrived at our Day Two camp at 6:30 p.m.

At one rest point, we hid in the bushes to avoid being "swept" into the bus for stragglers. We had one goal: to walk all 60 miles and make it to the end.

As we approached the final leg, with the Washington Monument in sight, a woman just ahead of us collapsed in the street. We had grown accustomed to the ambulances at every rest stop. But this terrified us, so close to the end. We stopped to gather strength for the last push.

Walkers who had finished ahead of us lined the path, high-fiving the new arrivals. We were sore and giddy with triumph. There were speeches and delays while we waited for the last walkers to assemble for the final parade up the Mall to the Monument, where our families waited excitedly.

I took so much from this experience — simple tenets that inform all aspects of my life:

Go at your own pace.

Listen to your body.

One foot in front of the other.

Stretch.

Commit, then decide.

Be in the moment.

Work through the pain.

You can do it.

Most of all, I learned the profound importance of being there for someone facing a life challenge. Strangers lined our route with signs of encouragement and support. It helped to know that my effort mattered, that I wasn't alone. I have tried to incorporate that into my life by sending cards and calling or visiting friends in crisis on a regular basis to assure them their struggle is not forgotten.

I learned the importance of kindness and looking out for each other. As the promotional literature said: "The 3-Day is based on the simple idea that if everyone stopped trying so hard to get ahead, no one would be left behind... Imagine a world that works for everyone for three days."

In May 2000, it did.

Sadly, in 2013, Karen lost a two-year battle with a brain tumor. I continue to walk, and I always feel that my best friend is by my side.

— Carol Randolph —

A Long Road to the Finish Line

Running allows me to set my mind free.
Nothing seems impossible. Nothing unattainable.
~Kara Goucher, Olympic long-distance runner

As my feet pound the pavement and my breath comes in shallow gasps, I pray that I won't collapse and lie in a heap on the side of the road. I want to finish my first real race.

And then I hit my stride. My breathing slows. My body glides low over the pavement. I am alone now, most of the pack having passed me in the first mile.

At 31, I am the oldest person in my running class. And I am the last to cross the finish line for every race. My coach waits for me every time. He has never asked, "Why are you in this class?" even though I wait for it.

My breathing is steady. My heartbeat establishes a rhythm with the swinging of my arms and the pounding of my feet. I am no longer tired. The air is crisp and smells of damp grass. I take a few deep breaths. The sun highlights the trees and flowers as they blur past me. The birds cheer me on with their song. The breeze ruffles my hair. This is why I love running. I am at the edge of my limits, but I am exhilarated.

My adrenaline has nearly reached its fever pitch. I can sense the end getting closer. I repeat my running mantra in my head: "Breathe easy, run easy, breathe easy, run easy."

Then I see the finish line, surrounded by people cheering and waving their arms. I do not know them, but their enthusiasm energizes me. I reach into my core and find a kernel of strength that allows me a burst of speed. My legs churn, and I imagine myself leaving a trail of smoke in my wake.

I cross the finish line, and my body stutters to a halt. I resist the urge to throw up. My husband finds me leaning on a garbage can. He hugs me tightly and wipes my tears. He is my biggest cheerleader.

This is my fourth real race outside of my running class — the kind where I pin on a number and get a T-shirt as a souvenir. In class, I just get the satisfaction of finishing each race, which is enough. It is an incredible challenge — one that I never thought I'd be up for.

When I was 17, I was in a car accident. The doctors told my parents I wouldn't make it. I broke my collarbone, pelvis, and both legs. I suffered blunt-force trauma to my knee. I lost a lot of blood and needed a transfusion. I developed an embolism in my lungs. Yet, I survived.

Then my parents were told I would never walk again. But I did. Every afternoon, I placed my hands on a walker and forced myself to put one foot in front of the other. Stairs were a nightmare. But I pushed myself. Hard. I graduated to crutches. And then to a cane. And finally to my own strength.

I spent months in physical therapy. They said I would see the light at the end of the tunnel. They were good to me, even though I was a crippled teenager who could be a little angry at times. I spent a lot of time wondering if I'd ever be the same — and whether "the same" would be good enough.

And then I was limping as if I was walking on a boat in rough seas. The physical therapist was perplexed. It became physically painful. At one point, the physical therapist put a book under my foot, and then I stood level. One leg was shorter than the other!

A few days later, I sat down hard at the bus stop on my way to work. I heard a pop. My leg went numb. I expected pain. I'd already dealt with so much pain in the past three months that it wouldn't have been a surprise. But the pain didn't come. I got on the bus when it came.

I worked at the mall, as did my dad. I stopped in at his store and said, "I think I broke my leg." He didn't hesitate. He told his employees we were leaving, and we drove straight to the hospital. An X-ray proved I was right. My leg was broken. Again.

The rod in my femur had been too thin. The rod and the bone had been bending until the stress had been too much and they both broke. That also explained why one leg was shorter than the other. As the femur bent under pressure, that leg shortened.

A new rod and six months of intense physical therapy later, the limp was gone. The rod was removed, and I was back to normal. It was a reason to celebrate — marching-band-level celebrate.

I was active from that point on. I walked, rode my bike, hiked with my husband, and worked out at gyms. And then, 13 years after the accident, I started running. I'd had arthroscopic surgery six years prior, but my knee was doing so well that I thought I'd try it. And I loved it! I made a goal for myself of working up to running three miles. I met a gal on the track at the gym who was an avid runner. She cheered me on several times. She encouraged me to enter an upcoming 5K race. I'd never run in a race, but I thought, *Why not?*

I started at the line with everyone else, but I was a slow runner. I was sure everyone had already passed me by the time I crossed the finish line. But it didn't matter because I'd done it! I'd finished my first race ever! Me! Someone who'd been told she'd never walk again! And it felt so good that I did it again. And again. The Race for the Cure in two states. A Fourth of July fun run. Even the running class!

Today, I'm running a 10K. Over six miles! But it doesn't scare me. Nor does the fact that I cross the finish line behind all my classmates. They know my story, and they wait for me anyway, cheering me on. And I burst into tears every time I cross the finish line because I know how lucky I am to be running at all. That girl who was told she'd never walk again proved that doctor wrong. And I will continue to run, walk, and live every day with gratitude that I made it through. I'll do it with a smile on my face and the breeze ruffling my hair.

— Kristi Cocchiarella FitzGerald —

For Kenny

The best way to not feel hopeless is to get up and do something.
~President Barack Obama

It's a cold October day in Toronto. I should be anxious and even a bit afraid, but I'm neither. I secure the pockets of my pack. I strap the 30 pounds to my back. I have extra layers to fight the cold.

I'm running in a weighted one-man half marathon, a fundraiser. I have the route mapped out. Two friends on bicycles stand ready to follow me for safety.

No need for pomp or ceremony. I face forward and step off.

Lake Ontario's shore is an indifferent shade of grey. The sidewalk is dirty slush. I can see my breath. I have no training for this kind of run. I'm banking on years of Army time to carry me through the pain. It's supposed to hurt. The feeling of hurt gives meaning. My only job is to finish this run.

I let my mind drift back.

***

The burning sun pushes heavily against my skin. I'm grunting under the weight of armour and weapons, struggling to keep up with the soldier ahead of me. I eat the dry dust of the grape rows and mud walls of Kandahar.

Snap-snap! Snap-snap-snap!

Bullets zip wildly over us. My body drops like a sack of potatoes before I tell it to. I swallow dirt, which tastes like granules of metal. Soldiers move and yell. I don't know what they're saying over the gunfire, but I see them forming into a firing line. I'm supposed to be there. It takes great effort to get off the ground and move. My God, here we go.

***

The first sign of drama brings me back to the here and now.

The load in my pack starts to shift. I feel the ends of a dumbbell and other items dancing across my back. Uh-oh. They're not strapped in tightly enough. Stupid. Now the loose objects will wobble against whatever little momentum I have. Each kilometre will only exacerbate the issue and will develop into abrasions and chafes. Stupid. Shut up and deal with it. Muscle through with aggression.

My mind goes to another time and place again.

***

The battle dwindles into a silent lull. The enemy disappears like a ghost. Smoke rises in the distance from our wanton release of destruction. All is quiet save for the distant thrumming of a helicopter. Adrenaline fades. My body relaxes. A cool breeze kisses my face. I begin to feel the notches and ridges of my rifle.

Poof!

Someone pops a smoke grenade. A flowery red plume forms into a rising spire. Radio chatter. The Medevac homes in. Hand signals. We hold our ground. This is a vulnerable moment. Helicopters are prime targets for any insurgent bravo to shoot at. The distant, mechanical thrumming grows louder. We have a new job. Defend the helicopter.

Chugga-chugga-chugga-chugga!

Spinning blades and turbines dominate the environment. Dust forces me to cover my face. I sneak a peek between fingers at the powerful machine. A Blackhawk. American. Red cross on the fuselage. Thank God for allies. I watch as a helmeted crewman slides the door open.

***

My mindless run in the cold is rudely interrupted.

An inattentive driver pulls in front of me as I trot across an intersection. I see him cross the line without checking the sidewalks. Silver-coloured sedan. Immediately, I'm angry. I slap the trunk of his car. Hard. I move around and carry on with the run. I hear him yelling. I don't look back. I don't care. Finish this run.

Defend the helicopter.

***

My rifle sits on the lip of a berm like a tamed animal. I dig the butt into my shoulder. I bury my chin into the stock. Now is the time for grit.

Fellow soldiers are hunched over a stretcher and struggle toward the roaring machine against a blast of wind. They're carrying a wounded man. It's Kenny, my God. The rotor wash blows his trauma blanket away, revealing a pile of humanity. His mangled body is so charred and broken that it's impossible for me to tell if what I'm seeing is real. I want to crush the rifle with my hands.

I see a sign of life. Kenny uses a hand to pull back on the blanket. It's his final act as a soldier in combat, covering his wounds from the world and finding some dignity in the grape rows and mud walls of Kandahar.

***

My run devolves into a weak shuffle.

So pathetic. I'm disgusted with myself. My calves cramp badly like someone is punching the meaty parts of the muscles. Violent twitches shoot up and down the legs. I should be wearing boots with ankle support, but I opted for running shoes, and now my legs are giving up. The slush from the pavement is inside my socks. My feet are frozen. A reservoir of tears rises up behind my eyes.

"Are you okay?" asks one of my safety cyclists.

"I'm good."

I'm lying.

I keep going. It's damned painful, but I keep going. I have to finish this stupidity.

I drift into a quieter place.

***

Surrounded by his family and friends, Kenny sits on a hospital bed and receives me as a visitor. The sheets are white. The walls are white. His bandages over his stumps are white. Sterile. Clean. Safe from bombs and bullets but not permanent disability. Kenny is visibly missing two legs above the knees.

He's a Canadian soldier of Kandahar. That's how he defines himself to me, beating his chest. A Canadian soldier of Kandahar. He talks. I listen. I dare not utter a word. This isn't about me. This is about him. This visit is the last time I see him.

***

The final steps at the end of my run are a sluggish shuffle of wet shoes barely clearing the ground.

I drop my pack and take a look behind me. It's done.

"It's his journey now," says a fellow veteran about Kenny.

I sigh. "Yes, it is."

The thought of Kenny's journey is painful, and there's nothing I can do for him other than raise money for his second life and tell people about his last walk in the grape rows and mud walls of Kandahar.

Anonymously, I send the funds I raised to his regiment. Kenny doesn't need to know our names anymore. He needs to live. After all, life is the daily opportunity to express the best of ourselves. We have our lives. Most of us have our limbs. We're supposed to be appreciative and move on. But I'll never, ever close the door of memories with our dead and wounded on the other side.

Lest we forget.

—James Barrera—

Go, Girl, Go!

Instruction does much, but encouragement everything.
~Johann Wolfgang von Goethe

I was determined to run the whole thing! It was my first 5K, and I had been practicing for about 10 weeks. I wanted so much to be able to run the entire race without walking, but I had no idea if it was possible. Running was new to me. In high school, one lap around the gym would have meant side cramps and stopping.

The sun was shining on that spring morning, and a brisk breeze blew. The weather couldn't have been any better. We gathered at the starting line, and my heartbeat sped up with anticipation. The gun went off to signal the beginning of the race, and I started a slow jog. I knew to pace myself and not use all my energy at once. I knew to breathe evenly and maintain good posture.

I felt like I had good control on the physical aspects of running. Mentally, it was a whole other story.

My mind was all over the place. I had thoughts going through my head like:

What if I die right here on this street?
I've never run this much uphill before!
Can people hear how loudly I'm breathing?
I haven't even passed the halfway point yet!
Did I really just pass gas?
Why did I think I could do this?

I think my mind was exhausting more of my energy than my body was.

After what felt like hours but was really about 30 minutes, I rounded a turn and could see the finish line that would follow a final lap of the high-school track. It was a relief, but it still seemed a million miles away. My breathing was all over the place. Spit dripped out of my mouth and onto my chin. My lungs gasped for air.

Suddenly, from somewhere to the left of me, I heard a tiny voice yelling three little words: "Go, girl, go!"

I glanced over and saw a little girl, around seven or eight years old, standing on her porch. She watched us with so much excitement that she could have burst. Her brown hair bounced as she screamed her encouraging words.

They were the exact words I needed to keep going.

I don't know why she felt compelled to shout those words out to me that day, but I am grateful she did. Those very words got me to the finish line. And those words have carried me through other parts of my life, too. I need people in my life who will notice me on the verge of giving up — whether I'm in my job, trying to eat healthy, finishing a project, or chasing a dream — and, with a big smile and bubbling excitement, say, "Go, girl, go!"

She made me want to be that person for other people, too. I want to see them well into their race, whether it's literal or figurative, and be the one screaming for them to keep going, reminding them that I believe in them.

The world would be a much brighter place with more of that kind of encouragement.

— Jen Chapman —

Training My Mind

Turn down the volume of your negative inner voice and create a nurturing inner voice to take its place.
~Beverly Engel, The Nice Girl Syndrome

A few years ago, when I set a pie-in-the-sky goal to qualify for the Boston Marathon, I followed a training plan, did everything I should have, and worked hard, but my mental confidence was never really there. Some days, I was strong, but most of the time I was exhausted — not by the miles, but by the fight with my thoughts. After missing my goal by a matter of minutes, I decided it was not my body that needed to train harder. It was my mind.

So I set out to do a little experiment in my local 5K. I vowed to keep track of every negative thought that came in, and replace it with a positive one, just to see what happened.

I love the 5K distance because it always pushes me to run a little faster than I am used to. The most challenging part of a 5K for me, though, is the runners around me. There have been countless races in which I *should* have finished first, but I let the other competitors and my negative self-talk get the best of me. I have always had issues with crumbling under pressure.

So I decided to try out this strategy. So simple, right? For every negative thought that came in, I would replace it with a positive one. I just needed to be aware of all of my thoughts. That was my only goal for this race — not a personal record, not to win — just to control my thoughts.

As I lined up at the start, I put myself behind a sea of what had to be the local girls' cross-country team. Great.

My first negative thought came in... *I am at least 20 years older than these girls.* I followed it with a positive one... *Yup, and you have 20 years of experience on them. They don't stand a chance.*

As I stood there anxiously, I felt my heart start to pound and my legs get shaky. *Good, use that energy.*

The gun went off, and three girls sprinted like a bat out of hell ahead of me. Negative thought: *Crap.* Positive thought: *Don't worry, you know how those young ones can be. They don't know how to pace. Get close to them, but don't worry.*

About a half-mile in, I checked my pace: 6:15.

Negative: *I can't keep that!* Positive: *Says who? You feel fine. Relax your shoulders and settle here.*

I ended up being right behind the lead girl by mile 1, and I decided to just hang there. But shortly after that decision, I noticed she started to lose a bit of steam.

I started off negative: *Don't go now. Just stay here where it's safe.* And then I recovered and thought, *What? You feel strong right now. Give a little push here.*

So I surged past her and had a serious boost of confidence and energy as I took the lead. As far as I knew, she was the only other girl who was close to me.

Well, look at me! I am so fast! I cannot believe I am going to win! I am awesome! I am...

A little teenybopper no older than 14 flew past me out of nowhere after mile 2. *You have got to be kidding me. Well, there goes my lead. I knew it was too good to be true.* I quickly corrected my thoughts: *There it goes? Don't just give it up, you pansy! You can stay with her! You got this!*

She was legitimately sprinting. I became frustrated, and I felt myself falling to defeat and self-hate on the inside.

My legs are dead. Correction: *They are alive.*

Who did I think I was to actually win a race? Correction: *You are a fast runner, that's who. Stay with her.*

Then I found myself looking at this girl ahead of me in comparison. *Look at her butt. That is a runner's butt. I couldn't even fit one cheek in those shorts. Who am I kidding here?* But I reminded myself, *You have a strong butt. That is an advantage.*

For what seemed like an eternity, I stayed right on her tail as best I could, huffing and puffing along the way, replacing every negative thought that came my way with a positive one. At one point, we passed a bank sign that read the current temperature: 91 degrees.

It's too hot to be running this fast. You really should play it safe. Slow down. Second place is still really good. I corrected that to *Oh, shut up. You love the heat, and you know it. Stay here. First is better. You know you want first.*

At one point, one of my favorite Fall Out Boy songs came on in my headphones called, "The Mighty Fall." I found myself repeating: "She will fall. She will fall. She will FALL." (Of course, I didn't want her to actually fall—just fall back.)

Then somewhere around mile 2.7, she stopped abruptly from her sprint and started walking. I literally almost tripped over her. I could not believe it.

Worried somebody else was going to threaten my potential victory, I put on the best pump-me-up song I could find and pushed on.

My body feels so heavy. I changed that to *I feel like a feather.*

What if somebody is right behind me? That turned into *So what if they are? They can't catch you.*

I can't do this turned into *You ARE doing it.*

Then I crossed the finish line as the first female, with a time of 21:16. This may not seem like an Olympic victory, but in my head it really felt like one. This was the first time I was ever able to control my thoughts during a run, and it was powerful. This was not a personal record for me, which is what makes it even more profound. Had I let those few girls beat me, I would have looked at my time and been confused and frustrated, knowing I could have run faster. But instead, I let my head win the race and let my body do what it knew how to do. This was not a matter of just trying to stay positive for the sake of it; I literally felt my body responding with each strong thought. It was a surreal experience.

Now here comes the comical part. At the awards ceremony, I was handed my fancy glass "First Female Finisher" plaque, and I was beside myself. Awkwardly, I asked a stranger nearby to take a picture of me with it. As soon as I gave her my phone, I dropped the plaque, and it shattered into a million pieces. Yup. A couple of people standing around me gasped in horror and waited for me to burst into tears. But I laughed. Because this is me, folks. And nothing could steal the joy of that victory. NOTHING! Not even a pathetic yet typical clumsy act that I would normally beat myself up about in embarrassment. Today, I was a champion. Shattered plaque and all.

—Jill Diaz—

That Marathon Mindset

No One Runs Alone in Boston

The greatness of a community is most accurately measured by the compassionate actions of its members.
~Coretta Scott King

Around mile 20 of the Boston Marathon I was struggling through injury and frustration. With only a few miles to go, I was focused on just making it to the finish line. So the last thing on my list of priorities was answering a phone call from my father, who was near the finish. After ignoring the first few attempts, I answered angrily with an annoyed, "What? I'm trying to run a marathon here!" and hung up. I pressed on, only to notice strange things happening along the course, including more runners answering their cell phones and slowing to a walk. Then suddenly we were diverted slightly off-course by officials.

An ambulance went by, and information soon trickled down to us that an explosion had occurred at the finish line and they had stopped the race. This perplexed me as, in all my years of racing, I had never once heard of a race being stopped. As we were ushered off the course and led to the closest medical tent, at mile 21, we were given broth, foil blankets, and water, but very little information.

At the medical tent, I found a cot and tried to contact my family and some friends who lived nearby. While part of me was glad to have a break from running and finally be sitting down, the reality began to dawn on me that the finish line seemed farther than ever. I regretted not taking the insistent calls from my father. I think we all were in a state of shock, between stopping abruptly, having little nutrition or change of clothes, and having no information. I did worry that, once I sat down and rested, I might not have the energy to get back up. And somehow, I had to meet up with my family.

Since cell-phone service was tied up, Twitter became my only form of communication with my family and friends. They were safe and knew that I was safe, but no one knew how to get to me. All of us runners were stranded on the course. It became clear that the only way to meet anyone was to proceed backward. But as I started walking back the course all alone, I realized that the street was now blocked off. I had no idea what was going on, but was now convinced that it was going to be impossible for me to meet my family or friends, and virtually impossible to get my feet to take me back to the medical tent. So, there I was, stranded farther down the course — cold, exhausted, and alone.

As I stood by the side of the road, a couple appeared beside me. They seemed as confused as the rest of us. They asked me how I was doing. I explained that my family was near the finish line, and that my friends, while closer, also could not reach me. At this point, they noticed that I was visibly shaking from the cold (as even three foil blankets provided no warmth). So Lauryl offered me her sweater. She absolutely insisted, and I took her up on the offer. Then she and her husband, Steve, did the most selfless and generous thing: They helped a perfect stranger. They offered to take me to their home so I could get warm and use their landline to contact my family. I accepted gratefully.

After a long and slow walk, we arrived at their home, where they offered me their bathroom, some warm socks, a jacket, food, and a seat to finally rest. I called my family, and we tried to arrange a way for me to get home. Again, Lauryl and Steve generously offered to drive me to the train station to meet my family. As we left their home, they loaded me with bags of extra socks and food for an army, gave me a jacket to keep me warm, and provided Lauryl's contact information so that we could keep in touch. They are the absolute example of what makes the Boston Marathon special. The people of Boston accept everyone, especially the runners, as family, and take care of them.

One year later, after waiting for the chance to finally finish the marathon that so many of us had started, I was back. As we had planned during a lunch meeting the day before the race, Lauryl and her family saw me along the course, once again around mile 20. And once again, as I struggled up Heartbreak Hill, Lauryl helped me through. Just as promised, she was waiting for me with her son, holding a special sign that she had made for me. As we took a picture, she asked me how I was doing and assured me that I would finish. She handed me a banana and her water bottle, which gave me the strength to get through the rest of Heartbreak Hill.

I cannot express how joyful it was to pass by the mile 21 medical tent and be able to focus, beyond it, and toward the finish line. In 2014, I finally crossed that finish line, but only with the help of so many others. With my hand on my heart and head raised to the sky, I thought about those who could not physically finish with me, but who carried me along the way.

Even today, when I reach for the comfy socks that Lauryl and Steve so graciously gave me, I think about that tragic day, when two kind people spotted me, stranded and alone on the side of the road, shivering in foil blankets, and offered their home and generosity to a stranger. I know that I am forever their "Boston runner," and I am forever grateful for their warmth and kindness.

Marathon running may seem like a solo sport, even lonely at times, but no one runs alone. We take the love and support from those around us, including family, friends, and even strangers. Especially in Boston, the city carried us runners and we, in turn, carried the weight of a heartbroken city to the finish line.

— Kelly L. Swan Taylor —

Beyond the Right Turn

Adversity causes some men to break;
others to break records.
~William Arthur Ward

I was about to discover how one moment would change my entire race. Twenty-two miles into the 2018 Chicago Marathon, I was on world-record pace. My splits were recording consistent 6:45 miles, and then I took a right-hand turn….

I had prepared for the race of my life with an unparalleled will and sheer determination. Hours of training had me up long before dawn every morning, seven days a week. Now after months of work, everything was coming together perfectly. The day was overcast and cool. I knew from the moment the starting gun went off that it was a day to break records. In a race as long as a marathon, anything can happen.

But then, at mile 22, my race took a turn that no one could have predicted.

The years have left many childhood memories hazy, almost dream-like. However, one memory is seared into my brain. It will never be forgotten, as it changed the trajectory of my entire life. After weeks of lying in a hospital bed, I emerged from a coma. My body had been ravaged by a rare form of meningitis called meningococcemia. I was four years old.

Though I survived, the price was high. As I slowly emerged from the coma, I knew that something was wrong. My legs felt heavy, and

I could not feel my toes. My parents explained that the doctors had to amputate both my legs to save my life. It was my first lesson about the harsh realities of life.

That double amputation helped shape and mold me. It gave me the drive to persevere when everyone else quits, and the determination to prove to the world and myself that any obstacles can be surmounted.

The following years blurred by as if they were on fast-forward. It seemed as though, in a single heartbeat, I found myself standing at the start line of the 2018 Chicago Marathon. Waiting for the starting gun can be one of the longest and most painful parts of a race, so I had time to think. I stood there contemplating all that had happened to put me on that line.

Running is a relatively new pursuit for me. I started training seriously as a runner in August 2016. From the start, it seemed to be a sport tailored to me. It required long hours of training. It did not matter if it was hot or cold, raining or snowing. There was always training to be done and new goals to surmount. The lessons of overcoming and triumphing in the face of adversity and obstacles were familiar to me.

The marathon is a difficult race. Anything can happen in a race that depletes your body both physically and mentally. The 2018 Chicago Marathon was my fifth attempt at the distance. The starting gun cracked, and a grin spread across my face as a chill raced up my arms and down my back. I surged forward, powerful and confident in my ability to run the exact race plan I had formulated with my coach. The goal was any finish time that started with a 2. Breaking the magical three-hour barrier in the marathon is not something that I ever thought would be possible for me. For most of my life, I abhorred any sort of endurance exercise. In college, I struggled to walk a mile and was often seen driving my car short distances around campus.

As the miles started to click by, the sound of my running blades was hypnotic. I stopped paying attention to the mile markers. The noise and energy coming from the crowd were infectious; it was hard to stay on pace. I wanted to race forward faster and faster. It became even more difficult as the elite men and women flowed past. My pacers reminded me patiently to keep it slow and hold on to my energy for the later stages of the race. My heart and mind were bursting with exhilaration.

The race dragged on, and with less than 10 miles to go, my body started to feel the effects of running at a fast pace for a long time. I knew that I did not have the level of running training I had hoped for coming into the race. I despaired slightly as I thought of the hour of running I had left to reach the glorious finish line. Seeing that I was starting to struggle, my pacers jumped in and made sure that I was consuming enough energy chews, salt tablets, Gatorade, and other horrendous nutritional options that can only be considered worth eating when running. Over the course of running for hours, one's mood can swing drastically. I knew that this low moment would pass with each mile and I reminded myself to smile and think of the good moments. I thought often of my three-year-old son, whom I had spoken to right before the race.

"Dada, I know you will win the race," he said. It gave me the desire and motivation to push on.

Finally, I was starting to regain my composure and good mood. Shortly after mile 22, I was making a right turn when disaster struck. I stepped in a pothole, and my right blade caught the edge of the hole. The phrase "my leg got torn off" is not something that is common when speaking of a marathon. A person hearing that phrase might naturally think of a war zone or some other grisly accident. However, this is exactly what happened to me. As I felt my leg coming off, I panicked and grabbed it with my right hand while frantically reaching out to grab the shoulder of one of the pacers. I missed and came down hard on my side. As my head hit the pavement, my whole world went dark.

I didn't know if it was seconds or minutes before I came to with people helping to drag me off the ground. My head was swirling. I was so dizzy. I couldn't focus my eyes, and my vision was blurry. I couldn't even tell if I was standing upright. My hearing was like a poorly tuned radio that was under a pillow.

Somehow, I managed to pull my leg back on and balance by myself. Then, I forged ahead with my pacers. At first, I staggered, and then I walked. Finally, I began a shambling run. I made it to the 23-mile marker and needed to walk again. My whole body was cramping. I had never considered dropping out of a race more seriously than at this point. I was at the lowest moment ever in my running career. I knew that I was strong enough to finish the race if I could just manage to stay upright. Those tottering walking steps turned into running again. I made it to the 24-mile marker and started to walk again.

The final 2.2 miles may as well have been a trek across America. The dizziness was worse, my vision was blacking out periodically, my hands and arms were numb, and my legs felt like lead weights. I was scraping the bottom of the barrel when an aid worker asked if I wanted medical help. Oh, such a sweet temptation! All the pain could end right then instead of having to complete the final 2.2 miles! I knew if I lingered a moment longer, I would walk right off the course. Though my body screamed at me, and cramps wracked my body, I did not walk again from that moment on. I ran.

For some cruel reason, one of the only hills over the entire course of the marathon comes in the final half-mile. As my pacer and I turned onto the hill, my body rebelled. Hurriedly, I grabbed his arm. Without him by my side, I would have been crawling to the finish line. Together, we churned our weary legs up that hill and made the final turn to the finish line. He steadied me and then turned me loose to run the final, seemingly endless 0.2 miles. For a while, it looked as though the finish line was not getting any closer.

Finally I crossed the final time mat. I immediately collapsed, my body having given everything that it could. I had battled the inner darkness harder than ever before and emerged on the other side, a husk of what I was going into the race. As weariness and pain overtook me, I was escorted to the medical tent in a wheelchair for evaluation.

By some miracle, I finished in three hours, three minutes, 22 seconds — a new personal record by a mere 13 seconds. This was a new double amputee world record. I had battled with everything I had on the streets of Chicago, and I arose victorious.

— Brian Reynolds —

Gold Star Day

The marathon never ceases to be a race of joy,
a race of wonder.
~Hal Higdon

As a long-time runner, I never had the desire to run Boston or the NYC marathon. For me, it was always the Marine Corps Marathon (MCM) in Washington, D.C. My dad was a Marine, my uncle was a Marine, and my husband was a Marine, so we are a USMC family! Named "The People's Marathon," the race is famous because civilians get to "run with the Marines" through Washington, D.C., and have a Marine Corps officer place the medal around their necks at the finish. The finish is at Arlington, at the base of the famous Iwo Jima Memorial. How incredible is that? When I saw Oprah run the MCM in 1994, I just knew I could run it one day, too.

In 2014, my dream came true when my name came up in the MCM lottery. I trained all summer, which is a big deal because summers are miserable in Phoenix. It was one of the hardest training schedules ever. I had to run at 4:00 in the morning to try and beat the extreme heat. I ran hills because my uncle (who had run the MCM before) advised me of all the hills on the course. As a result of all the hill training, I injured my calf muscle and had to rest. I obeyed the doctor's orders and was ready to run the marathon of a lifetime by October.

My husband and I flew to Maryland and stayed with friends. We picked up my race bib and packet the day before the race and toured

Mount Vernon. It was a lovely day until we drove back to Maryland. Fifty feet away from my friend's driveway, we were hit by a car.

Blessedly, no one was seriously injured in our car. My knee was banged up, but I wasn't going to let that stop me from running. "If you have pain tomorrow, you're not running," my husband said.

"You're cute," I replied. Of course, I would run. A car accident wasn't about to stop me from making my dream of running with the Marines come true.

The next day, I was fine. No pain. So we drove to Washington, D.C., but got lost on the way to the starting line. Finally, we found our way (after an hour of searching) to the start. The race started, and I was on my way through hilly Georgetown and then through the Mall, past the Lincoln Memorial and all the other special monuments and memorials. I stopped to take many pictures along the way. The weather was crisp and cool, complete with brightly colored fall leaves gently tumbling to the ground before me as I ran by. It was perfect, exactly how I always imagined it would be.

The only hindrance was the mantra of "Beat the Bridge." Participants are warned about The Bridge beforehand. All runners of the MCM have to get to the mile-20 marker before the five-hour mark or else the drawbridge over the Potomac will rise and prevent them from finishing in time. The psychological pressure of "Beat the Bridge" was daunting. It was worse than the seven miles of hills through Georgetown. The pressure made me run faster than I usually did, so I was spent by mile 15. I stopped to walk and wasn't sure if I could beat the bridge in time. I was sad, tired and cranky, and wanted to give up. I didn't think I could do it.

And then I came upon Memorial Way....

In this part of the race, a section of the course was lined with family members of the fallen Marines from the wars in Iraq and Afghanistan. Enlarged color photographs of Marines killed in action lined the street, adorned with beautiful American flags. The Gold Star families cheered us on as we ran by them. It was overwhelming! With tears in my eyes, I studied each photograph carefully. Some Marines were pictured in their dress blues, others were in combat gear, while some were in civilian clothes, holding their children. It was so difficult to run and cry at the same time, but I did. I thought, *What if I had lost my husband when he served in the First Gulf War?*

I'll never forget those cheering families encouraging us to keep going. I wanted to hug and encourage *them*! How could I complain about the pain? How could I even consider quitting after that moment? Those families can't quit. They must carry on through their pain. They must endure. I made a concerted effort then and there to beat the bridge and complete the race in their honor. And I did.

Of course, at mile 25, there was one last hill. Gotta love those Marines. They just had to make us work for the finish. Marines lined the street, cheering and clapping for us at the end. And then, finally, I crossed the finish line and received my medal: The Eagle, Globe, and Anchor. I shook the young Captain's hand and thanked him for his service as he placed the medal around my neck. "Good job!" he said with a wide smile.

I walked over to the base of the Iwo Jima Memorial and located my husband for our reunion. "I had a hard time, but it was nothing compared to what you had to endure to earn that title of United States Marine," I said as I hugged him.

The Marines have a saying: "Earned, never given." Yes, I earned my medal that day, but I was given so much more.

—R. A. Douthitt—

Cones, Curbs and Cracks

Faith is the quiet cousin of courage.
~Judith Hanson Lasater

It was an unusually frigid January morning when my friends and I lined up for the Mobile Marathon. I hopped up and down in nervous excitement as the wind whipped through my multiple layers of clothes, double checking my iPod, ear buds, gel packs and water bottle. Months of training had culminated in this moment. Had I put in enough time and pushed myself hard enough? Could I finish the grueling 26.2 miles?

In my left hand, I clutched 13 index cards. Thirteen more cards were in my jacket pocket. I had read about this idea in a running magazine. I had written one Bible verse per card, each beginning with a different letter of the alphabet. Twenty-six letters in the alphabet equaled 26 miles in the marathon. The plan was to meditate on a verse for each mile of the race from A to Z.

The starting gun went off, and we began to run at a slow pace.

"What's your first verse?" asked my friend Lisa, jogging beside me.

I fumbled with the cards in my gloved hand and read, "Ask and it will be given unto you." With my eyes on the card in my hand, I didn't see the orange cone covering a hole in the road. Before I could stop, I had fallen over the cone and was on the asphalt, my Bible verse cards strewn across the pavement!

This was not the first time I had found myself on the ground over the past 15 years of running. Cones, curbs and cracks in the sidewalk have caused me to tumble many times. Although I've been fortunate not to have any serious injuries, the battered ribs and twisted ankles have been aggravating, interrupting my training and daily life.

Often, decisions that seem insignificant at the time can ruin my training run or race: eating an extra helping of almond chicken at the Chinese restaurant the night before my marathon; wearing new shorts that rub in the wrong places; walking through wet grass to get to the starting line so that my shoes and socks are wet for the race. And, of course, not watching for the orange cones in the road.

Those cones have come to represent the small problems in life that often throw me off course. A minor irritation, such as a long wait for customer service or someone cutting me off in traffic, can cause my blood to boil and ruin my day. Just like the crack in the sidewalk that causes me to trip, these annoyances can become huge if I'm not careful.

But often in running and in life, the little things can make a positive difference. During the last few miles of a Disney marathon when I was down to my last bit of energy, I heard someone call my name from the crowd of onlookers. I turned, confused, wondering if someone I knew was there. Then I remembered that my name was printed on my race bib. I felt a tiny rush of adrenaline that pushed me through those last miles. I will always be grateful to that unknown cheerleader!

I've learned to look for and appreciate the small gestures that remind me that a Higher Power is watching out for me. It might be a phone call that comes just when I need it, a child's hand in mine, or my cat curling up in my lap after a long day at work. They give me the boost I need to keep going. Sweet moments like these bring a layer of joy and depth to my life when I take the time to look for them.

On that bitterly cold morning in Mobile, I scrambled for my Bible verse cards, dusted myself off and continued the marathon, reading my verses each mile while keeping one eye on the road. I persevered to the final mile — "Zacchaeus, hurry and come down, for today I must remain at your house." Once again, the little things got me through.

— Millicent Flake —

A Year at a Time

If you want to be happy, set a goal that commands your thoughts, liberates your energy and inspires your hopes.
~Andrew Carnegie

I had always avoided risk—that is, until my mid-thirties, when I resolved to get out of my safe, comfortable rut. I vowed that each year on my birthday, I would set a new goal: something that would make me stretch and grow. I made sure to pick something that I thought was hard—beyond my abilities, even—and gave myself a whole year to accomplish it.

One of my early goals was to complete a marathon. I had been that girl who would do anything to get out of gym class, so running the Marine Corps Marathon was the scariest thing I could think of tackling.

I began training a year in advance. First, I bought a book on how to train for a marathon. Then I drew up a schedule and stuck to it religiously. My training started with a short, gentle run every other day. I had to force myself to get out there until running became a habit. Once the simple runs became routine, I incorporated gradual increases in mileage, plus some hills and sprints for strength and stamina. And after outfitting myself with the recommended equipment, I began to feel more like a runner.

I made numerous sacrifices in pursuit of this goal: my long hair and my social life, to name two. As the year wore on, my training became all-consuming. Other interests were put on hold as one entire day each weekend was devoted to a long run. I found I enjoyed its solitude and rhythm. And though the mileage increased each week, I gradually became more comfortable running.

That's not to say it was easy. On those days when I dreaded going out in the cold or lacked the energy to run, I'd make a deal with myself: If I just got out there at all, I could make it a short workout. And by the time a mile or two had passed, my lethargy had usually passed too, and I'd end up going the whole distance.

Even when I went on my summer vacation, I allowed myself no vacation from training—not even when the temperature reached 110 degrees on the day I was due for a 20-mile run. I questioned the wisdom of running in that heat, but stuck to the program. Completely wiped out after that brutal run, I barely made it back to where I was staying. I had to lie on the bathroom floor for 20 minutes to cool down before I felt strong enough to walk shakily to the beach and jump in the ocean, where I stayed submerged until my core temperature returned to normal.

The day of the race, in late October, was cold and rainy in Washington, D.C. They lined us up by average speed, with the fastest runners in the front of the pack to avoid a bottleneck. That meant I was way at the back. In fact, once the gun went off, it took me several minutes to even inch my way to the starting line!

In addition to the threat of hypothermia, the gray, drizzly weather was demoralizing. I don't know which was harder to bear—the mental torture of completing a five-hour footrace under those conditions, or the physical pain. Of the 18,000 who registered for the race that year, 4,000 didn't finish.

The chill and fatigue got to me around mile 16. I felt weak, my energy reserves were depleted, and I gulped the sports drinks that were offered along the way. As the miles wore on, my body felt like its structure was crumbling, and there was nothing holding me upright. Every footfall rattled my bones as my shoes pounded the streets of Georgetown. Even worse was the lonely stretch of the course past the Kennedy Center on an isolated peninsula with wind whipping off the water and no spectators to cheer on the runners. But quitting was not an option.

Incredible as it would have seemed a year prior, I made it the full 26.2 miles… the last yards of which were uphill! Trudging up that hill, I felt like I'd never make it. But I just kept putting one foot in front of the other and reminding myself that's how I got to this point — by focusing on the next step, not on the top of the hill.

Of all my "birthday goals" over the years, that one probably had the most impact on me. It's not because I became a runner. I don't do marathons anymore; I don't need to because now I know that I can.

What mattered was the side effect. The confidence I gained by setting a nearly impossible goal and then achieving it propelled me to be fearless in other areas of my life. I applied and was selected for a job I wouldn't have dared pursue before. I became braver in my personal relationships. I felt there wasn't anything I couldn't do if I put my mind to it. Thanks to my marathon training, the formula for success was there: break the task into manageable pieces and make incremental progress — a series of minor goals leading up to the major one. Each year, and with each new goal, I continue to reinforce this.

I don't have to run a marathon again, but I plan to find other "marathons" to complete — more impossible goals — ones that have nothing to do with running. I'll just keep putting one foot in front of the other. Because now I know that I can.

— Susan Yanguas —

Dreams Come True

So many people crossing the finish line of a marathon look as happy as when I won. They have tears in their eyes. The sport is full of winners.
~Gary Muhrcke, winner of the first NYC marathon

Before you can have a "dream come true," you have to have a dream. Running a marathon was never really a dream for me, but more like a bucket-list item. All my running friends had done them, and I figured I'd eventually have to do one myself. When I did, it was an amazing experience, but not really a dream come true.

But yesterday I worked the finish line at the Long Island Marathon. My job was to place the medals over the heads and around the necks of the people who ran the 10K, the half marathon, and the full marathon. I wasn't the only volunteer, so I'm going to estimate that my share was about 1,500 heads. I witnessed an awful lot of "dreams come true" yesterday.

Running a long distance requires focus. There's no room for emotion while running. There's no time to express the anxiety felt at the starting line; the gratitude felt for the cheering crowd; the frustration when there isn't a water stop near enough; the inspiration when a runner in a wheelchair passes you; the disappointment when you know you won't make your target time; the elation you feel when you pass someone; the incentive or despair when someone passes you; the delight when the running is going well; the fear that you may not finish; and, finally, the joy when you spot the finish line and hear the announcer call out your name. After that long, challenging run, peppered with an array of mixed emotions, both good and bad, who is the first person the finisher encounters? Me.

Some of them hug me. Others blurt out, "Thank you, thank you," or "I didn't think I could do it." They are exhausted, panting, out of breath and often stumbling, but they all express gratitude that I am there to acknowledge their triumph. More than a few told me, "I've been waiting to see your face for over five hours." "I'm a winner!" "I made it!" One runner did a somersault; another did 26 pushups right at the finish line. Sometimes, pairs finished together with hands held high. There was an engaged couple dressed in a bridal veil and tuxedo T-shirt. Fathers and sons, mothers and daughters, sisters and brothers all ran.

There were also many who were strangers at the start, but after finishing the last miles together, became soul mates, comrades. One woman told me she signed up for the half marathon but realized that her friend needed help, so she did the full marathon with her. Now that's a friend! There were high-fives and hugs. There were men with bloody nipples and shirts stained with salty sweat. There were chafed thighs and cramps that required ice or a massage at the medical tent. None of that diminished the exuberance of the participants.

The overweight people are the most inspirational to me. If that 300-pound man can run a marathon, what am I doing standing here? The large teenage girl tells me, "I did it! I lost 50 pounds already! I did it, and I'm gonna keep doing it." There are all types of people, all races, ages, sizes: those with runners' bodies and those with beer bellies; the Asians who give me a "wai," bowing deeply to receive their medals; the people in costumes: the Hulk, the clown, the man in the suit, the waiter holding a tray of drinks. Teams finish together: New York Road Runners, Black Girls RUN!, Greater Long Island Running Club, We Are Athletes, Fred's Team, Friends of Karen. Most are running to raise money for charities; some are running just because it's fun.

If I hang the medal and don't hear a "thank you," it's because they are crying—men and women both. They are the emotional tears of joy that we shed at weddings, births and graduations, and when we see soldiers coming home or look at old photographs. They are the deep, emotional tears that connect us to our loved ones, to our brothers and sisters who shared this experience with us, and to the rest of humanity. "I'm okay," they all say, and their emotional equilibrium is restored by the time they see their families. I'm the only one to witness the tears. Their families hold signs, scream their names and applaud them. They hold up their children and say, "Look at Mommy," and sometimes they pass the baby over the fence to finish with her mom.

The marathoners are handed Mylar blankets as they come through the chute. The silver capes make them all look like the super heroes they are, invincible, at least for now. And, for some, it's a dream come true.

— Eileen Melia Hession —

Becoming Exceptional

Make sure your worst enemy doesn't live
between your own two ears.
~Laird Hamilton

The very first time someone told me they aspired to run a marathon, I thought to myself, *Who does that?* Although I was very impressed, I was convinced this type of running adventure had nothing to do with me. Marathons were reserved for exceptional individuals.

I grew up in Flint, Michigan, where a great majority of my youth was consumed with basketball. And if I was told to run without a ball being involved, it was because I failed to follow instructions during practice. Running long distances for me was a form of punishment.

Nevertheless, as a high-school athlete, I stumbled upon running as a method of conditioning during the off-season. Running became a means to improve endurance and stamina. In fact, I credit running with giving me the "edge" I needed to land a spot on the basketball team. I realized running could have some benefits, but I still wasn't convinced it was an enjoyable thing to do. Later, as my athletic career vanished and my life moved on, I decided to hang up the old running shoes, still viewing them as punishment.

During the winter of 2005, life began to deliver a series of blows. First, I received a pink slip from my employer. I was doing what everyone else was doing—average work, but not performing at an elite level. Only co-workers who were willing to go beyond what was expected remained.

The second blow came in late 2006, when I was served divorce papers at my new job. I came home to a house that was cleaned out. Suddenly, my newly constructed dream home became a bachelor's crib. I thought to myself, *I'm doing what all the other young husbands are doing. Why is this happening to me?* I was reacting to life's circumstances instead of being proactive in creating the life I desired.

The third blow came in 2007 when I was no longer able to pay my mortgage. Although I agreed to put the house on the market, it eventually went into foreclosure due to being deeply underwater.

I let these negative events define my life. I was losing complete control. I decided to move back to my hometown of Flint, Michigan. While trying to recover and rebuild, I stagnated. Soon, I realized I was just going through the motions.

I began searching for something that would renew my strength and change my circumstances. I lent my full attention toward my faith with a daily morning routine of prayer. As I prayed, I felt in my spirit that I needed to be active and moving. It was as if God was telling me that I had to move forward. I had to take control and own my life. I was the only one who could change it.

So, in my restlessness to figure things out, I started running to relieve stress. Slowly, I began to incorporate a short run as a part of my meditation time with God. Running became symbolic of how I was moving forward with my life. Quickly, I noticed how I felt more alert, energized, and less stressed after each run.

With my new habits of running and prayer, things began to turn around. One day, I encountered a lady standing in line at the bank, wearing running apparel. Intrigued, I inquired about her attire and was informed she had just completed a daily run. Because I was a novice at running, I was curious to hear from someone with experience. She was thrilled to share her passion and invited me to join her running group.

The group met once a week in various neighborhoods throughout the Flint area. Their purpose was to prepare for the annual 10-mile Crim race. As a novice runner, I never gave such a race a thought. But as a member of the running group, I was encouraged to give it a try.

The group provided support, insight, and tips. I learned what shoes to wear and what food to eat. I discovered techniques for pacing myself during a long-distance run and became confident that I could actually complete a 10-miler. Most importantly, I learned the power of drawing from the strength of other like-minded individuals to help me not only pursue my running goal, but to go beyond my limited expectations.

One day, I came across an online trivia quiz about the history of the marathon. One lucky winner would be selected to win a free entry into the Chicago Marathon. The accommodations included a high-rise, luxury hotel in downtown Chicago. I took the quiz for the fun of it, and I won the prize! I was so excited about being the winner — until I realized that I had won a prize to run a marathon! Huh? As I deliberated over accepting the reward, I thought, *This is an opportunity to stay in a beautiful hotel on the Magnificent Mile in Chicago.*

So, just before my 30th birthday, I embarked on a mission to complete my first marathon. I put in hours of training, including a series of smaller races leading up to the big race. While training, I learned to put one foot before the other and to keep moving. I stayed focused by using the three Ps that I use in every area of my life: pray, prepare, and pursue!

On the day of the race, I experienced a range of emotions. I wasn't sure if I was capable of this task despite all my preparation. I began having negative thoughts. In fact, before the race, I decided that I would run about 10 miles, and then veer off-course to catch a taxicab.

But then I realized that the only thing stopping me from reaching my goal was *me*. I began to change my mindset by changing my self-talk. I prayed for strength and was well prepared for the race; now it was time for me to pursue the quest I was sent to complete. As I ran, I felt the push from the crowd and the other runners. In that moment, I said to myself, "I got this!" This simple phrase pushed me across the finish line.

Running that marathon taught me invaluable lessons. I learned that once we take ownership of our lives, we gain control to complete our goals. We may have to seek the support of other like-minded individuals to help build our courage and stay inspired, but the only person standing in the way of our own victories is ourselves. It's time for us to show up and be exceptional!

—Sherrod C. Schuler—

Semper Fi, Sister

The marathon is not really about the marathon;
it's about the shared struggle.
~Bill Buffum

I felt myself fading again as my head dropped, and I began to lose consciousness. Pungent smelling salts startled me awake as I started to slump out of the kitchen chair.

"I can't believe you drove home from the gym!" I heard Annie say.

My woozy head nodded in agreement. What the heck had just happened? All I did was finish the longest run in my marathon training.

"Maybe I'm not up to this. Maybe I can't pull it off," I said, my voice breaking.

I'd come so far from my "can't run to the end of the driveway" days. Thirty-two years after hanging up my Marine Corps running shoes, I'd started training in earnest for the Marine Corps Marathon. I completed my first half marathon at 57, but gave my tired knees a rest. Days turned into weeks, which turned into years. I thought my dream was dead.

Ten months earlier, I came across a woman online who was training for an Arctic Adventure. *How cool,* I thought. *If she can do that, maybe I can brush off my Marine Corps Marathon dream.* I reached out to wish her good luck and let her know she inspired me.

I started training slowly, not sure my knees were up to the task. When I told my new friend, she suggested Jeff Galloway's run-walk-run program. With this new approach and my impending 60th birthday, it was now or never.

I needed motivation and a commitment to something bigger than me, so I registered to run and raise money for the Semper Fi Fund, supporting our wounded warriors. Before I announced my intention to the world, I needed some solid training months under my belt.

During this time my inspiring friend Annie became my life partner and motivator-in-chief. Saturdays were spent training. While I racked up the running miles, she racked up mountain-bike miles.

I threw myself an epic 60th birthday bash, enticing friends and family to support the Semper Fi Fund through raffles and a drawing. I "earned" my race bib, raising more than $2,400. All that was left were four months of training, running longer distances than I ever had before.

Things were going great. Then, eight weeks before the event, I got bronchitis. Four weeks later, painful shin splints reappeared from my boot-camp days. The following week, I did my long 20-mile training run/walk on a treadmill. That's when Annie found me fainting in the kitchen.

But I couldn't quit. *I've trained too hard and come too far*, I told myself. *I'm just going to do the best I can.*

The weekend of the 40th Marine Corps Marathon finally arrived. After a Runner's Brunch near the Iwo Jima statue in D.C., Annie and I walked through Arlington Cemetery so I could pay my respects at the gravesite of Major Megan McClung, the first female Marine Officer killed in Iraq. A triathlete and accomplished marathoner, I had long admired Megan's legacy and was humbled by her sacrifice. Silently, I asked her to be with me during the marathon because I didn't think I could do it alone. I fell into Annie's arms sobbing. "Megan was the marathoner, not me. She should be here running instead of me."

"Megan will be with you. You can do this," Annie assured me.

I wasn't so sure, but I collected myself while Annie laid a 40th Annual Marine Corps Marathon challenge coin on Megan's tombstone. We returned to the hotel to fuel up with Team Semper Fi. Later, while setting out my clothes, nutrition, and gear, my stomach churned.

Marathon day dawned, and I woke with quiet confidence that I had done my homework. If I started slowly and ran my race, I would finish.

Spirits were high as 30,000 runners settled into place at the starting line. With a cannon blast, we were off. As I shuffled forward with the rest of the back-of-the-packers, the adrenaline rush made it hard not to try to keep up with faster runners.

"Run your race. Put one foot in front of the other," I kept reminding myself, listening for the vibration and audible beeps that reminded me to either walk or run. "That's the only way you'll beat the bridge and make it through the 26.2 miles."

It was motivating to see the throngs of people holding funny signs and Marines lining the route, shouting, "You can do it!" I soaked it all in and pinched myself. Reality was certainly sweeter than any dream could have been. Wounded warriors running with prosthetic legs and operating adaptive hand cycles inspired and motivated me. I thought, *I have nothing to complain about.*

Around mile 3, a younger woman pulled up on my side and asked, "Are you doing run/walk intervals?"

"Yes, 30 seconds running and 30 seconds walking," I answered.

"Would you mind if I ran with you? I started training, and life got away from me, so 10 or 12 miles is the farthest I've ever run. If I don't pace myself, I won't finish."

"Sure," I responded half-heartedly. On one hand, it would be great to have someone to talk to. On the other hand, I always ran alone, listening to music. But I felt her sincerity and appreciation for the opportunity to pace herself.

"I'm old, and I run slowly," I warned. "If I'm holding you back, you've got to go for it and run your race."

"Okay, if I feel that way, I'll go on ahead," she agreed.

We settled into a 30-second run, 30-second walk rhythm with casual conversation thrown in. She was married to a Marine Reserve Officer and had two boys and one girl, who we would later see along the course. I explained that my partner was bicycling nearby. As we came down a long, straight stretch, I saw Annie on her bike, official-looking with her yellow safety vest and race map attached to the handlebars. She yelled, "Looking good. Way to go!"

When I asked my running friend her name a few miles later, she said, "Meagan Mead." The hair on the back of my neck stood at attention. I relayed the story of having visited Arlington and told her about Megan McClung, the Marine marathoner. At mile 12, the Blue Mile, runners solemnly pass photos of Fallen Warriors posted along the flag-lined mile. Meagan noticed Megan's photo, and we paused to pay our respects.

From the time Meagan joined me to mile 26.2, we ran, walked, talked, ate, drank, laughed, and kicked it to the finish line together. We were awestruck that she had chosen me to run with out of 30,000 others, especially since she started 13 minutes later than I did. Clearly, there were three of us crossing the finish line of the 40th Marine Corps Marathon.

Major Megan McClung's gravestone bears the signature phrase she always signed off with as a Public Affairs Officer: "Be Bold. Be Brief. Be Gone." Gone, but never forgotten, Megan. Thank you for your inspiration, and Semper Fidelis, Sister.

— Deb Sinness —

Bee-utiful Run

Run when you can, walk if you have to,
crawl if you must; just never give up.
~Dean Karnazes

I spent four months on the trip of a lifetime. I sold my house, threw a few duffle bags into my old Jeep Wrangler, and set out to see the 18 states I hadn't been to yet. Along the way, I watched a sunset from the top of a dormant volcano, ate pie at the Pie Town Café in Pie Town, New Mexico, threw a snowball in July in Colorado, and near the end of my trip, adopted a dog I named Annie Oakley Tater Tot in honor of both her western heritage and the state where I found her.

What I didn't do much of was run, and by the time I was back in New Jersey at my mom's place, figuring out my next move, the New York City Marathon was less than a month away.

So I plugged along on a mid-week eight-miler and was just about to turn home when what felt like an ice pick plunged into my back. I screeched and swatted at the spot, and knocked a bee out from under my shirt.

I sprinted back to my mom's house. I'd been stung twice in my life—once when I was three and tried to pet a bee, and again when I was 13 on the day I also got my first period. I hadn't had too bad a reaction, but I knew my allergies had changed as I aged. Plus, the point where it stung me burned.

"Bee sting! Bee sting!" I cried as I threw open the front door. My mom was in her pajamas making oatmeal and rushed over. I threw off my shirt and struggled out of my sports bra, which was still suctioned to my body with sweat.

"Benadryl!" she yelled.

"Meat tenderizer!" I called back, which is what she'd used on me when I was 13.

I lay down on a beach towel on the floor out of both deference to her carpet and modesty, which was ridiculous since this is the woman who had given birth to me. I choked down two Benadryls while Annie, oblivious to my pain and happy that I was on the floor at her level, licked my face. Mom spread a paste of water and meat tenderizer on my back.

"It looks like you got out the stinger," she said.

"But it hurts!" I cried.

"I know," she said and patted my head in a tone that made me feel three again. "Are you having trouble breathing?"

"No," I said.

"Any swelling in your fingers?"

"No," I said again.

I lay on the floor for about a half-hour while the sting started to burn away. My mom talked constantly as she got ready for work to make sure I wasn't having a reaction. Annie settled back into her favorite spot on the couch. As the adrenaline receded, I started to feel like, yes, I'd just run eight miles on a warm day and should probably eat and drink something. She gave me a baggy T-shirt, and I sat up to drink a glass of water and eat some granola. I still felt shaky and a bit drowsy, but not like I was in any dire need of help.

"You sure you're going to be alright?" she asked as she walked to the front door.

"Yes, I'll be fine. I'm going to take a nap," I said.

"Good plan," she said and left.

I sat at the dining-room table, which was my temporary desk, and figured maybe I'd get some work done. I'm a writer who can take her job anywhere, and I could at least answer a few e-mails while I drank more water before taking that nap.

But just as I sent out a tweet about the bee sting, the edges of my vision started to blur, and a chill blew through me. *Oh, no,* I thought and tried to grab the table.

Next thing I knew, I woke up on the floor.

In more than 10 years of running, I've injured myself in a lot of weird ways. I snapped a branch halfway through a 50K ultramarathon and ran the rest of the race like I was stepping on glass. I fell down a mountain while running by myself on a trail along the Blue Ridge Parkway. I even flopped off a treadmill at the gym. But getting whiplash after knocking myself out because I passed out after taking Benadryl on an empty stomach now occupies first place on the pedestal.

When I came to, I pulled myself up the chair and grabbed for my phone off the table. I called my doctor's office, and they advised me to come in. I called my mom and asked her to turn around and pick me up. I lay back on the floor and checked my phone. Based on when I sent the last tweet, I'd been out for 15 minutes.

My dog stared at me from the couch, where she'd sat the entire time I was passed out. Lassie, she is not.

"You fainted," said my doctor, who admitted that he faints every time he gets an injection. He ordered rest, water and ibuprofen.

I never got back into a running groove after that. My neck hurt too much for me to get in a planned 20-mile run that weekend, and then, three days before the New York City Marathon, my grandfather died after a long illness. There was no funeral, and I know he'd have wanted me to run, so I did. My race started to fall apart around mile 18, and when I saw a friend at mile 23, I started to cry.

"It's okay!" she told me as she walked with me for a block. "You've had a rough time of it. But this is what marathon of yours?"

"My ninth."

"Your ninth. You got this," she said, and that was enough for me to start running again.

"At least all the bees are gone for the year!" she cried at my back as I shoved off to the finish line, which helped. I did finish my ninth marathon, and then my 10th the next year. I run mostly on trails now, and have been swarmed by mosquitoes and biting flies, but I haven't been stung by a bee since. But if it happens again, I won't let it keep me from running. I will reach for the Benadryl — but with a big glass of water and a protein bar, too. And then I'll get back out there.

— Jen A. Miller —

Walk On

There are two ways of spreading light: to be the candle or the mirror that reflects it.
~Edith Wharton

Mom was in the throes of breast cancer. We sat outdoors with her little dog Kati, listening to the birds chirping, and watching the bumblebees darting from flower to flower. I studied Mom's face, wondering how I could take her mind off the pain she was experiencing. Her strong faith had always inspired and encouraged me. It was my turn to do the same for her.

"Aren't the dandelions in the field over there beautiful?" Mom smiled wanly, gazing at the countless clusters of vibrant yellow. She managed to find beauty in all God's creation, even weeds.

Suddenly, I had an idea.

"How would you like to go get some flowers we can plant together in front of the house? It's a nice day for a drive in the country, too."

Mom's face slowly lit up like the afternoon sun.

"I think I'd like that." The three of us slowly climbed into the car, Kati's tail wagging in anticipation of a ride.

Soon, we were wandering through rows and rows of colorful blooms. Mom's pain was forgotten temporarily as she bent over to choose a potted red chrysanthemum.

"Oh, how glorious," she murmured, pressing the flowers against her cheek.

A young lady approached, her dimples welcoming, her eyes bright.

"Hello, ladies. Isn't it a beautiful day for planting flowers? My name's Jenny, and I'm here if you have any questions."

"She's young and beautiful and has no idea what we're going through," I whined silently, wondering if the girl was even old enough to be in college yet.

Mom winced. I hurried to her side, reaching for the pots she clutched in each hand.

"I think we have enough flowers to plant for now, Mom. Do you want to wait in the car while I pay for these?"

Kati hopped happily into the back seat.

"I'll come with you." Mom placed her arm through mine.

"Let me carry those for you," Jenny smiled, taking the flowers from me.

"Thank you so much. Mom tires so easily now with this breast cancer."

Suddenly, Jenny froze in her tracks. Her expression was compassionate, loving.

"I'm running on Saturday for breast cancer… Well, it's really more of a fast walk. My mom has it, too. May I please add your names to hers? I'd be proud to walk and pray for you both!"

My eyes teared up as I reached for my wallet.

"We'd love that. Wouldn't we, Mom?" I sniffed.

Mom reached out, patting Jenny's arm.

"Thank you, beautiful one…."

Ringing up our sale, Jenny carefully placed the pots of flowers in cardboard cartons before reaching for a pen and paper.

"Now I just need your names so I can remember you both during the marathon. By the way, you're both invited to come and have hot dogs and ice cream on Saturday. We'd love having you there."

"I'm afraid I'm not quite up for that, dear. But thank you for praying for us; you don't know how much that means. My daughter is named after me so it should be easy to remember us. Two Marys."

It was Jenny's turn to choke up.

"You'll both be able to wear these bracelets then."

Reaching under the counter, she retrieved two pink rubber bracelets, placing one on each of our wrists.

I took in the words printed across the bracelets: "OUR MARY."

"It so happens that's my mom's name, too. And you know what Jesus says, 'For where two or three gather in my name, there am I with them'" (Matthew 18:20).

Mom reached for my hand, placing hers and mine with Jenny's. Together, we lifted them in triumph.

Mom whispered a prayer for Jenny's mom, for us, and for all the women out there suffering from such a terrible disease.

We headed to the car, hope in our hearts.

"Roll down the window," Mom whispered.

Jenny stood waving, brushing a tear from her cheek.

Mom waved back. Then, gathering all the energy she could muster, she cried, "Walk on!"

Jenny lifted her hand once more in triumph.

Mom glanced in my direction, a smile creeping slowly across her face.

"What do you say we go plant those flowers?"

— Mary Z. Whitney —

Step by Step

Never underestimate the power of dreams and the influence of the human spirit. We are all the same in this notion: The potential for greatness lives within each of us.
~Wilma Rudolph, winner of three Olympic gold medals

It seemed about as plausible as strutting in quicksand. When my caregiver first suggested I complete a half marathon several years ago, I thought he might be a tad crazy. I am a full-time wheelchair user, and I had not walked with canes or braces since I was a kid. But that evening we'd had a conversation about some options I might have for exercise, and we both had to admit that my options were limited, at least compared to those in the typical population.

However, I could see the imaginary light bulb switch on over his head by the look that came over his face. Several years previously, I had acquired a set of parallel bars, but had used them about as often as the sun shines in Seattle. However, on that evening in the middle of our conversation, he had an idea.

On what seemed like a whim, he got the tape measure out of my toolbox and figured out the length (down and back) of a lap on my parallel bars. Once he had that calculated, he sat down with a pencil and paper and went to work. After a few minutes, he said, "If you walked 5,050 laps on your parallel bars, you will have walked 13.1 miles, a half marathon. If you completed 50 laps a day, then you could finish the whole thing in a little more than three months. What do you think?"

I was intrigued, but also intimidated. I could think of numerous benefits. Walking those laps might reduce my spasms, improve my kidney function and decrease my back pain. In addition, changing position several times per day might make me more comfortable. On the other hand, I knew that I didn't use my parallel bars often, and I also understood how quickly putting that much effort into this kind of exercise would wear me out.

Still, I couldn't help but think about the days back in high school when I was part of a sports team for people with cerebral palsy. At first, I wasn't a good athlete, and I was weary after every attempt in every event. Endurance only came with time and practice. After thinking it through, the warrior wannabe in me was convinced that I could complete this goal if I put some effort into it. I realized I wanted to conquer this parallel-bar challenge.

At first, I couldn't walk more than five laps without getting winded. It became obvious that it was going to take a while to work up to 50 laps per day.

I would like to say that I worked at it consistently every day from the beginning, but I don't like to lie. Life has no manners sometimes, and it interrupted my process with health problems more than once. But my body battled back, and after a while I got used to walking 50 laps per day on my parallel bars. I completed the 5,050 laps in May of that year. The process took about five months. One would think I would have been satisfied with that accomplishment, but as a long and uneventful summer lay before me, a strange thing happened. I was hooked.

I decided to double my goal and walk 26.2 miles, the distance of a full marathon, in the three months ahead. Pretty soon after I started on the second goal, it became apparent that if I were going to complete this goal by the end of the summer, I would have to seriously step up my game.

I wanted to make sure my posture was good most of the time, so I hung mirrors at each end of the parallel bars. That way, I could watch myself while I was doing my laps and focus on my form, just like real athletes do. Fifty laps per day had become my standard, but I slowly began to increase the number of laps I would complete at one time. Sixty laps. Breathe. Seventy-five laps. My endurance was getting better. Ninety laps. I wanted to believe that I could do this. 115 laps. Eventually, I started walking an average of 150 laps per day.

My caregivers and I kept track of my progress in prominent black marker on a dry-erase board in my living room. Every day, they changed the number of total laps that I did so I could see the number increasing. My excitement spilled over to them, and everyone was thrilled to see me get closer. Every morning, I put completing my laps on my to-do list. Even if I accomplished 15 other things in a day, I didn't feel like I had done what I was supposed to do until my laps for the day were complete. Over time, I noticed that my balance was better, and my transfers were easier. I also had more stamina when I had to stand at my grab bars that are located throughout my house.

The exercise was good for my mind-set as well. Sometimes, I would listen to good music when I walked, which would quiet my mental clutter. Sometimes, the rhythm of completing my laps would help me think through a writing project when I was stuck or help me come up with the perfect phrase to articulate what I was thinking.

But in walking my laps, I also proved to myself that I could look at a huge challenge and break it down into manageable pieces. That way, I could get closer to accomplishing it by focusing on just a little bit at a time. For someone who has been known to get overwhelmed fairly frequently, that was an excellent lesson.

On August 25th, I got it done. I finished walking 10,100 laps on my parallel bars for a total of 26.2 miles.

My Facebook post about this accomplishment got 103 likes and 28 positive comments. As active as I have been on Facebook since I joined in 2008, I have never had a post get so much attention. I realized that I could not only be proud of what I had accomplished, but people who care about me were proud of me as well. Feeling that love made me as happy as an Olympic athlete when she knows she's won the gold.

Most of the time, when people look at me, they assume that I can't do much physically, and for the most part they would be right. But in terms of exercise, I have learned to look outside the box to accomplish the things that I want to do. I have learned to set goals and achieve them.

Now I know that attaining any goal is possible as long as I do it step by step.

—Lorraine Cannistra—

Oh the Places I've Been

Belonging

There is no greater reward than working from your heart and making a difference in the world.
~Carlos Santana

When my 14-year-old daughter Ellie lamented that she'd "only ever lived in one bedroom," I mentioned it to my wife, Jane. She responded, "Isn't she lucky to have a stable family?" But something else rocketed through my mind: *Let's chart a new course.*

Ellie sparked a fire in me. iPhones, Whole Foods and fancy soccer teams were not the be all and end all. I quit my comfy Creative Director job in San Francisco, and Jane and I began to design an adventure. She suggested that if we were going to embark on something new, we should do community service everywhere we went.

Jane is Greek, so Greece became our first destination. She found an NGO—Yoga and Sport for Refugees (YSFR)—on the island of Lesvos. They were looking for a running coach. And since I run, they wondered if I might help out. Our stay in Greece matched their needs, so we committed instantly.

Soon after we arrived on Lesvos, we met YSFR's founder, Estelle Jean, at a coffee shop. A new yoga volunteer, Maria Clare, from Argentina, was with her. After a few minutes, Estelle excused herself to go and say goodbye to a refugee heading to Athens. It dawned on me that Estelle's relationship with each refugee was personal. She needed to give a hug and wish the refugee safe travels.

My commitment to Estelle was to coach running on Mondays, Wednesdays and Fridays. I didn't know what to expect the day of that first track workout. I'm a distance runner — slow, steady and long. I am no track guy. Estelle led us in stretching and warm-ups, and I relished the sweat above my brow. By the end of our session, I knew these young athletes didn't care if I was slow or fast. What they wanted was someone to spend time with them, someone to lead them, someone they could count on.

With each passing lap, more young refugees arrived, some in flip-flops, most in jeans. Eventually, Estelle needed to turn people away. We didn't have enough running shoes, shorts or socks to share. I caught my breath. I just couldn't accept that some guys had to sit out because they had no shoes. We needed running gear — immediately. I whispered to Jane, "These guys only have what's on their backs. It's not right."

I wrote a fundraising video script. Within days, and with generous help from VidMob Gives, our family recorded, edited and posted a call for help on social media. Our goal? Raise $10,000 in two weeks. We hit our goal in six days. Within two weeks, we neared $20,000. Boom!

We bought running shoes, shirts, socks, water bottles and more. Our new friends received things that we take for granted. Even more importantly, they were accorded dignity and respect. And they had a spot on the track. Slowly, we were building a band of brothers who ran for the sense of belonging. They were a part of something good.

As my days with these wonderful men piled up, my heart melted. I learned about their lives, where they came from, and the miles they'd walked. I heard about the trucks, boats, and rafts that brought them to Lesvos. I heard about dead brothers, sisters, mothers and fathers, and about people who lived for two years in a bombed-out stadium. One young man was subjected to carrying rocks in a quarry when he was just eleven years old. Early on, my family and I fell in love with this young man, Majid, a soft-spoken, warm-hearted teen from Afghanistan. Something about his presence lifted us. He was kind, gentle, and appreciated everything. Most of all, he gave us purpose and sowed seeds of affection and love.

We saw Majid often at the track, on the trails, and across the dinner table. Although we didn't share a language, our communication was crystal clear. He became the big brother my girls didn't have. He was their protector, superhero and inspiration. I took him to doctors' appointments, bought him a watch and, at training, pushed him to run harder and faster. Jane cooked for him, doted on him and encouraged him to study English. As he let go of some of his innate caution, he accepted our love. For our part, his tenderness, humility and vulnerability were palpable. He'd been dealt a tough hand, and we accepted him for who he was and respected him for all that he'd endured.

The days passed quickly. Our time with Majid, Estelle, Maria Clare and all the guys was coming to an end. At dinner on our last night on Lesvos, we celebrated a cherished month together. We laughed, cried and hugged. We promised that this would not be the end but a beginning. We were family now, and family doesn't let space and time erode it.

To our astonishment, Majid, Estelle and Maria Clare were there to say one final goodbye when we got to the Lesvos airport. Tears, photos and hugs were exchanged.

As we were going through security, I was told, "Your knife's blade is too long. Drop it here or go back out and stick it in your checked bag."

Damn! My knife was always with me. On long runs — 50 to 100 miles — I used it to pop blisters, carve off unwanted pieces of skin or make alterations to my clothes. My dad gave me a similar knife when I was a boy. With a lump in my throat, I ran back and searched for Majid. I found him outside peering through a frosted window at our gate. Since I didn't speak Dari, I asked Estelle to translate. "Tell Majid I love him, and I want him to have my knife — forever. May it always keep him safe."

She replied, "No, you do it."

I turned to Majid, looked him in the eyes and held out my hand. Without saying a word, he took the knife gently from my palm and closed his fingers around it. Words were not needed.

— Burr Purnell —

52 Marathons in 52 Weeks

The real purpose of running isn't to win a race.
It's to test the limits of the human heart.
~Bill Bowerman, track-and-field coach
and co-founder of Nike, Inc.

As I was blasting through yet another of my six-mile runs down the rugged dirt-and-gravel roads of rural Hocking County in southeastern Ohio, the thought occurred to me, *Ordinary people can accomplish extraordinary things!* It came as no surprise to me that I should think this, as over the years of reading and studying, I had become a student of what I like to call "Positive, Possibility, Power Thinking." I wasn't necessarily an extraordinary runner, but I truly loved to run, especially long distances.

The brilliant rays of summer sunshine lit up the vapor that hangs low over open country fields in the early morning. I felt vibrantly alive, running strong, and then the thought hit me: *I'll run 52 marathons in 52 weeks to raise money and awareness for leukemia!* The statement looped over and over in my mind as I finished the rest of my run, and I absolutely knew I could do it!

It had only been a few months since I had joined the Leukemia & Lymphoma Society's national marathon training group called Team In Training. Not only was I trained to run a marathon, but I also had to raise money to help find a cure for leukemia, plus choose a marathon to run with the group. I chose the Honolulu Marathon. And to help every runner understand the brutality of this disease known as leukemia, we were each matched with a local leukemia patient. I was matched with a five-year-old boy named Glen. When I first met him, he looked like any other youngster. But as the months flew by, his health declined quickly. Despite undergoing a bone-marrow transplant from his older sister, which was then his best hope of recovery, the procedure was not successful. A little more than a year after I first met this healthy-looking little boy, his mom informed me that Glen had passed away. She told me that his entire family was around him, and she spoke the words to him, "Go to Jesus, baby."

Already stoked by the fires of my "Positive, Possibility, Power Thinking" life philosophy, little Glen's passing was like pouring gasoline upon a bonfire. The flames of my passion and commitment to run 52 marathons in 52 weeks burned brighter and hotter. I had worked for 16 years as a disc jockey at WHOK-95.5FM in Lancaster, Ohio, and I was a super healthy, wild and crazy bachelor. My lifestyle was ideal for me to head off into the unknown to pursue something that many people described as crazy.

Weeks and then months passed as I started to up my weekly running miles and intensity. I began to do at least one 20-mile run every weekend so that my body would become accustomed to going that kind of distance. On every run, the fire to accomplish this gargantuan running feat burned brighter and hotter within me.

This was the mid-1990s, and the Internet was in its infancy. In order to set up my sponsorship, find officially organized marathons to run, and arrange lodging and travel plans, it was all phone calls, faxes, press releases, and a lot of chutzpah. Many nights, I would fall asleep after a long day of running, working, and tirelessly promoting what I called my "Super Run for the Cure."

Finally, it was time to run, and I loaded Bo, my Golden Retriever, into my car. I locked the door to my home in Hide-A-Way Hills, Ohio, and headed to Cleveland to start my run at the 1996 Cleveland Marathon. It was the perfect start to my year of running since Cleveland was my hometown, and my parents still lived there. Cleveland would be where Bo would live over the next year with my parents.

I finished the Cleveland Marathon in a little more than four hours, feeling great. But then the thought hit me on the drive back to my parents' house, *Whoa! I have to do this 51 more times!*

As the weeks, months and miles flew by during my Super Run, I ran across almost all of North America, including the continental U.S., Alaska, Canada, and Hawaii. I drove 65,000 miles in my trusty SUV, and flew 60,000 miles to complete my year of marathoning for a cure. I ran a trail marathon around the Kilauea volcano on the Big Island of Hawaii; a marathon on a track in Dayton, Ohio (104 ½ laps); on the streets of Montreal; through the rain of Olympia, Washington; and finished up with number 51 being the Holy Grail of Running—the Boston Marathon. I concluded with number 52, the Big Sur Marathon in Carmel, California. I raised thousands of dollars for leukemia research along the way. I also spent thousands of my own dollars to make it all happen. And on yet another 14-hour drive by myself through the heart of America on my way to run yet another 26.2-mile race, I would say to myself with all the intensity I could muster, "I can do this!"

Although to date they have yet to find a cure for leukemia, the rate of remission for most leukemia patients is better than ever, and I know that I played a small part in this. With a burning passion and the ability to do so, I truly learned that ordinary people can accomplish extraordinary things. From May 5, 1996 to April 27, 1997, I unleashed my inner champion to successfully run 52 marathons in 52 weeks to help find a cure for leukemia. And I thought about that five-year-old boy the whole way.

—Karl W. Gruber—

Boston Love

If you are losing faith in human nature,
go out and watch a marathon.
~Kathrine Switzer

As I arrived for my first marathon, I saw a sign that said: "The person who starts the race is not the same person who finishes the race." I wondered who I would be once I crossed the historic Boston Marathon finish line. What would change? What moments would fuel my mind, body and spirit while running? What part of the 26.2 miles would stay in my soul forever?

The journey of a marathon starts long before the starting gun goes off. The voyage starts when you ask yourself a few questions. Can I complete a marathon? Do I even want to complete a marathon? What does it take to finish a marathon? For me, the motivation to run a marathon came in November 2015 while sitting around a table of 13 women in a New York City brownstone rented by iconic runner Kathrine Switzer. Kathrine is known not only for breaking barriers as the first woman to officially enter and run the Boston Marathon in 1967, but also for creating positive global social change for 50 years. Millions of women are now empowered by the simple act of running because of her fearlessness.

As each woman introduced herself, explaining why she was there and why she runs, I was surprised to learn that only two us had never run a marathon. I was a 15-year, two-mile-a-day runner with a couple of 5K races under my belt.

Kathrine inspired us that day with her dream to create 261 Fearless, a global nonprofit organization, to use running as a vehicle to empower and unite women globally. She asked us to get involved and launch the organization in our own cities and countries. It is hard to say "no" to Kathrine because she is the most amazing woman I have ever met. She is electric and gracious all rolled into one. After bonding with these 13 women from all over the world, I left New York City changed, wishing I could stay and run with my new friends and help Kathrine with 261 Fearless.

In late summer 2016, I received an e-mail from 261 Fearless asking women to apply for charity bibs to run in the 2017 Boston Marathon with Kathrine. It would be the 50th anniversary of her historic feat. My hands shook as I contemplated the decision, thinking there was no way I could run a marathon and yet deeply wanting to do it! Next thing I knew, my roommate from the New York City trip—the other non-marathoner—posted a video where she said in her southern drawl, "I'm doing this!" I opened the invitation, filled out the application and sent it in.

Nine months later, on April 17, 2017, as I walked toward the starting line in Hopkinton, my roommate was at my side for this once-in-a-lifetime experience. As we walked behind Kathrine with 125 other women (and a few men), we grabbed hands and said a prayer we would finish. The gun went off, and we started to run.

I felt great looking ahead at the colored hats and shirts of thousands of runners. The energy of the crowd swept me up for the first seven miles as I ran downhill and uphill with hundreds of people cheering me on. Then I started feeling the tightness in my legs, the slowing of my pace, and the reality that I had 19 more miles to go. I was not discouraged because I had trained well, but I knew it would take every ounce of tenacity to complete.

I was also running for the 100 people who donated $8,000 to my charity so I could run the Boston Marathon. I knew there was nothing to stop me from finishing that race even if I had to walk part of the time. The generosity of my donors fueled me in the doubtful moments. As I approached the beginning of Heartbreak Hill, a blind woman and her coach ran next to me on the left and a man with blade feet ran on my right. My spirit soared as I witnessed these two incredible individuals.

Heartbreak Hill was "Heartfelt Hill" for me because my son Thomas graduated from Boston College in 2014, and that was the last hill until his dorm. I loved that hill! Just as I ran down the hill onto the "Haunted Mile," a flat part of the race in Newton, my husband and younger son hugged me. A mile later, a member from my company, Women TIES, and her sister-in-law, an Ironwoman I supported, hugged me and inspired me to finish the last few miles.

Down the hill and the big left turn onto Boylston Street, the crowd noise was louder than if the Boston Red Sox had just beaten the New York Yankees. I couldn't believe how loud that crowd was and how many people stayed to cheer us on. The elite athletes had finished. Kathrine Switzer finished an hour before, at the age of 70, realizing her big dream. I didn't feel like a charity runner when I heard that crowd. Someone called my name, and it was my friend Dawn. Miraculously, we had caught up to each other the last mile of the race. Was it fate? I say it was our prayers that helped us cross the finish line.

At the end of the race, I was happy and proud. During the race, I had tried to give back to the crowd as much as they gave to me. I stopped to take photos, danced for them, acknowledged them, and shook their hands. I gave hugs to people who held up a "Do You Need a Hug?" sign, slapped as many little girls' hands as I could to make them happy, and slowed down to bask in the true love of Boston.

In the end, I realized how much people really care about each other. The nightly news doesn't always remind us about the good in everyday America. I felt it that day. People do believe in each other. We want to love others. We show our love the best we can. We are there in service and support, from the youngest of us to the oldest.

I am changed forever by my family, the financial supporters who gave to my charity bib, and my new expansive Boston family. The road sign was right: I am not the same person as when I started the race. I'm a proud, female Boston Marathoner filled with love.

— Tracy Chamberlain Higginbotham —

Storms and Strength

There are some things you learn best in calm,
and some in storm.
~Willa Cather

As a runner of many city races, I decided to register for a lakeside half marathon, a first for me. I could hardly wait to escape work and woes, and enjoy the beauty of Lake Powell in Page, Arizona. There's nothing like running on a shady forest path or along a beautiful beach to help one forget about one's troubles.

When I registered for the race, however, I had no idea that this half marathon would take on so much more meaning to me than any other race would.

In October 2014, my sister Tammie was diagnosed with stage 4 liver and colon cancer. Because I had lost many friends to cancer, I knew what the diagnosis meant. With treatment, she would have a year to live. Without treatment, probably six months. At age 55, she decided to fight and have the treatment. We all supported her decision.

That next year, her two adult daughters set aside their lives to help their mom get through the treatments. I did my best to help as much as I could. My running took a back seat during this time, as there would be no escape from the inevitable: My sister was dying. One night after work, I tried to run two miles, but had to stop halfway. The thought of losing my older sister overcame me, and I broke down and cried on the side of the road. Tammie fought hard, but in October 2015 she lost her battle.

I knew I still had the Lake Powell half marathon to complete that month, but my heart just wasn't in it. My nieces, however, urged me to go because they understood how much I love to run. "Mom would want you to go!" they told me. They were right. She loved Lake Powell and would want me to see it. She was genuinely happy for me when I had told her about the race months before. So my husband and I packed up the car and headed north from Phoenix. It was the first time I would see the famous lake.

As we approached Page, Arizona, I noticed dark storm clouds hovering over the small town. How appropriate. The clouds matched my mood. "Looks like rain," I said. I searched the weather apps frantically on my phone. Sure enough, a storm with cold rain and wind was in the forecast. Running a half marathon is hard enough without the cold rain and wind. "Oh, no!" I cried. "It'll be so difficult to do a trail run in the rain. The rocks will be slippery!"

"What do you want to do? We can turn around and head back if you want," my husband said, leaving the decision up to me.

Strangely enough, at that moment, the story of the biosphere in Tucson, Arizona, came to mind. In this science experiment, a group of scientists had built a sealed ecosystem that was supposed to lead toward replicating the perfect environment outside the sphere. Inside the sphere, they included a manmade ocean, rainforest, and wetlands to study. They grew their own trees and harvested their own food. After a while, the scientists noticed that the trees were dying. They would grow only so high and then fall over. Alarmed, the scientists studied the water, air and soil, hoping to find a cause. Finally, they figured out that the trees were dying because there was no wind inside the dome. Trees need windstorms to make them stronger. The wind makes the roots dig into the soil deeply. The beating of the wind on the tree trunks makes them grow thicker, able to withstand the next storm. Without the storms, the trees never matured. Instead, they grew to be top heavy and fell over.

As we approached Page, I couldn't help but remember the "storm" my family had endured over that year. Cancer had swept over us like a violent hurricane, taking Tammie from us and altering our lives forever. All of us wish we could have avoided it. Yet all of us came through it stronger, more mature, and more prepared for the next storm. Isn't that how it is with storms? We fear them because they can destroy everything we hold dear and even kill those we cherish. We would love a life without any storms, yet, ironically, we need them. Just like the trees in that biosphere, storms make us stronger. Afterward, the air is cleaner, and the earth is replenished. Life goes on.

"Let's keep going," I told my husband. "A little rain won't hurt."

The day of the race was cold and cloudy. We had a few sprinkles at the starting line, but it didn't rain. Lake Powell was as beautiful as I had heard. With the sun barely peeking over the mountains, the run around the lake was as tranquil as I knew it would be. During the race, I paused to watch the sunrise through the dark clouds. I felt my sister's spirit with me, and I knew she was glad I was there. With each step along the rocky and uneven trail, I thought of Tammie's brave battle with cancer. Like the rocky trail, each step of her cancer journey was unpredictable and sometimes dangerous. She could no longer run, so I ran for her.

The clean air and desert scenery were exactly what my ailing spirit needed. As I crossed the finish line, I felt renewed. Later that night, the rainstorm hit. We listened to the downpour and watched the lightning show from the safety of our hotel room. The storm was breathtaking. As we headed home the next day, the sun rose over the lake, and the air was crisp. I was grateful that I had decided to stay and run the Lake Powell half marathon.

It's true that we want to avoid the storms because they are frightening and powerful. We fear them because we cannot control them. I often think of what I would have missed had we turned around and returned home after seeing the threatening storm clouds over Lake Powell.

Running has always been a way for me to escape my troubles, but now I realize that running can also be a way to endure the storms and come away stronger on the other side of the proverbial finish line.

—R. A. Douthitt—

Racing into a New Life

Few things in life match the thrill of a marathon.
~Fred Lebow

I decided to run my first marathon—Honolulu—while going through a divorce. Training for it gave me hope and kept me motivated during a time of sadness and loneliness.

Training began in the blazing summer heat, but the weather began to change as weeks and months rolled by. As the runs got longer, the days grew shorter and colder, pushing me out of my comfort zone more and more.

My 20-miler was in late November, and I ran it with determination. It was snowing, and there was no one else on the streets that morning. It was so quiet! So still! And my sneakers were the only treads to hit the road.

Part of getting divorced meant working a second job as a server in a local restaurant. One night at work, I reminded the manager that I needed the first week of December off to go to Honolulu. Later that night, a fellow server asked me some questions about my trip.

Leanne and I were friends at work, yet we were quite different. She was a talented artist and the lead singer in a local rock band. She was (and still is) cool beyond cool! I envied her candor, free spirit and fierce independence. She was not an athlete at all. She loved eating chips and fast food, staying up late and sleeping in, and smoking cigarettes. Yet, a few days later, she asked if she could go with me to my race. I couldn't wait!

Next thing I knew, we were on a plane to Honolulu. She was excited and decided this would be a new start for her, too. By the time we touched the tarmac in Honolulu, she had decided to do the 10K walk.

The next day at the Expo, we each picked up a race packet—mine for the marathon, hers for the 10K, her first event ever! We both left the Expo feeling wildly excited. It was the start of my marathon career and the start of her health kick.

After a restless sleep, we made our way to the start line. We gave each other pep talks about how proud we were of each other and watched in silence as fireworks lit up the pre-race sky. This was the moment I had worked so hard for, the test of my physical and mental endurance. Could I make it through all 26.2 miles? Survive this painful divorce?

The starting gun sounded, and off we went. The terrain rolled up and down hills and wound through cozy neighborhoods. Miles later, I passed an elderly man running in wooden sandals. I was told later that he was in his nineties. His grace and power have become an inspiration to me.

After four hours and 48 minutes, I swung into Kapiolani Park, and crossed the finish line into a sea of people. I had made it! And, somehow, Leanne was right there. Both of us were glowing from our victories. Quickly, we gathered ourselves and our cherished medals, made our way back to the hotel and hit the beach!

We relaxed on the sand, listening to the rhythmic waves of the ocean. We took swims in the cool, salty water while stretching out our well-used bodies, melting away the aches. Relief. Pride. Confidence. We didn't know it at the time, but that's what that trip brought to our lives, along with a friendship that would weather any storm over the years to come.

We spent a few days exploring the island. Oahu changed us. It brought us to life. A week later, we flew home to the snow-covered farms of the Mohawk River Valley and went back to work.

The following summer, Leanne and I went for a hike in the Adirondacks. On our drive there, we wound around the Great Sacandaga Lake heading north, chatting and catching up. In a desolate area, she pulled over beside a chain-link fence with the lake looming in the distance. Suddenly, she cut the engine and got out, which caused me alarm. Had something happened to the car? Was she sick?

She called to me, "Get out of the car." With wide eyes, I got out and met her beside the car, its maroon paint glistening in the sunshine. She turned to me and said, "Do you know why we stopped here?" Seriously, I had no idea. She asked, "How long have we been driving?"

I didn't know exactly, so I replied, "A while. A pretty long time." That's when she gave me a gift I don't think she had intended.

She told me, "We drove 26.2 miles. That's how far you ran in Hawaii. You rarely give yourself credit for anything, and you need to know that what you did is pretty incredible."

I was silent, amazed because she gave me the gift of reflection. I ran 26.2 miles, and she put that feat into physical and mental perspective. To this day, I am grateful for that pause on the side of the road. It is one of my fondest memories. We both stepped it up in Hawaii and became healthier, happier and stronger versions of ourselves.

When the going is rough, the tough get running. From divorce to dynamic duo, we healed our hearts through running in Honolulu. It brought out the best in us, and we inspired each other. The self-confidence, pride, and focus we learned at the Honolulu Marathon continue to deliver in abundance and for years to come.

Who would have thought that 26.2 miles would give me a forever best friend, too? Fifteen years later, we are both still on our health kicks!

— Sarah A. Richardson —

Believing in Myself

In every walk with nature, one receives
far more than he seeks.
~John Muir

My husband and I were on a vacation. He told me about a hidden lake that was on top of a mountain nearby. Seeing that lake was on his bucket list. The distance was 10 miles round trip, and it was rated an intermediate to difficult hike. Right away, I began to panic because I didn't know if I had the capacity to make it. I hadn't been exercising, and I had fallen into the mindset that because I was getting older it was only natural that I would have less energy and drive.

Early the next morning, we began our ascent. Right away, I knew this was going to be very hard. About halfway up, we met a discouraged couple who had given up trying to reach the lake. I noticed how disappointed the husband seemed to be, and I determined right then that I would continue no matter what.

Strangely, as we walked, I stopped thinking about not being able to endure the walking. Instead, I began to enjoy the beauty of the area and our conversation. What I had considered to be an unattainable goal had become a source of fulfillment.

As the day progressed and the trail became more challenging, I could sense that my husband was growing concerned about our timing. We had to get off that mountain before dark, or we would have to find refuge from the cold and the many animals in the area.

At last, we reached the top. The hidden lake was enchanting. Birds were singing and flitting from tree to tree as if they were welcoming us. The tranquility of the water was overwhelmingly serene. Too soon, it was time to depart, because we had to make it down before nightfall. We didn't even have time to rest on the way down. We did it, and we were safely in the truck heading back to our campsite while it was still light.

Over the next few days, I noticed that my perception of myself began to change. I realized that I could do many things that I had been fearful to do. I also made the decision to exercise every day so that I could stay healthy and strong. There are so many things that I want to do and places I would like to see. I am excited to know that many adventures are in store for me now that I have my new attitude. I intend to enjoy life to the fullest!

— Ruth Roy —

A Marathon Waltz

There is nothing so momentary as a sporting achievement, and nothing so lasting as the memory of it.
~Greg Dening

A New York City Marathon banner flapped overhead, beckoning runners to the starting line on the Staten Island side of New York's Verrazzano Bridge. On a crisp November morning, I waited to tour the city's five boroughs by running 26.2 miles with more than 45,000 other runners.

I have run marathons in a variety of states and countries, but on this particular morning my usual pre-race jitters were different. I was serving as a guide for a disabled athlete, a 41-year-old blind runner.

Physically, I felt in shape, having trained at local parks and nearby running trails. But as we waited for the official start, I suddenly had the sinking feeling of being ill-prepared. My running partner for the next 26.2 miles was totally blind and completely in my care. I had to rise to the occasion.

So here we were, his muscular five-foot, nine-inch frame next to my slight five feet. A rope connected our wrists, his right to my left. As I triple-checked his shoelaces, I asked him if he was ready to "rock New York City."

He responded with an enthusiastic shout, "Let's do it!"

As we began to run, I worried about potholes, uneven road grades and clothing — a hat here, a sweatshirt there, all discarded by fellow runners as they warmed up.

Running together was difficult. We needed to find a mutually comfortable pace. I felt like we were two preteens at our very first dance.

My running partner was donned in a bright neon yellow shirt denoting his first name followed by the words "Blind Runner." He smiled graciously as spectators continuously screamed his name and cheered for him.

As we logged the miles, I explained in vivid detail certain landmarks that were integral to the running course: famous streets in Brooklyn, the 59th Street Bridge, and First Avenue in Manhattan. As we entered Central Park at mile 24, I tried my very best to describe the beautiful foliage. When I saw the finish sign and clock, I told my running partner just how close he was to attaining his goal.

Somewhere along the way, our awkward first dance became a synchronized waltz. At the finish line, we raised our wrists in triumph. I realized that our shared determination was our real tether.

My partner turned to me and said, "Hey, same time next year. What do you think?"

I was exhausted, more mentally than physically, but I answered, "Yes, definitely."

And so we danced again the following November—and many more.

—Patricia Ann Rossi—

The Roots of Barefoot Ted

Don't ask what the world needs. Ask what makes you come alive, and go do it. Because what the world needs is people who have come alive.
~Howard Thurman

Human beings are amazing critters with amazing stories... each and every one of us. We are all on a unique journey, trying to form the best version of ourselves, step by step, in a never-ending parade of potentials, new heights and insights. And the vehicle of our journey, the veritable temple of our being, is our body. And what a body! What a marvelous work of ingenious complexity, so capable, so well suited for the world in which we live... or so it should be.

Anyone who has read Christopher McDougall's book *Born to Run*, an all-time bestselling book on running, already knows a great deal more about me than they probably care to remember. Chapter 25 starts out with the infamous line: "Barefoot Ted was right, of course." But what was I right about? For me, the solution for finding the path forward in my running required getting rid of the shoes and learning how to operate the original equipment. It required re-examining my roots, both literally and figuratively.

I grew up mostly barefoot. I explored the world barefoot. I even wore clothing that had bare feet embroidered on the chest! The bare foot had always been my first best choice for outdoor adventures from my childhood on.

Growing up in Southern California in the 1970s had some rare benefits. The formative period of my life was filled with images of hippies and surfers, of Nature Children and a sense that the simple things in life are not so much about what we own, but rather where we are and what we can do. The beach and beach life always rose to the top of ideal locations to just be. Next, the mountains and the paths that went on forever. Wild nature and all her majesty were always regarded as the supreme good, and the legs and feet the primal vehicles to explore the world.

On top of this, I had a truly remarkable grandmother whose magnetic personality and grand vision of the good life had everything to do with turning her modest suburban yard into orchards of paradisiacal proportions: avocados, pomegranates, figs, oranges, lemons, guavas, plums, etc. Sunlight, water, bare feet and love combined to create an endless harvest of the best things in life: living food. At the core of her being was a deep pride in the Choctaw Indian blood she inherited from her cherished grandmother. She made it clear that this combination of native roots was to be regarded as the part most valuable, the gift of the best my ancestors had passed to me. I paid attention to her when she spoke.

The trajectory of my life set me up for a unique approach to mastering the art of running long distances. In 2003, I was on the verge of turning 40... and my mind was occupied with a promise I had made to myself 20 years earlier. In 1984, I attended a party for the 40-year-old son of a U.S. Senator who ran the Los Angeles Marathon as a birthday challenge. I was impressed and thought I would revisit this concept as I got closer to 40.

During the years between 20 and 40, I made small forays into the art of running, but one hour was always my limit. I was never overly exhausted exactly; rather, I could not handle the building pain in my feet, legs and back. I was dumbfounded. How did those people go farther? My quest endured, but my experiments in running were not working out for me. After exhausting nearly every avenue of running technology, I was about to give up. I was certain that some newfangled running shoe would help me transcend my personal limitations. Yet, one hour remained the limit.

My solution came with a leap of faith in late 2003, but the outcome proved to be superlatively perfect for my own goals. I took off my shoes and rediscovered the light, quick and smooth motion that truly efficient runners know. If a foot has been trained through years of exploration and use like mine had been, the foot alone can do amazing things. And when I learned that I could master a way to run better, smoother and more joyfully without shoes, I knew I had to share it. At the time, hardly anyone imagined it possible. My generation had been conditioned on the idea that the human foot was by no means prepared to handle the stresses of running without help or support.

As in my youth, this "No Trespassing" sign did not stop me from experimenting. When I found that I was able to run smoothly and light in my bare feet on hard surfaces, I was overwhelmed with excitement. As I studied the history of modern running, I started to see athletes pop up from the not-too-distant past who had been barefoot at elite levels. A whole new world was opening up to me. And as I studied more about our shared ancestors and their primal capacities, it became crystal clear that we as a species were, simply using our default equipment, the preeminent long-distance running animal on the planet. The bare foot was a marvel. It was one of the most important survival tools that we had inherited.

Yet clearly the bare foot was not ideal in every situation, not the perfect solution every time. Humans had also been clever about inventing things to help them go farther and do more. That's when I started studying what I call the natural selection of footwear in human culture. My curiosity was piqued when I found that humans all over the planet had solved the problem of footwear in many different ways, but most paid homage to the foot first. This led me to seek out places in the world where the most basic and ancient of footwear, the simple sandal, was still being used in daily life. I found them!

My dream to find a living culture of sandal runners led me down into the Copper Canyon of Chihuahua, Mexico, in 2006 to meet and run with the Tarahumara tribe, the Rarámuri, considered to be among the greatest long-distance mountain runners in the world. It was on this trip that I first met Caballo Blanco, Luis Escobar, Scott Jurek, Eric Orton, Jenn Shelton, Billy Barnett and Christopher McDougall, whose book highlighted the experiences we all shared in those deep canyons. It's also where I first met Manuel Luna.

That meeting changed my life. It inspired the creation of a sandal company and the introduction of sandal running to a much wider audience. Today, like surfers making surfboards, we make LUNA Sandals in our own factory. We take pride in keeping alive the art of sandal making, and we celebrate with our fans all over the world the simple joy of running free!

— "Barefoot Ted" McDonald —

Family Ties

Running in Circles

We can only be said to be alive in those moments when our hearts are conscious of our treasures.
~Thornton Wilder

The fog was thick at daybreak as my son and I gathered at the starting line with 100 other racers. We were about to embark on our first ultramarathon. Nervous energy filled the air as runners set up their personal aid stations and made trips to the portable toilets. Although I had run dozens of marathons, I had never run a race like this… for several reasons.

First, this was a "timed" event. Every race I had run prior had been a "distanced" event. Whether it be 100 meters or 26.2 miles, I always knew how far I had to run. This particular race was six hours long. The goal was to show up and run as many miles as possible in the allotted time. I had set a goal of running 40 miles, but had never run that far, and honestly didn't know what to expect. Despite having run many marathons, I couldn't imagine running any farther. After each and every one of those races, I was completely spent, sometimes taking days (or weeks) to fully recover.

Second, those six hours would be spent running in circles on a .355-mile cinder track. I was no stranger to a cinder oval, as my high-school years had been spent training and racing on a similar track. I am sure there were days I even spent two hours doing so, but *six* hours was a whole new level of crazy!

Third, and most notably contributing to my elevated level of anxiety,

I was set to run that race with my seven-year-old son, Shamus. Shamus would not be so much "running" the race as he would be rolling in a stroller in front of me. Shamus was born with cerebral palsy and uses a wheelchair as his primary means of mobility but throughout his young life he has run thousands of miles with me as I trained for marathons.

One month prior to the Sweltering Summer Ultramarathon, we had run our first race together—a four-mile race on the 4th of July. Shamus had enjoyed that race so much that he asked if he could run my next race with me, which he knew would be my first ultramarathon. After much discussion with my wife, Nichole, and after reaching out to the race director to gain permission for wheels on the course, I agreed (reluctantly). I was hesitant because I wasn't sure if I could run for six hours on my own, let alone while pushing Shamus. However, I knew that we would be on a closed course, Nichole would be there, and Shamus was bound to get bored running in circles. I figured he could stop whenever he wanted. The race director was on board with the plan and excited to have us there on race day.

As we were given the one-minute warning, I leaned down and gave Shay a kiss on the forehead. He gave me a fist bump and said, "We got this, Dad!" I was glad that at least one of us was confident. As we waited for the starter's pistol at the front of the pack, my last thought was, *What did I get us into?*

Luckily, my legs remembered what to do, and we set off together at a steady pace. Many experienced participants started at a walk or slow jog. I had no idea how to pace myself for a quarter day of running, so I ran at a pace that felt comfortable. I knew Shamus didn't want to be out for a stroll, so we settled in at about 7:30 per mile. I quickly realized that many participants had no intention of being on the track for the whole six hours, planning to stop at a set "goal distance" of their choice. I was in it for the long haul but I figured Shamus would only last a few laps.

As those laps ticked by, Shamus entertained me by telling me about the latest chapters he was reading in *Harry Potter*. I had read all the books several times, but loved hearing it from his perspective. The details he gave provided me with a welcome distraction from all the running in circles we were doing. However, I frequently interrupted Shamus's storytelling by checking on him.

"Shay, how's it going? You want to take a break?" I asked. He gave a quick "No" and then proceeded with his conversation. After an hour and many laps, I could tell he was getting irritated with my interruptions. Together, we rounded the track. I listened and put one foot in front of the other. Shay chatted and enjoyed the wind on his cheeks.

The sun had burned off the fog, and though the temperatures were rising, Shamus and I found a steady rhythm. As time passed, I noticed that most runners were resting, rehydrating, refueling, stretching, and finding shade. I hydrated and fueled on the run, grabbing what I needed as we passed the aid table we had set up that morning. I knew many of these runners were much more practiced at ultrarunning than I was, but I was feeling okay and decided that if I stopped, I might not start again.

Finally, after about four-and-a-half hours of running, Nichole stepped in and told Shamus he needed to take a break to eat, stretch his legs, and use the restroom. He agreed unenthusiastically, but insisted that I keep going. By then, it was 90 degrees, and I was exhausted. I would have loved to lie down in the shade, but I obliged my "teammate's" request.

There was no respite from the sun on the track, and my legs were screaming at me to stop. Without Shamus to entertain and encourage me, I had a hard time finding a groove. I plodded along, took some walking breaks, and simply tried to keep moving in a clockwise direction, one step at a time. Fortunately, Shamus took only a 30-minute rest. Nichole loaded him in his running chair, and we were together again. I leaned on him for support, worked through muscle cramps, aches and sore feet, and simply did my best to continue forward. I found motivation in knowing that stiff, sore, cramped legs were a daily occurrence for Shamus. He persevered through each day in spite of the physical limitations imposed by his cerebral palsy. Quickly, I found my stride with him leading the way.

As the race clock neared six hours, we decided to squeeze in one more lap. The sun was high in the sky and we were drained, but as we completed our final and 125th lap of the day, we felt accomplished as we realized we had covered 45 miles! Even more surprising was that no one else had run over 115 laps. Shamus and I had won… by *10* laps, nearly four miles more than our closest competitor. Onlookers and runners were impressed with our feat. They patted me on the back and congratulated me on *pushing* Shamus. However, I corrected them immediately, because there is no doubt in my mind that Shamus was the one doing the *pulling*.

— Shaun P. Evans —

A Double Blessing

Exercise should be regarded as tribute to the heart.
~Gene Tunney

After my mother-in-law Judy said she'd love to go to Israel with us, my husband Eric had to warn her. "This trip requires a lot of walking. To see everything, you'll need to be able to walk several miles each day." Eric paused, trying to be sensitive. "We're concerned about you being able to fully enjoy the trip."

I stepped in. "Judy, we're going to start training to get in shape for the trip. I need to start exercising, too, so we're going to do it together. Let's make a walking schedule."

We decided to walk three mornings a week. My sister-in-law Lori planned to join us. She and Eric's brother, Jeff, were going on the trip as well.

That first morning, I laced up my Nikes and clipped the leash on our dog, Piper. The two of us walked across the street to Judy's house. She and Lori, along with Judy's dogs, met us in the driveway, and we started walking. We planned to start off slowly, walking just to the end of our road and back.

As we walked, we talked mostly about nothing—the dogs checking each other out, what we planned to make for dinner that night, even the weather.

As Judy spoke, I listened carefully to her breathing. She was in her seventies, and she hadn't exercised for several years. I didn't want her to get too winded, but I was pleasantly surprised by her stamina.

Just a few weeks into our training, I knew it was time to tackle the big hill not far from our homes. When Lori and I suggested it, Judy balked.

"In Israel, the land isn't flat," we said. "You'll need to be able to manage stairs and hills in order to see everything."

Judy nodded with determination and headed toward the big hill. As we climbed it, Lori and I encouraged Judy to take breaks when needed. When she stopped to rest, I was secretly relieved. I could use the breather, too.

As our trip to Israel inched closer, Judy's endurance improved noticeably. So did our conversations. We talked about marriage and family, matters of faith, and how much we were looking forward to our upcoming trip.

I loved our walks. They were designed to train our bodies for all the walking we'd be doing in Israel, but I realized they were also good for my spirit. I'd always been close to my husband's family, and the time we spent walking reminded me how blessed I was to have married into such a special group of people.

We talked about Larry, my father-in-law, who'd passed away the previous summer. He'd suffered several incapacitating strokes during his last two years of life, and Judy had been his primary caregiver. It had been so hard, and I knew she missed him. We all did. But we also knew how happy he'd be that Judy was getting to take such a special trip.

The walks were good for all three of us—not just for our bodies but for our emotions. It was a double blessing.

We walked a bit farther each time, and by the week before our trip, even the big hill wasn't as daunting as it once was. The first time we made it to the top without stopping, we felt like throwing a party.

I grinned, so proud of the progress Judy had made over the past few months. Her stamina had increased. She looked younger, and I'm sure she felt younger, too. Honestly, I was proud of all three of us. I'd lost a few pounds, and I could tell my calf muscles were more toned from all those mornings of walking up the big hill. I just felt better on the days we walked than on the ones we didn't.

When our plane finally touched down in Israel, I was so excited that I could hardly sit still. I couldn't wait to walk up and down the streets of Jerusalem, visit the Jordan River and the Dead Sea, and see all of the sights I'd spent my whole life reading about.

I smiled at Lori and Judy, knowing that we were ready to experience it all. For months, we'd been putting in the work, and now nothing would stop us from having the trip of a lifetime.

— Diane Stark —

Muddling Through

Your children get only one childhood.
Make it memorable.
~Regina Brett

What were we thinking? I was standing at the starting line for the Marine Mud Run—a 5K that includes a trek through a stream, hill climbs, and a course of obstacles to finish in a long, soupy mud pit one has to low-crawl through. The USMC sponsored this "fun" run, and they took it seriously. At every challenge, they stationed a Marine to do his best drill-sergeant impersonation as the challengers ran by.

My family had decided to do the team run. The rules: no man left behind. Teams start together. Teams finish together.

As we crept to the starting line, I glanced around at the competition. There were warrior teams in matching uniforms. Young adults prepared themselves for combat. Some wolfed down an energy bar. Others warmed up with a quick set of jumping jacks.

And then there was my team. My wife was busy chatting with another runner, oblivious to the world around them. My daughters, ages eight and three, were sitting on the ground playing with a butterfly.

An old-fashioned air-raid siren screamed out. War whoops sounded all around us as the mass of runners started forward. My daughters brought me the butterfly so it wouldn't get stepped on. Our team with the butterfly mascot riding on my shoulder started off with a shuffle but gathered speed, hitting our stride of a walking jog.

Teams of runners passed us on all sides, many slowing to give my daughters a high-five as they ran by.

The first challenge was running up a stream. The autumn water was cold but not unbearable. But with each step, the water got deeper. My wife and I each grabbed a girl in our arms to keep her from drifting downstream. Dripping and giggling, we climbed onto the bank to start the hill climbs.

My wife was keeping pace with our older daughter, encouraging her to push to the top. Our three-year-old fell behind the pack. I could see her spirit crashing as her big sister pulled away. Someone had to do something quick.

I took a knee as the three-year-old climbed onto my back. With a kick in my ribs and a strangling choke around my neck, she pointed her steed to the top of the hill. We were off at a full gallop, my daughter squealing out her warrior cry as we caught up and passed the others.

At the top of the hill, we sidestepped through tires, climbed a rope ladder, and leapt log hurdles. Then came the six-foot wall. As we approached, the Marine stationed there saw our team charging his way. He waved us to go around the wall. My girls were having none of it. They were warriors. They wanted to go over the wall.

I went up first and straddled the wall. Then my wife handed me one daughter and ran to the other side as I passed our daughter over the top. The process repeated with our younger daughter. Finally, my wife scrambled over the top. As a team, my family topped each obstacle.

As we started down the backside of the hill, a lady near us slipped and fell. My little girls scrambled to her side to make sure she didn't hurt herself. Then realizing all the obstacles were behind them, they asked if they could roll down the hill. The girls screamed out in laughter as they tumbled down the hill.

There was just one last obstacle — the mud pit. As we waded into the muck, I knew we were in trouble. One of my daughter's feet got stuck deep in the mud. I pulled her free only to see that the sticky stuff kept both of her shoes, and she was not happy about it. I passed her over to her mother and fell to my hands and knees. My wife draped our daughter across my back, and away we went.

Side by side, laughing and spitting mud, we crawled. Climbing out of the pit and crossing the line was an event. Our team of warriors was on as we crawled out by a hundred other mud-caked victors of the pit.

Our team didn't finish first, not even close. But in the spirit of the team event, we crossed the finish line hand-in-muddy-hand. This was our first time competing in the Mud Run, but with the encouragement of the girls, this became a yearly event we shared. The Mud Run taught us that we wanted to live our lives together. It also taught us that there will be plenty of mud pits and high walls to climb. We learned that we can always count on family and never leave a man behind, no matter what the obstacle. And we also learned that towels are good. Lots of towels.

— Larry Hoy —

Running on Empty

Don't forget to cheer for yourself
when you reach the finish line.
~Charmaine J. Forde

For the past three years, I have been working full-time, attending school, and raising a family. To say I am tired is an understatement. My teenage daughter has signed up to run a 5K this Saturday morning, and I intend to return to bed once I drop her off.

I drink my coffee and scurry around to pick whatever I can find to wear off the floor of my bedroom. I put on the wrinkled clothing, pull my hair back in a sloppy ponytail and rush out the door with her. When we arrive and I see the crowd, it occurs to me that I am going to miss her first race. I am overwhelmed with the feeling that I should run with her, even though I believe that I cannot do it. I have never run a race before. In fact, I haven't been physically active at all during the last three years. In addition to the obvious fact that I am not conditioned for a race, I am not dressed for it, nor have I had the proper nutrition and hydration. Despite these barriers, I find myself registering for the race as if I am under the influence of some power other than my own will. "I'll just walk it," I reason to myself. I don't even know what the rules are, if there are any.

I tie my sweat jacket around my waist and stuff my keys in my jeans pocket. Standing in a crowd of people dressed in running clothes, I hear the gun go off to signify the start of the race. Everyone else is running, so I run too. I am dead last. The crowd pulls ahead quickly, and I no longer see my daughter. The sea of runners vanishes over a hill, and I am left with only one other woman.

It isn't long before I begin to walk, and the other woman has done the same. I can tell she is older than me by roughly 20 years. She begins to run again. I cannot let her beat me, so I begin to run too. We continue this series of running and walking, and I pass her. I see a group of women running with a small child. They cannot go any faster because the child is running at a child's pace, which involves a lot of complaining by the child. I pass them. I come upon my daughter's pregnant teacher, and I tell myself that I cannot let a pregnant woman beat me. I run and walk and run and walk until I pass her.

I keep running and walking until I see one of my daughter's classmates. I pass her in my steady run-walk pace, and then I do the same with another one of her classmates. I come upon an area that is set up for the runners to get water, and I take a paper cup. It is impossible to run and drink, so I wet my mouth and throw out the rest. The course is set in Amish country, and the smell of farms is stifling. If I didn't need to breathe, I would just hold my breath.

Amish children line up to watch the race in their lawn chairs. I tell myself that I won't be able to make it up the last hill before the finish, but I keep picking goals such as a telephone pole or a mailbox to run or walk to. I have figured out that if I make my strides long when I walk, I cover more ground. I crest the top of the hill and see a truck parked in the road to stop traffic for the runners. I run through the intersection and to the finish line to find my daughter waiting for me.

I finish in 42 minutes, which is less than my age. My face is burning red and my hip hurts, but I made it. My daughter and I pose for a selfie wearing our numbers. I am so proud of both of us.

Sometimes, life teaches us lessons when we least expect it. I learned that I can complete a 5K without training. Just imagine what I could do if I had actually trained. I learned that, in the end, my daughter will be there for me. I learned that nobody cares if I run in jeans. I learned that it's okay not to know the rules; sometimes we have to figure it out as we go. I learned that running requires focus, which takes one's mind off other things. In this way, running is a healthy alternative to other unhealthy coping means. I learned that people will watch out for me and help me if I need it. I thought I was running for my daughter, but I got so much more than I gave.

— Heidi Kling-Newnam —

Outrunning the Hard Yards

There will come a day when I can no longer run.
Today is not that day.
~Author Unknown

Newlyweds are dreamers. My husband David and I were no exception—envisioning our perfect future with two kids and the stereotypical house with a white picket fence. Life might throw us challenges, we understood, but we were strong and smart.

We had life figured out, and six months into marriage we had begun building our family traditions. Our first one, we decided, would be running the annual Thanksgiving Day 5K Turkey Trot. We believed it was an event we could share with our future children—pushing them in jogging strollers, and then years down the road all running together, side by side. It was our beautiful dream.

Three years later, on Thanksgiving Day, instead of lining up for the annual Turkey Trot, I was lying in a hospital bed in the middle of a different endurance challenge. After six excruciating days of trying to stop labor, our identical twins, Hayden and Holden, came into the world through emergency C-section almost 10 weeks early. Immediately, the boys were whisked from our arms and began a five-week stay in the NICU. We learned they suffered from a condition called Twin-to-Twin Transfusion Syndrome.

We watched as their little bodies endured tests and blood draws every few hours. Because of their fragile state, we could only hold them a few hours a day. Their weights dropped day after day—little Holden barely weighed three pounds. The first time Holden's monitor blared, I stood in horror as a nurse stimulated his little body to start breathing again. The boys fought every day against numerous problems. We fought with them. Life was not a dream but a nightmare—one we could not outrun. By the time they gained enough strength to come home, we were empty—physically and emotionally drained.

Bringing the boys home brought little relief as they were only slightly improved. My husband had gone back to work, and the twins' older sister, only eleven months old, now demanded more time and attention. Suddenly, we were raising three babies, two of whom had significant developmental delays. Three sets of diapers to change, three to comfort, three to shuffle back and forth to doctors (where we spent the majority of our time). For a marriage only three years in the making, it was daunting. The twins would not be comforted as they were sick and frail, while our daughter entered a period of sleep regressions and tantrums. The primary dialogue I shared with my husband was down to two-word phrases: bath time, make bottles, clean kitchen, change diapers.

Every day, we fought the hardness of life. It was a marathon of hard yards. The boys fought for life, my daughter fought for attention, and David and I fought for survival. In this fashion, winter changed to spring, which turned to summer and faded into autumn. Slowly, we found time to expand the two-word phrases into three, adding the word "please" back into our vocabularies. Our sons began overcoming some of their challenges, and I saw in our daughter glimmers of a little girl longing to be Mommy's helper.

Eventually, one beautiful fall day, I pulled out my old running shoes and went for a jog. Soon after, we bought two jogging strollers (a single and a double) and began to take the kids out on Saturday mornings. At first, seeing happy families hurt me, but we were on our way to the same—we were recapturing a little of life's normalcy.

Five days before Thanksgiving, with the kids recovering from their latest illness and with me ill with bronchitis and delirious from sleep deprivation, my husband asked, "Did you sign us up for the Turkey Trot?" No, I hadn't. It hadn't crossed my mind, but I lay awake that night thinking about that family tradition. Could we do it?

***

On Thanksgiving Day, I am standing at the starting line of the Turkey Trot. I am facing in the direction of the hospital. I feel a chill down my spine, so I focus instead on the man standing beside me. He looks older, tired, with a few more gray hairs. When he smiles at me, I notice wrinkles around his eyes that weren't there only a year ago. He leans over and kisses my forehead. We look ahead and notice the race has begun. I lean down into my husband's double stroller and kiss the boys, tears welling up as they look back at me with wide eyes. Looking down at the stroller in front of me, I ask my daughter, "Ready, baby?"

"Daddy come?" my toddler inquires.

"Yes, baby, Daddy come," I confirm.

"Babies come?" she responds.

"Yes, Daddy and babies will be with us, all of us running together." And with that, I feel my breath leave my chest and the tears seep down my cheeks as I push us off into the race.

The run is hard, the hardest of my life. My chest burns from bronchitis, the weight of my toddler in the stroller drags on me, and my legs ache from lack of use. My husband and the twins pass us by and disappear into the crowd. I want to quit at mile 2, knowing I've taxed my body more than it can bear. My feet slow. And then my daughter, who seems to have finally caught on to what's going on around her, looks up and says, "Running, Mommy?"

"Yes, baby. Mommy's running." No, I correct myself, "We're all running, baby." We've all been running for a year now. I think about those hard yards—my boys fighting for life and my daughter's desperate race not to be forgotten in the chaos. I think about us as newlyweds, three years prior, the victory we felt in our veins versus the ghosts of our prior selves that we are today.

I push the stroller faster and force my legs to burn. I feel the pain my boys felt and push harder. We go faster. I feel the defeat my husband felt and push harder. I feel the loneliness of my toddler, and I run harder still. I feel the exhaustion, the heartbreak, the overwhelming hardship of our lives. And with tears streaming down my face and my lungs on fire, I push harder and faster.

Then I push my daughter across that finish line and don't slow until I see my boys up ahead. I gasp for air, and my whole body shakes. I feel weak, empty and raw. But in this rawness, through blurry eyes, I see my family. We've come out on the other side. We've crossed the finish line, and the hard yards have been outrun. And though there isn't a white picket fence, there is something more: a family built of strength and love, a family tested, and a family survived. We are a beautiful dream.

— Kristin Baldwin Homsi —

Christmas in July

Peace on earth will come to stay,
when we live Christmas every day.
~Helen Steiner Rice

When my daughter was three and my son was six, we signed up for a local 1K fun run. My husband and I had already run a few 5Ks on our own, and we were hoping to make this shorter race a true family experience.

It was a brand-new race: the July Jingle Run, a fundraiser to benefit the Chesterfield-Colonial Heights Christmas Mother program. The organization's goal is to make sure no member of the community goes without food, toys, or clothing during the holidays.

We thought it was an excellent opportunity to give back to our community, practice making healthy choices, and have a lot of fun as a family. The real selling point for the children was that we were encouraged to dress up in Christmas attire.

We visited thrift stores in search of Christmas-themed clothing that we could wear in the hot weather of late July. It seemed unlikely until we realized we could buy long-sleeved shirts and cut off the sleeves. Perfect solution.

We arrived early on race day and saw that the park was decorated with Christmas trees, inflatables, and colored lights. The environment was festive; it was truly Christmas in July.

When the race began, my husband and son took off through the woods. My daughter, Delaney, and I were in the back of the pack.

She jogged at a speed that allowed her to chat the entire time. "Will we get a banana at the end?" she asked. "What about cookies? It's a Christmas race, you know!"

I told her I wasn't sure, and the only way to find out was to get to that finish line. She jogged a little, returned to a walk, and jogged some more. At one point, she tripped over a root, cried for a minute, and asked me to hold her. I did, but only until she calmed down. I wanted her to have the experience of crossing the finish line on her own two feet.

When she made it across, she looked so proud as the crowd around us cheered and clapped. She was the youngest race participant that year. She and her brother wore their medals as they walked to different booths, played games, and made crafts. They decorated banks to save for Christmas shopping, made beaded tree ornaments, and colored a few pictures. All four of us enjoyed taking pictures at the selfie booth with reindeer antlers, Santa hats, and elf ears. Plus, there was a booth for race participants to donate new books and toys. We were thrilled to participate in this as well.

The first annual July Jingle Run was a hit for both the Christmas Mother program and my family of four. And while my children are still very young and enticed by shiny medals and free bananas, they are also beginning to understand the bigger picture.

On the way back to our car, one of the race organizers stopped us to chat. "Thank you for coming and helping us out this year," she said.

"You're welcome," I responded. "We are already looking forward to next year!"

"Why did she thank us?" my son asked after she was out of earshot. "Shouldn't we have thanked her? We got to run, eat bananas, and make things to bring home."

My husband and I explained that part of our registration fees and donated items were going to help children in our community have a better Christmas. He thought for a moment and said, "I really like helping."

"We do, too," we told him. "That's one reason we run."

We run other races throughout the year as they fit our schedules, and we are grateful to be able to support various causes and charities.

But the July Jingle Run holds a special place in our hearts as the first one we ran as a family. It's a great cause, a festive theme, and a wonderful reason to celebrate Christmas in July.

— Melissa Face —

He Never Pushed the Baby Carriage

Walking is man's best medicine.
~Hippocrates

My mother had always loved my father, even though they'd been divorced for decades and lived on different continents. So I was delighted when my father came from Eastern Europe to visit us in Dallas. I had my parents under one roof for the second or third time in my life that I could remember.

They got along beautifully except for one thing: I guess she couldn't help it, but my mom would still bring up old grievances. So many years had passed since they were married that these grievances became almost comical.

"You never pushed the baby carriage."

"You never went for a walk with me."

Father looked at me and said, "Well, she's too old for a baby carriage now, but let's all go for a walk."

My mom wasn't ready for that answer.

"I can't. I'm too old. I'm too tired."

So I would go walking with my father instead.

We walked a couple of blocks on a residential street with no sidewalks at a nice, slow pace. When my father, who was in his late seventies, suggested we run, not walk, I thought, *Fine. I'll stop when I see him getting winded.*

Was I surprised! It started out great at first. Then, halfway down the block, I realized he was beating me. I had a hard time catching my breath, but I was too embarrassed to let him know. Finally, I fizzled out, only to see him flying past me effortlessly. Wow! I was an aerobics instructor and dancer/athlete, but I couldn't keep up with a man pushing 80.

When my father realized I was no longer jogging by his side, he turned around and ran back to me. We returned home where my mom had a couple of sweet rolls waiting for us. I passed.

I started thinking about our different lifestyles. Here was an Eastern European man who had spent his life walking. He had walked to work while employed; he walked to grocery stores and to meet friends. In his country, they walked everywhere. In America, we take our dogs for short strolls in the park, but mostly we are couch potatoes. When we go somewhere, we jump into our vehicles. Even if a 7-Eleven is a block away, we drive.

That first jaunt with my father changed my way of thinking about life, health and wellbeing. My way of life was going to lead me to an early old age, poor health and a diminished quality of life. Did I want to end up like my mother, who only walked from her room to the refrigerator and back each day?

While he remained in the U.S., my father and I made it a point to walk and eventually jog daily. Not only did I lose weight, but I felt stronger, healthier and happier.

Meanwhile, my mother was contacted by her surgeon. She had an aneurysm and needed surgery as soon as possible.

"But," the doctor said, "you are not in great condition. You have very little muscle tone, and you're weak. I won't let you have surgery in this condition. You must build up your strength. Start by walking."

Needless to say, that scared me. I hadn't realized how inertia had weakened her. I had tried to get her to walk with me before, but now her life almost depended on it.

My father took the matter into his own hands.

"Florencka," he sweet-talked. "You say I never went for walks with you. Let's start now."

Fortunately, his charm still worked on her. She grumbled and complained, but she made an effort for him. She put on her comfortable clothing, and the three of us hit the street.

It wasn't easy. We'd go half a block and then she'd stop and say, "I can't." I could see she wasn't faking. She was out of breath after a few steps. She was too weak.

Cautiously at first, we took it at her pace.

"Let's go see those beautiful flowers at that big house over there," my father suggested.

"Oh, no. I can't," my mother replied. We ended up walking halfway to that house.

The next day, my father urged a little more.

"Let me make up for the walks I never took with you." This time, we made it to the house with the flowers.

We never pushed my mother to exhaustion, but we did encourage her to try a little harder each day.

I laughed after a couple of weeks of walking when we three met at the kitchen table, my father and I ready for breakfast. My mother walked in, all showered and dressed, and expressed cheerfully, "Let's go for a walk first and eat later."

My father started to protest, "But can't we have a bite to eat first?"

My mother gave him a look and her age-old complaint. "See, you never want to walk with me," she said, smiling.

Without a word, my father got up, and we three went for an early stroll.

A couple of weeks went by, and at a return visit to her doctor, my mother was given the news that she was ready for surgery. There had been a noticeable improvement in her strength, blood pressure and endurance. Leaving the office, the nurse said to us, "By the way, both of you are looking better. Whatever you're doing, don't stop."

Thankfully, my mother's surgery was successful. My father stayed to see how she would do, which I'm sure aided in her recovery. When he returned to Europe, we three kept in touch by mail.

My mother would write: "Thank you for taking walks with me — finally."

After my father's visit and my mother's improved health, I decided I would take better care of myself. I realized I didn't want to end up getting old, tired and weak before my time. Now some 20 years later, I still walk, run and/or take fitness classes several times a week, improving my health and my mind-set. I find there's nothing more stress-relieving than physical activity.

As I grow older, I never want to become a burden to anyone. I want to be able to take care of myself. So I will continue doing what has kept me so healthy and feeling good as long as I am able to. I walk to clear my mind. I walk to think. Walking lifts my spirits. I'm happier after a walk. My energy levels go up, and my stress levels go down. Lethargy, fatigue and boredom are greatly reduced by walking and running.

I will always be grateful to my father for finally walking with my mother, helping to get her into shape for her surgery so she could no longer chide him by saying, "You never walk with me."

And although he hadn't always been a presence in my life, he did instill in me something valuable — the desire to walk for health and life.

So I forgave him for never pushing me in my baby carriage.

— Eva Carter —

The Bridge

A bridge can still be built, while the bitter waters
are flowing beneath.
~Anthony Liccione

The porch door creaked its welcome and then slammed with a thud. "Home, Mom!" my teenage son called. A moment later, he stood beside me in the kitchen, blond hair tousled, cheeks flushed, and blue eyes shining.

I smiled. "How was your day, Grant?" I wanted to hug him, but I knew better. These teen years had brought turbulence. My son had transitioned from home teaching to public school, and suddenly we stood on opposite sides of a gaping chasm. Grant was my second-born son, so I understood that as he stretched to grow, I needed to open my hand. But this was different. Grant was often distant.

"School was good. Track was great." The fridge door opened, and the top half of Grant disappeared behind the door. I chopped veggies and wondered what made this a sharing day. Usually, Grant would come in, nod, drop his backpack, and quietly make his way up the old, curved stairs to his bedroom.

"I'm glad," I said. "What made track great?"

Now the fridge door slammed. "I just love to run," he said, taking a huge bite of apple. "We have an at-home log. We need to run outside of practice. I'm starting in the morning."

"Wonderful," I said. I chopped. Grant chomped.

"Well, I'm going to do homework," my son said. He grabbed

his backpack and headed out of the kitchen. But when he got to the dining room, he stopped and turned. "Mom, want to run with me? It'd be good to have a partner."

I looked up. "Oh. Well, I haven't run in years," I said. Grant had three younger brothers, one just tiny. I wasn't in great shape, and I didn't know where to find my shoes. But my son had just asked me to share time. He invited me into his world. I'd been praying for this opportunity.

"I'd love to," I said.

"Cool," Grant said. And he was gone. *Thump, thump, thump* up the stairs.

And now my smile came straight from the soul.

As a little boy, Grant had been exuberant. He loved life and approached everything with wild curiosity and boundless energy. I spent most of my life chasing him. But the joy! One minute, we'd be pirates in the playhouse; the next, we'd fly down the hill on bikes. He'd throw his head back and laugh, and that laughter could soothe the sore out of anything life could throw. He knew how to test me, often putting his toe on the line of my limits. But at the end of the day, we were on the same side.

Lately, though, same-sidedness was rare. We argued about music. Movies. The holes in his jeans. We didn't let him have as many freedoms as his new friends had, and the friction was fierce.

But maybe running…

Maybe running would fix things. Return things to the way they were.

The next morning, Grant and I began. I crept out to the patio to avoid waking my husband and other children. I tried not to grimace as we stretched. I tried not to appear too eager as we closed the gate and took to the road.

"Ready?" Grant asked.

"Ready," I said.

Grant and I kept an even pace as we left our drive and headed toward the river. Our shoes tapped the pavement with cadence. We followed the bike path that paralleled the Mississippi, but when we reached the footbridge over the ravine, Grant moved ahead. His stride opened, and soon I was looking at the back of his yellow T-shirt. I tried to move faster, but my lungs ached. My heart beat fast.

I couldn't match his pace.

"Sorry, Mom," he breathed as he looked back. "Gotta move ahead."

And off he went.

Catching up was useless. Soon, Grant was a small figure in the distance.

So much for togetherness.

Running fell right in line with everything else about our relationship — me trying my best, but my son still moving away.

That night, under the safety of darkness, I made a confession to my husband, Lonny. "This running thing. It's not going to work. Grant will always be faster. The distance seems significant."

"It was the first day," Lonny said.

"Every day will be the same."

"You won't know unless you try."

So the next morning, I tried again. And the next. And the next. It wasn't easy to add a morning run to my schedule, but those first strides together kept me going. There were physical benefits. My muscles got stronger. My side stopped aching. I could run farther. I became more fit. But the healing. The fixing. That still seemed far off. Grant and I still disagreed about movies, activities and friends. The few minutes of morning togetherness hadn't solved that.

I wondered if anything ever would.

One morning, when I woke and pushed back the curtains, the sky was gray, not the warm pink-orange we'd found most of our mornings. Surely, we'd take the day off from running. I crawled back into bed and let Lonny's arms settle around me. I'd just drifted off when I heard a voice at the door.

"Mom? Mom? You ready? Time to go."

Grant? I sat up and looked toward the door. Sure enough.

"It's going to rain," I said.

"It's okay, Mom. My phone says later. Want to go?"

"Give me 10 minutes?"

Soon, we were heading down the familiar road. I kept Grant's pace for a longer time now. We ran along the river, but when we hit the first dock, Grant moved ahead.

"Grant, look at the sky. It's going to rain. We should go home."

"Just a little more," he breathed.

I looked up. The sky was darker. A half-second later, slow, fat drops began to fall. Then, in an instant, the sky opened wide, and rain fell in a wild rush.

Grant was by my side.

"Guess the rain came sooner," he said.

I nodded, and the two of us bolted. Drops pelted from the sky and drenched our clothes. Our arms and legs pumped. When we reached the footbridge, we stopped to catch our breath under the canopy of trees. Underneath, water charged through the ravine. I bent forward, hands on knees, and gulped air. Through the cracks in the bridge, I watched the mini-river roar. And in that moment, I understood.

Running was like this bridge.

Coming together on these mornings, running together even if we weren't side by side, connected Grant and me. It brought us together. Closed our chasm. Linked his life to mine in a way that was positive, strong and good.

Bridges span differences.

And running bridged ours.

I would've stayed in that moment forever, even in the downpour, but Grant reached over and tugged on my arm. "Mom, I keep telling you, you gotta move faster!" He laughed, and his beautiful face was bright even in the rain.

"Let's go!" we said in unison.

Then my son and I ran toward home.

— Shawnelle Eliasen —

The World of a Runner's Mom

I don't drive a car. I drive a portable locker room.
Who needs a garage when you've got a trunk?
~Author Unknown

Let me make my disclosure right at the beginning. I am not a runner, although I did spend several decades chasing after my six sons and two daughters. So, I cannot claim to be a member of the "Runners' World." I am, though, a proud member of the highly selective "World of a Runner's Mom."

One does not easily become a card-carrying member of this group. There are multiple initiation tasks to complete. To remain a sustaining member, a mother must exhibit dedication to and patience with the often-eccentric environment of runners.

Many children begin running as young teens. The first challenge to a runner's mom is the need to adjust to the emotional ups and downs of the runner child. These fluctuations are precipitous, intense and often dramatic. A runner's happiness quotient and sense of self-worth are strongly connected to the perceived success of the last race or workout. Mix a disappointing time into the cauldron of adolescent insecurity, and your runner has created a toxic potion.

The usual maternal psychology may prove ineffective in this situation. This is not the time to apply the comparative method. Your runner sees little consolation in looking back at past successes or in looking forward to the next opportunity to achieve a personal record. The present is what matters. I once read that a mother is only as happy as her least happy child. If you have several runners in your home, you may experience many unhappy moments.

However, a good race, a training PR (personal record), the camaraderie of a team or a running buddy—these can quickly offset the unhappy moments for a runner, and a mother. At times, the sport can be a harsh but nurturing teacher of life skills. Sometimes you win; sometimes you lose. Aim to do your best; be diligent in your preparation; enjoy the process. Gradually, a runner learns it can be just as rewarding to compete against oneself as to compete against others.

There are also physical challenges for a runner's mom. You must be ready to do lots of laundry—lots of *odoriferous* laundry. If you are a good trainer, you will insist your runner do his/her own laundry. However, even the best-trained children slip up—or out the door—now and then, and a mother can only hold her breath for so long. So be ready to do some extra loads of laundry out of self-defense.

Some of your happiest moments as a runner's mom occur at the finish line or at your front door. No matter how experienced your runner may be, it is always a relief to see them back safely. It is anxiety-provoking to be standing at the finish line knowing the expected time of arrival of your runner, but your child is not in sight. In panic, a mother's mind creates many possible explanations for the delay. As a veteran mother of runners, I have experienced the news of twisted ankles, dehydration, and falls.

One of my daughters provided a most original explanation for her delay. She was running a half marathon in torrential rain when she stopped to use a Porta-Potty along the route. Her spandex running tights were so soaked that she couldn't pull them up to leave. So, there she was stuck in the Porta-Potty with her tights glued to her ankles. It took minutes of distressed wriggling and tugging to get them up. How can people say running is a boring sport?

Weather can be a mother's best friend or her most challenging adversary. There is nothing more pleasant than standing at the finish line for a cross-country meet or a road race on a crisp, clear fall day. A mother must store that memory as a pleasant flashback as she shivers on a cold winter day or wilts in the heat and humidity at a summer race. There is always consolation in reminding yourself that at least you are only a spectator, not a participant.

At first glance, running seems to be a comparatively safe sport—and so it is. Still, a runner's mom may be called on to add some impressive medical terms to her vocabulary. However, with luck you will never need to deal with:

- plantar fasciitis
- Achilles tendonitis and insertional Achilles tendinopathy
- shin splints
- patella tendonitis
- high hamstring tendinopathy
- stress fractures
- runner's knee, aka patellofemoral pain syndrome (PFPS)

Dealing with the emotional repercussions of an injury is often more difficult than treating the physical issue, especially if your son or daughter is a "passionate" runner. Losing weeks of a season or a training program can be traumatic. However, it can be a period of enlightenment when a runner can learn that running does not define the person. The time-out experience often confirms the adage, "When one door closes, another opens." Personally, I have watched my runner children on the disabled list slowly gravitate toward involvement in a new activity—school newspaper, volunteering with children with disabilities, swimming, or a public-policy study. It is important to learn that there is fulfillment outside the running realm, although the call of the pavement may remain the most commanding in the end.

Eventually, your runner children move on—and out of the family home. Now, as the experienced mother of a runner, you have earned the right to rejoice in the good moments, while being less directly involved with the frustrating moments. However, I can still tell as soon as I hear one of my kids on the phone whether the most recent race was a good one or a not-so-good one. The mother of a runner retains her maternal ESP.

But what does the semi-retired mother do once there are no resident runners at home? I have been privileged to find out that, with luck, she becomes the grandmother of runners!

— Patricia A. Gavin —

Committing to Life

In Step Forever

What we have once enjoyed we can never lose;
all that we deeply love becomes a part of us.
~Helen Keller

I first met Gweneviere on Myspace (yes, that's how long ago it was). She saw a picture of me dressed in a Borat costume, complete with lime-green singlet, mustache and wig. Bravely (or foolishly), she called me one night. I was just around the corner from where she was out with friends in the East Village. We saw each other every night after that for two weeks, and we fell in love. Soon, we moved in together, and we were as happy as two people could be.

Two years later, in 2008, Gweneviere started having dizzy spells and, later, blackouts. She was diagnosed with a brain tumor—"the size of an orange," the doctors said. She had surgery, which was successful. But she also suffered a stroke during the operation.

When she finally woke up, she was really confused—not remembering basic things, like what city we were in. The diagnosis was anterograde amnesia, which meant that she couldn't form new memories that would "stick." In the early months, she was sometimes on a memory loop of 15 minutes, or even less. She also had something called "confabulations," where her memories would mix up bits of reality with bits of imagination. We'd laugh about some of these later—like how she thought Barack Obama was a personal friend of hers, when in fact she'd just voted for him. Or how she sometimes thought we'd broken up, and when I'd ask her why we were still living together, she'd say,

"I thought we were just cool like that!" It was always delivered with her buoyant, contagious laughter.

Over the next several years, we worked together on her memory and coping skills. That included living every day to the fullest, and making adventures and fun memories out of everyday tasks.

One of the strategies we came up with was to start running and training for a marathon. We had dabbled in running together before, but Gweneviere was never really interested in serious long-distance running.

But after the brain tumor, the idea of completing a marathon took on a different light for both of us. It became one of many symbolic goals that embodied what Gweneviere could achieve in her new reality.

As we approached our goal of running the 2010 New York City Marathon together, Gweneviere's sense of fun and humor always came through. She was my inspiration throughout our training. We laughed together about how her short-term memory issues helped her run extended distances. During a long training route, she'd often ask me, "How long have we been running?" No matter how many times she asked, I would always answer, "Just about fifteen minutes," and we would keep going.

When we crossed that finish line on the day of the marathon, she burst into tears when she realized we'd actually accomplished our goal.

Fueled by the success of our marathon training, we set other big goals that Gweneviere was able to achieve. Although her short-term retention of facts and details was still challenged, we found she could learn other skills that used different parts of her brain. We talked about it as an opportunity, literally a "do-over" of her life, to follow the path of what she was most passionate about. Gweneviere was a talented musician and writer, and she was able to complete a degree program at New York University on multiple academic scholarships, attend Juilliard for singing and songwriting, and was accepted to Columbia University's prestigious MFA in Creative Nonfiction program. We also crossed eight marathon finish lines (seven in New York City, one in Harrisburg) together in those years.

On one cold winter day—February 2, 2013—I dragged

Gweneviere into Central Park for a training run near that familiar finish line. I had spent several months picking out the perfect, unique engagement ring — but I also needed the actual proposal to be really outstanding so she would be able to remember it.

We came to a clearing, and Gweneviere was surprised to see our friend Elaine there — apparently teaching an aerobics class (not something Elaine would ever do). Then the "class" turned around to reveal that they were all our friends, wearing costumes and disguises, and shirts that spelled out: "GWEN, WILL YOU MARRY YASIR?" After stripping off my tracksuit to reveal the original Borat lime-green singlet, I got down on one knee and proposed.

She said, "Yes!" And a little over a year later, on June 14, 2014, we were married on one of the most amazing and happy days of our lives. Elaine (the faux aerobics instructor) was the officiant, with all our friends and family gathered around. And I knew that Gweneviere would always remember that day.

Fast-forward to May 2018. We had just purchased our dream house, a big, two-story home with a yard in the Bed-Stuy neighborhood of Brooklyn. But only a few weeks after we moved in, Gweneviere developed a recurring cough that became persistent. She was diagnosed with stage 4 lung cancer — a very rare form of lung cancer found mainly in non-smokers.

We both thought this was just another hurdle that we would conquer together, as we had with her brain tumor. But it did not turn out that way.

Despite our aggressive efforts to get the best care, Gweneviere's health went downhill rapidly. We made a road trip to the Dana-Farber Cancer Institute in Boston. We had always loved traveling and having adventures together, and despite the circumstances, we still made it fun. It turned out to be our last road trip.

As Gweneviere grew weaker, I still held on to the impossible belief that we would beat this thing, so I ran an idea by her to create a nonprofit foundation that would raise awareness and provide screenings for both brain tumors and lung cancer. She loved the idea. I was still hoping we'd do it together.

Gweneviere passed away on July 22, 2018, in our new home. She was 47 years old. I was beside her, with many close friends and relatives nearby. Her last words to me were "I love you, too," and I treasure that memory.

After her death, I felt lost. I didn't know what to do. I didn't have a roadmap for grieving. So I fell back to what I always count on: finding good "coaches" (in this case, therapists and friends who had experienced loss), and then setting a "training" schedule. I also started work on our foundation.

Once again, running was key to my healing. I came up with the idea to run 50 marathons in 50 states in a single year — "50 in 50" — to honor Gweneviere, and to raise awareness and visibility for the newly formed Gweneviere Mann Foundation.

I knew from the start that running the races would be the easiest part for me.

When sitting at home on the couch alone, it can feel like there's nowhere to go but down. But when I'm running, I can work mentally through the hardest and darkest parts of my pain and fear. The repetitive left-right, left-right — the ongoing progress through the miles — allows me to go deep into processing these thoughts and feelings, while always moving forward. I don't spiral downward when I'm physically moving toward a goal.

Running a foundation is turning out to be more challenging. But I'm surrounded by friends and advisors, and we're working on building this thing together.

As I write this, I've run 12 marathons so far on my road to 50 — nearly one a week. If I get through this year without an injury, I'll log over 1,300 miles in marathon races — while processing what has happened, thinking about Gweneviere, and honoring her memory on every mile.

I'll finish the "50 in 50" year at the New York City Marathon in November 2019 — where Gweneviere and I completed our first marathon in 2010. And she'll be with me every step of the way.

— Yasir Salem —

No Feeding Tube

Be positive, ignore the critic, follow your heart,
invest in your passions, believe in your dreams
and get busy making them reality.
~Josh Cox, U.S. 50K record holder

I ran over 30 miles the week I was diagnosed with throat cancer, and eight miles before sunrise the morning I met with the doctor.

"There's no easy way to say this. You have base of tongue carcinoma. The good news is we can fix it, but you'll probably need a feeding tube. Most people lose 10 to 15 percent of their body weight during treatment. You only weigh 145 pounds. It's dangerous if you drop below 130 pounds during treatment."

"What's a feeding tube?"

"Nothing to worry about. We make a small incision in your abdomen and insert a plastic tube into your stomach. You pour liquid nourishment into the tube."

I said, "You can't imagine how much I'll hate that. I'll make myself eat."

The doctor replied, "That's what everyone says. But when you have second-degree radiation burns inside your esophagus and are constantly nauseated, you won't be able to make yourself eat. How old are you, 64? Your blood pressure's 82/60, and your heart rate is 52. Those numbers are great for any age."

His assistant, Jana, said, "I bet you run. How long have you been running?"

"All my life, but I took three years off when I approached the big 5-0. Life was pretty good. I stopped running and celebrated by trying to drink all the beer and wine in New Mexico. I put on 103 pounds."

"You aren't overweight."

"No, I carried my hard-earned Pillsbury Doughboy physique to my annual physical. I asked my doctor if she would still see me after I registered for Medicare. She said, 'You aren't asking the right question. Your waist is over 44 inches, your cholesterol is pushing 300, and your triglycerides are through the roof.'

"'Sounds like I hit the trifecta,' I joked.

"'The question you need to ask is whether or not I'll attend your funeral. I'm going to prescribe some medication to help you.'

"'Give me six months. I did this to myself. I'll fix it.'

"'I'll give you three months. If you aren't dead, we'll re-check your vitals.'

"When she weighed me in three months, I was 30 pounds lighter. She said, 'No one does this. Everyone lies to me. They try for about two days and then eat a quart of ice cream. What did you do?'

"'I eat 2,000 calories a day, and I run 30 miles a week. I keep logbooks.'

"'No offense, but you're still too fat to run that much.'

"'I didn't say I was fast.'

"'Your blood work's better, but it's not okay. See you in three months.'

"It took 18 months and five appointments, but I ran off the 100 pounds, and my vitals were back in line. I didn't go on TV or post it on Facebook. I didn't write a diet and exercise book. I wasn't proud of it. Actually, I was ashamed I needed to lose the weight. I haven't told anyone before today."

Jana asked, "Do you race?"

"I ran the Duke City Marathon two weeks after my 50th birthday. I ran it again the next year and the year after that. Work got in the way of racing, but I still ran five or six days a week. I remember those years as the years I ran in the dark. Rain or snow, hot or cold, I ran. I ran when it hurt and when it didn't. When you're over 60, it always hurts somewhere."

I remembered mornings in subzero weather and blisters. I remembered getting up after tripping and running three more miles with two broken toes. I finished my first marathon with blood streaming from my nipples.

That brought me back to my cancer doctor's warning about a feeding tube. "I'll make myself eat. How bad can it be? I can stand anything for five minutes."

"Your call, but if your weight drops below 135 pounds, we'll revisit the feeding tube. Two more things... First, eat everything you can for the next two weeks. You need to put on a few pounds. Second, stop running until the treatment is over. I don't want you to burn calories you need to survive."

I thought I was lying when I agreed. Three weeks later, I could barely walk. I missed running, but the combination of chemo and radiation sapped my strength, and I was terrified of falling. A case of road rash might be deadly to my drug-ravaged immune system.

Two months later, the doctor said. "Your treatment went really well. It was easy for you because you're a runner. You started treatment in great condition, and you have a decent level of pain tolerance."

I spit up pink slime from my burnt throat. "If this was easy, I'd hate to see hard."

Jana checked my weight after the last treatment. I stared enviously at her running shoes. She said, "138 pounds. You'll lose a couple more pounds before your throat heals, but you made it through this with flying colors. I remember you run. Good for you. This treatment is harder on most people. Almost half don't survive."

I rasped, "Nice shoes. I'm going to treat myself to new shoes and start running again. I can run, can't I?"

"Whenever you're ready."

"How long will that be?"

She smiled. "That's not for me to say. You'll know. Trust me. You'll know."

I promised myself I'd be running in two months, but it didn't work out the way I wanted. I walked my first mile a month after the last treatment and added a 10th of a mile every day after that. On my two-month treatment anniversary, I walked the blocks and ran across the streets. A week later, I walked across the streets and ran the blocks. Three months after treatment, I ran three miles without stopping. At mile 2, I realized I was going to finish and started to cry. I could run again. It was a dusty New Mexico day, and the grit stuck to my face. I walked in the house. My wife took one look at me and screamed, "Are you okay? I'll call an ambulance. Sit down. Sit down."

I could barely speak because I was so choked up. "I'm fine. I've never been better. I ran the whole three miles. I never thought I'd be able to do that again."

She cried with me.

I'm over 70 now. I ran 30 miles the week I wrote this, and unless I cripple myself, I'll probably run 30 miles the week you read it.

Whatever challenges life after 70 has in store for me, I'll face them with double-knotted running shoes, a water belt, sunglasses, and a sweat-stained baseball hat. I'll break troubles down into bite-sized pieces, put on my headlamp, and chase them back into the darkness. After all, I can stand anything for five minutes.

— Robert Allen Lupton —

Three Words of Advice

It's never too late to take your heart health seriously and make it a priority.
~Jennie Garth

I never gave walking much thought. Thanks to my parents' genetics, I was tall and thin, so I rarely exercised. When I did walk, it was generally in four-inch heels from the parking lot to my office and around the building during my nearly four-decade-long business career.

Last year, however, walking up a flight of stairs made me feel more winded than I remembered. Surely, it was a sign of getting older and a little too much time sitting—or so I thought. An echocardiogram and subsequent stress test revealed that I had a severe leak in the mitral valve of my heart that required surgery to repair. I wasn't prepared to hear this news. The last time I was in the hospital was when I had my tonsils out at age six.

But this story really isn't about me. It's about the people I had the great pleasure to meet in a gym that doesn't do any advertising, has no memberships, and doesn't require any fancy workout clothing. It's known as Cardiac Rehab.

Its patrons range in age from 30 to nearly 90. They are dressed in street clothes with comfortable shoes. One would never know the connection between these individuals if they were seen on the street. But each one risked stroke, arrhythmia, and even death from their cardiac conditions and the surgical procedures that were required to correct them. Some were victims of their own bad behaviors, while others were simply affected by chance and circumstances beyond their control. Regardless of the cause, we all found ourselves in the same place.

Three words of advice are routinely provided by surgeons and cardiologists to cardiac patients. Walk. Walk. Walk. It seems easy enough until walking across a room after a cardiac event or surgical procedure feels like a mile. This extreme exhaustion can be created by a number of different cardiac conditions and treatments to mitigate them, but for the most part, there's no escaping it. That's why we heart warriors are referred to this exclusive health club.

The first day in cardiac rehab can be intimidating. We introduce ourselves by replacing our last names with our conditions. "Hello, I'm Susan Mitral Valve Repair." Some people have an easier time than others. It's not easy to introduce oneself as "Joe Aortic Aneurysm" or "Jane Emergency Cardiac Catheterization." Saying these words can be surreal.

In the first three months, cardiac-rehab patients wear heart monitors the entire time they are involved in the rotation of exercises. Our heart rates are displayed on monitors around the facility, and alarms sound as patients get out of their targeted ranges. Initially, participants are very tentative; some are downright horrified, especially walking on the treadmill, as it represents the most physically demanding of the initial workout routine. Blood pressure is measured before, during, and after each session. At my facility, some individuals are asked affectionately to go to the "Penalty Box" (a seating area) when their numbers are too high or low to safely continue exercising.

The team of medical professionals is acquainted with each person's medical history and fears. They are also well versed on the risks of exercising after cardiac treatment and the swift action that will be needed if anything goes awry. Nonetheless, they keep spirits high and patients motivated. In the three-times-per-week regimen, the cardiac-rehab staff is keenly aware of the progress that will be necessary for patients to get back to daily living, which includes walking, walking, walking. Treadmill speed, incline, and duration are slowly increased as individual blood pressure and heart rate indicate that more challenge is warranted.

The more seasoned participants encourage the newbies and do their best to restore their confidence that life does go on after traumatizing cardiac events. Observing their brisk walking speed, endurance, and pleasure in their achievement keeps everyone focused and looking ahead to reaching their own goals.

Walk. Walk. Walk. These words of advice are still relevant, even at the conclusion of the initial 36 visits. Some leave and maintain their routines on their own. I suspect some go back to their old habits, hoping that lightning won't strike twice. Still others opt for an extended rehab program that offers a twice-per-week workout routine.

Upon joining the extended class, I met an entirely different group of cardiac workout buddies. These people possessed a level of dedication and commitment like no other individuals I had ever met. One woman has been attending for 26 years since the event that brought her to this program. Another has been involved for 15 years and yet another for 13. An 88-year-old woman said, "I never thought I'd still be here. I know I wouldn't be alive if it weren't for cardiac rehab." She jumped on that treadmill and walked like she wasn't a day over 55!

In a world of immediate gratification and people who abandon their fitness goals as soon as they get too challenging or inconvenient, these participants seem to exist in another dimension. Not only do they continue participating for years, but they embrace the opportunity to walk like it is a precious gift.

I never thought I would appreciate walking until I had the pleasure of doing so with my new friends. Whether our heart conditions were months, years, or decades ago, we all understand that walking doesn't just keep us active and independent; it dramatically decreases the probability of becoming heart patients for a second time.

The most recent medical research indicates that sitting is the new smoking. So, take it from this cardiac-rehab participant: don't wait until a cardiothoracic surgeon or cardiologist is giving you this magical advice. Walk. Walk. Walk. Engage your own group of walking buddies and enjoy long, healthy lives together. Your hearts will be glad you did!

— Susan Lynn —

Healthier Ever After

Lack of activity destroys the good condition of every human being, while movement and methodical physical exercise save it and preserve it.
~Plato

I had been single for about a year when a charming, handsome gentleman entered my life. After being in a one-sided relationship for nearly six years, God sent me someone when I wasn't even looking, and he was my blessing.

It was refreshing to have someone who wanted to spend time with me and truly loved me for me. We became best friends. We worked together; we talked and laughed together; we traveled together; we experienced great food together… We experienced great food together… We experienced great food together. It was all about the experiences with us. When it came to food, no experience was the same. We dined in places that I didn't know existed. I was getting fed both spiritually with love and physically with food. But then came the shift.

One day, I looked in the mirror and didn't recognize myself. Who was this person with fat cheeks who looked like she was in her first trimester of pregnancy? Oh, my God, it was me! What had happened? I had gained over 20 pounds in a year. When I went to the doctor for my physical, it was confirmed. I remember the visit like it was yesterday.

"You look so well and happy," my physician stated. "You are just glowing. What seems to have you so giddy?"

I proceeded to tell her about the new man in my life. In the midst of congratulating me and going over my vitals, I asked about my weight. "I know I've gained a little weight…," I said reluctantly.

When the nurse had taken my weight earlier, I turned my head quickly to avoid the disappointment.

"You've only gone from 140 to 161 pounds," my physician stated kindly as she combed through my chart. "That's understandable. You're just happy, and women tend to gain weight when they are happy."

"Girl, I don't need to be *this* happy!" I exclaimed with a laugh.

I had sprouted from a size 8 to a size 12. I had never been a size 12 in my life. I had to get out of the double digits.

After hearing that disturbing number, I was determined to shed some pounds. Although I looked healthy, I felt heavy. It became imperative for me to start feeling healthier.

Nearly a month after that physical, I decided that I was going to exercise more consistently and make it a lifestyle. I made a promise to God and myself that I would take better care of my "temple."

I started with baby steps by walking briskly for 30 minutes during the afternoons. Soon, I began to track my steps daily and got up to 10,000 steps. After I felt that my body was conditioned to walking, I graduated to walking and running. That decision took me about two weeks.

Fast-forward to my routine today. I begin my workout at 5:30 every morning, excluding the weekends, which is my break. I walk and run in intervals on the treadmill for 30 to 40 minutes. During the first three minutes, I do a brisk walk and then run at a high intensity for two minutes. I continue at this rate until I've reached the full 30 minutes. Frequently, I increase the resistance to 10.5 or higher, which provides an uphill challenge.

In addition to the treadmill in the morning, I also continue to walk for 30 minutes in the afternoons. I have become accustomed to working out twice a day. And I have increased my steps to 15,000 a day.

The results are encouraging. Although I have not stepped on a scale, I can feel the difference in my weight. I am now able to fit into some pants that I couldn't get into two years ago. I've found that the combination of running with walking is working for my body.

Now that I've become an avid runner and walker, I eat what I want, but in moderation. I don't starve myself because that's a road to failure. If I get an urge to overindulge, I'll pull up a picture of myself when I was a little heavier and compare it to where I am now. When I examine the here and now, I push away the extra food. The self-discipline has also been advantageous for my partner, who has made exercise a part of his lifestyle, too. We are both on our way to living healthier ever after.

— Kimberly Nichelle —

Getting Back on Track

You've done it before and you can do it now....
Redirect the substantial energy of your frustration
and turn it into positive, effective,
unstoppable determination.
~Ralph Marston

My calf muscles are killing me, I'm struggling to breathe, and I'm waging a war against negative self-talk as I continue a slow jog on the treadmill. I compromise today's goal of jogging three miles by quitting at one. Feeling defeated, I leave the gym thinking that running is hard work and takes discipline. I don't want to work that hard. But I know I will.

I remember how good it felt to run a few years ago — the delicious feeling of well-used muscles after running, the camaraderie and excitement of running in community races, hanging out with physically fit people, and the happy atmosphere. I was actually proud when I got a shin splint — my first athlete's injury — that unfortunately stayed with me throughout the summer.

It's not like I was a prize athlete or someone for whom exercise played a steady and important role. The majority of my adult life has been spent as an overweight, sedentary person. My exercise consisted of walking in and out of malls and fast-food restaurants.

A few years ago, things changed. My teenage daughter challenged me to run with her in the Crim Festival of Races, now called the Health Plus Crim Festival of Races — an annual event in Flint, Michigan.

Typically, over 14,000 people participate in the running and walking events. Determined to make a permanent, positive lifestyle change, I accepted her challenge to run the 5K.

For one wonderful year, I was a role model for a healthy lifestyle — at least among couch potatoes. I considered myself a card-carrying member of an exclusive group of fit and healthy people. My very slow jog worked up to a fast jog — six miles, five days a week, in 50 minutes. I actually enjoyed running.

By the way, something amazing happened along the way. My body seemed to grow smarter. When running, my body let me know that the burgers, pizza, Coke, and cupcakes I consumed weren't a good idea. After eating them, I felt sluggish and weighed down. Eventually, I didn't eat as many of those unhealthy foods. My body didn't want them — and over time, neither did I.

My weekly social calendar included participating in local road races. My speed was consistent, which I attributed to training on a treadmill for months. And me — a former middle-aged couch potato — actually placed in three races in the small age-group category of 45- to 50-year-olds.

That was an exhilarating year. I ran in 13 consecutive weekly races. By the time the Crim race came around, I had months of training under my belt. So, I surprised my daughter and ran in the 8K, not the 5K.

Running in the Crim was the high point of the summer. After all, it was my daughter's challenge to run in the Crim that started me on my athletic journey.

I remember lining up at the starting line with hundreds, maybe thousands, of runners, along with the nervousness, anxiety and urge to go to the bathroom again. (I had already gone two times.) Family, friends and enthusiastic spectators cheered us on. Some thoughtful people ran their lawn sprinklers on the curb so water drizzled on us while we ran on that hot, August day. Running in the Crim was exhilarating, and I planned to continue my new lifestyle!

Unfortunately, I stopped running three months later and returned to my former lifestyle. My last race was the Halloween race, an event that took place at a fall festival in Davison, Michigan.

The festival was a fun family event. Pumpkins, haystacks and corn stalks decorated the small town, as well as vendors selling baked goods and crafts. Laughing children with painted faces ran around, and runners enjoyed cider and donuts after the race.

That race was definitely different from typical races. Some runners wore costumes and took on the persona of their characters while running. This was a race in which some runners didn't take their running times seriously. How could they, when their costumed character, Mickey Mouse, was skipping and playing to the spectators? I ran as a witch in a black, cotton gauze dress with a handkerchief hem over my running tights. I also wore a black wig that trailed past my bottom.

In spite of the festivities, my spirits were down, and I didn't experience my normal "runner's high" after the race. As usual, my friend's husband was there to cheer her on. Mine wasn't. My marriage was crumbling, and I was on the brink of getting a divorce. Depressed, I resorted to my old coping patterns — staking my claim on the couch, eating a lot of comfort foods, and ignoring my running shoes.

My depression ran its course after my divorce, and I came to my senses. I remembered the fun I had at the weekend races, but I knew that to get into that lifestyle again, I would have to do the work. First, I banned junk food from my diet. Then I reintroduced running — actually slow jogging — into my life with the goal of participating in the local races. Just like the first time, I made small, manageable goals and am on my way to a healthier, happy me.

This brings me back to that day at the gym when I compromised my commitment. Yes, running is hard work, takes discipline and battling negative self-talk. I did it once. I will do it again. Actually, I'm doing it now.

— Michele Sprague —

The Dawn of a New Day

If you don't have answers to your problems after a four-hour run, you ain't getting them.
~Christopher McDougall, Born to Run

The fall of my sophomore year found me struggling through life. My mother already had me on antidepressants, and I was attending regular counseling sessions. My days blurred together. Life was passing me by, my own world moving on without me. Nights were spent wide-awake, staring at the ceiling, waiting for a quick demise. The demise never came, but my best friend AJ did.

She dropped by without notice and barged into my room. As usual, I was lying on my bed, listening to macabre music. She plucked the earphones right out of my ears and plopped on the bed next to me.

"You're wasting the best years of your life," she told me, looking me straight in the eyes.

I closed my eyes, avoiding her piercing gaze. "These are the best years of my life?" I barely recognized my own voice at that moment. It sounded so heavy and strained, like speaking was such a huge task. Living itself was such a huge task.

"Every year is potentially the best," she said, with a touch of finality in her voice. She grabbed my wrist and hauled me into a sitting position. "Enough slugging around. I know, tough times, lots of problems, but that's no reason to let your life get ruined like this."

"AJ," I said, slowly. "Look, I..." I pulled my arm away from her grip. "I really don't want to..."

"Did I say you have a choice?"

True to her word, she rang the doorbell to my apartment at 5:00 the next morning. I was awake, plagued by a sleep cycle that had become erratic thanks to nightmares. I dragged myself to the door before Mom could wake up, and I opened the door. There she stood in her black-and-pink tracksuit and gray jogging shoes. AJ always looked great—pulled together—while I was a mess, with zits and fat hanging out.

"AJ, what are you even..."

"Shhh!" She held up a finger to her lips, and I stopped talking. She went on, "I was going for a jog, and I didn't want to go alone. You're my best friend, are you not?"

Trick question. "I am, but..."

"No buts. Get dressed."

Long ago, I had learned that a determined AJ was not to be argued with. There was no one I hated more in that moment as I struggled into my old running clothes. They fit far too snugly than my self-esteem would have liked. I remembered that they used to fit perfectly when Dad bought them for me a year ago. So much had changed in just one year. So much had been lost.

I tried to prolong the dressing process, thinking that if the sunlight became too strong, AJ would call off the jog. But she was not to be deterred. She started banging on the door. Scared that my mom would wake up, I dressed quickly and got out.

We left a note for my mom in case she woke up, and we hit the road. Within the first two minutes of walking at a normal speed, I started to realize that AJ had set me up for an impossible task. Whether it was the toll depression had taken on me, or the lack of use of muscles, I was soon out of breath. We took a route from my apartment complex to a nearby park. AJ paused and started doing stretches. I watched in breathless horror.

"Um, are we going to..."

She grinned. "Yes!"

She grabbed my wrist again and pulled me along. Slowly at first, then jogging, and finally running. I tried to keep up, but it was impossible. My legs felt wobbly, and my knees felt like they would snap at any moment. Muscles stretched in ways they were not used to. Lungs expanded like they had never done before.

And then, suddenly, I felt liberated.

I was running free, heart pumping hard and fast. All the blood gushed through my veins, like life coursing through my being. It was amazing. At some point, I realized that AJ had dropped my hand. That was okay; I didn't need her hand to guide me anymore. I was happy running on my own.

My euphoria didn't last too long that day, as my unused body didn't align with my soaring free spirit. AJ was, however, really pleased with my performance. She whooped and hugged me, despite how sweaty we both were. She told me that I had done great and she would bring me the next day, even if she had to force me again.

She didn't need to force me; I was willing on my own.

Running became a habit, a routine escape from my dreary life. Every day, I looked forward to it. It left me feeling energetic for the rest of the day. I even went to sleep early most nights because I liked running when the sun was rising slowly above the horizon. Before I knew it, people at school were commenting on my improved appearance, how I appeared much livelier than before. Even my counselor commented on it.

I ran and ran and ran, and life took a turn for the better.

This morning, I woke up at 4:30 a.m., left a bright note for my mother and walked over to AJ's house. I rang the bell thrice until her mother opened the door, looking disheveled.

"She's still sleeping, sweetie," she told me, barely controlling a yawn.

"No worries!" I told her. I walked past her into the house, straight to AJ's room.

She was lying on her stomach, snoring lightly. I jumped onto her bed, jostling her awake.

"Let's go!" I said, loudly.

She groaned. "I don't want to… Not today…"

I grinned from ear to ear. "Did I say you have a choice?"

—Runeha Sneha—

A New Label

What seems hard now will one day be your warm-up.
~Author Unknown

The excuses came quickly and all-too-easily to my tongue, but I could tell that my doctor was unimpressed. The reality about my weight was staring me in the face — in the numbers on the scale, in my lab results, on the tags of my clothes — but somehow I had managed to convince myself otherwise. By carefully curating photos that appeared of me online (bad angle, bad outfit, delete, delete, delete) and completely avoiding scales, I had managed to delude myself for a long time. Now, the truth came crashing down like an anvil as I sat, vulnerable in my crinkly paper gown, and wavered under my doctor's steady gaze.

She was kind but clear: Things needed to change.

I was only 25 years old, but that had been long enough for me to become so fully entrenched in my lifestyle that change seemed utterly impossible. Even as a child, I preferred arts and crafts to playing in the back yard. Any attempts by my parents to involve me in sports were met with resistance, tears, and — if I was forced to participate — stubborn apathy or exaggerated failure. Make me play tee ball? I'll pick flowers and have a seat in the outfield. Sign me up for swim team? Enjoy my dramatic flailing as I pull myself along the lane marker.

Eventually, I was allowed to drop all athletic endeavors entirely.

I found success in my own way in painting, writing, baking, and caring for animals. I was perfectly happy to avoid breaking a sweat.

I just couldn't see the appeal. Watching runners slogging their way down the sidewalk from the driver's seat of my car, my only thought was, *Why?*

Unfortunately, my wide range of hobbies did not do much for my health. As I got older and moved from college to a desk job, I became fully entrenched in a daily routine: shower, work, couch, Netflix, dinner, bed. Most of my week revolved around sitting or eating, and it began to take its toll. I had to buy larger clothing. I started to get winded from just a few flights of stairs. At one point, I decided to "go for a run," and I barely made it to the end of my street.

I sat there in that doctor's office, my face burning and my eyes fixed on the doctor's hands to avoid meeting her eyes. And I swore to myself that this was not how I'd remember my young-adult years—tired, sick, and sad.

And so I gave running—that hobby that had always looked more like a punishment—another try.

The next few months passed in a blur of sweat and emotion that cycled from pride to discouragement to dejection back to determination and pride again. I was slow—and my "runs" contained a lot of walking. But as the weeks passed, I found I could go farther and farther without stopping, and I started to understand why people do this for fun.

Once I had a few 5Ks under my belt, I decided to jump in with both feet and signed up for my first half marathon. Words can't do justice to the fear that roiled my gut as I stood awaiting the starting gun, or the exhilaration that surged through my veins when I realized around mile 9 that I was actually going to finish. When I crossed the timing mat at the end, I found myself weeping openly with a mixture of relief, pride, and joy.

Since that race, I've done countless more—including marathons, triathlons, and even a few obstacle courses. I've found my favorite paths and trails around town, where I chase mental clarity, pound out my frustrations from a long day at work, and simply breathe deeply in a multi-hour moving meditation. Running gives me agency over my own body. It makes me feel at once powerful and humble, invigorated and at peace.

Two years after that initial, uncomfortable doctor's appointment, I changed insurers and found myself under a new physician's care. She performed the routine annual exam and began to chat with me as we finished up.

"Well, I can clearly tell that you're an athlete. What sort of activities do you do?"

An athlete.

For a moment, I was too confused to respond.

But I quickly beat back the tendrils of self-doubt and answered, "I'm a runner."

It's a word that still feels foreign. After two years, I still wear the label like an untailored suit. But it's mine to claim, and I'm learning to do so proudly.

I am still a painter, writer, and baker. But I am also now a runner. Stepping out of my comfort zone did not mean losing a piece of myself; I simply gained another that I did not even know I had room for.

— Michelle Anderson —

If I Can, Anyone Can

At the end of the day, your health is your responsibility.
~Jillian Michaels

After the birth of my second child, I was the largest I had ever been. A combination of crippling postpartum depression and teaching myself to cook by watching the Food Network led to an astronomical weight gain.

I hated myself and decided enough was enough. It was time to get my ducks in a row and feel better.

In January, I decided to get a personal trainer through my community recreation center. I had had some bad experiences in the past with personal trainers wanting to work me so hard that I would throw up. I needed a trainer who understood larger bodies. I researched and pored over the rec center website with the trainers' bios and finally decided on Brenda. Brenda was probably older than my mom, and I just knew that she would take care of me. When Brenda came into my life, she came as a trainer, psychologist and friend. She helped me to heal.

On top of strength training, Brenda put me on a walking interval routine. I was supposed to fast walk for one minute and then slow walk for one minute.

I laced up my shoes, put on my headphones, and got on the treadmill. I started fast walking.

I felt ridiculous, but I got through 15 painful minutes. I kept up like that for about a week. At the end of that week, though, I was fed up. So, on my fast walk I started to jog. As I continued, I gradually increased the amount of time I was "jogging"—first bumping up to 90 seconds, then two minutes, and then five minutes. Eventually, I was hitting a 10:1 run-to-walk ratio.

March came along and the snow was melting. I started to see all the runners getting out on the streets. I wanted to be out there, but I was afraid of being seen. People would stop and stare. My husband must have been reading my mind because he suggested that I get out there. I expressed my concerns, and he, in a matter-of-fact tone, told me that people don't actually do that, and I should just do it anyway.

So I did. It was the most amazing feeling I have ever had. No one stopped and stared. No one called me names. One lady stopped once just to tell me that I inspired her.

Every morning, I would get up and run. Most mornings, it was hard, especially at 5:30 a.m. I would wake up grumbling and moaning, but by the time I was done with that run, my attitude would become so much better. Those morning runs became my meditation, peace, and joy. I saw more of my community than I ever would have, all while experiencing incredible sunrises.

In June of that year, I enrolled in a fun race for multiple sclerosis. It was the first time I would be out in a group of runners. I wanted to show myself that I could finally do this. I wanted to see where I fit in the world of runners.

When I showed up, I realized that most of the entrants were half my size. Skinny, fit people. I was ready to back out because I was about to make a fool of myself. My husband, always my hero, told me to stop being a baby and get out there and do what I do. I lined up at the start line, put in my earbuds, and away I went. I finished that 5K race in under an hour, and I was not the last person to cross the finish line.

As soon as I crossed the line, I collapsed—not from exhaustion, but from the sheer joy that I was able to do it. I could run a 5K at 300 pounds, faster than some of the other, smaller competitors. It was a feeling I will never forget. Thinking back, it still brings tears to my eyes. It also reminds me that it's time to go for a run.

—Annie Randall—

Boston Strong

Boston is a tough and resilient town. So are its people.
I am supremely confident that Bostonians will pull
together, take care of each other and move forward.
~President Barack Obama

The Boston Marathon is a sort of mythic beast, akin to the unicorn that is its chosen symbol. It's a race steeped in history, an emotional, transcendent experience where one lines up with the best of the best to tackle the notoriously capricious course. You feel the spirit of the crowds who line the course every inch of the 26.2 miles.

I'd been a runner in high school, but I didn't lace up another pair of running shoes until I was in my mid-thirties. I enjoyed some success in local 5Ks and 10Ks, but soon the lure of longer distances was pulling at me.

In late 2005, my father was battling terminal prostate cancer, and I spent a lot of time with him, either at the hospital for his treatments or else at home, just keeping him company. I'd talk to him about my running, and I shared with him my secret ambition to train for a marathon. At the time, I found solace in my long runs. Simply putting one foot in front of the other helped allay the feelings of impotence, fear and anger as my father deteriorated before my eyes. Whenever the effort became painful or taxing, I would try to put things into perspective, reminding myself what my father was going through, and the courage and strength he was drawing on simply to survive.

My father passed away on February 11, 2006.

In May 2007, I ran my first marathon. The last few miles were tougher than almost anything I'd ever experienced, but I felt my father there with me, and I remembered his courage and grace. I crossed the finish line with a time of 3:35, and the tears began streaming from my eyes as I found my husband. My first words to him: "We're going to Boston."

He had no clue what I meant.

I had to explain the whole notion of qualifying times, and age- and sex-based standards. That was easy enough. But trying to explain to a non-runner the concept of chasing the unicorn—that was more challenging!

In April 2008, I ran my first Boston, and it lived up to all of its promise and then some. Bostonians treat runners like royalty, and the course is a non-stop party of sights, sounds and characters. It's said that an average of half a million people find a spot alongside the course. They have impromptu barbecues, hold up encouraging signs, and play instruments or stereo systems. They hand out orange slices, wet wipes, small bottles of water, and even beer when you pass by Boston College. Just before the halfway point is Wellesley College, where the students are renowned for setting up a scream tunnel; you can hear them long before you see them.

For this small-town girl, the experience was overwhelming to the point that I moved toward the center of the road to shield my senses a little bit. But it is absolutely exhilarating. After the race, runners are invited to ride the T (subway system) for free. They proudly wear their medals and jackets, and Bostonians everywhere stop to congratulate them and ask them how their race went.

I have had the good fortune to qualify for Boston every year since my first race, and barring an injury or two, I've been at that starting line in Hopkinton every third Monday in April.

Patriots' Day 2013, Monday, April 15th, dawned like any other. I got up at about 5:00 a.m., had some breakfast, and dressed in my marathon gear, covering myself with throwaway clothes that would keep me warm in the hours before the start. My husband drove me the couple of miles from our B&B to the Common, where the endless line of yellow school buses waited to ferry us out to Hopkinton.

I am a very introverted person, so my typical strategy is to snag a window seat and zone out. But this particular year, something clicked with my seatmate Susan, a woman my age who was running her first Boston. A recently widowed Chicagoan, she had a teenage boy and girl at home. We talked about everything and nothing all the way to Hopkinton. My wave was before hers, so we eventually parted ways, but I wished her all the best and told her to remember to savour the experience.

My race was pretty typical; I finished at around 3:30. Volunteers massed around us in the finish chute, dispensing sustenance, medals and heat blankets. It took a while to navigate out of the organized chaos.

I'd learned that the best thing for me after a marathon is to keep moving. I headed back toward our B&B, which was in Brookline, about two miles upstream, on a side street parallel to the marathon course. I followed the marathon route back, going along Commonwealth Avenue to the 25.5-mile mark to check in with some friends who were watching the race and cheering on various other friends who were still on the course. But despite the heat blanket, I was beginning to get chilly in my sweat-soaked clothes, so I didn't linger long.

I went on past Fenway Park and along Beacon Street, cheering on the runners. As I turned onto the side street where the B&B was, a police car went peeling away. I didn't think much of it at the time.

Entering the B&B, I found our room door locked; I could hear the TV on inside, but my husband did not respond to my knock. I went to find the concierge, and as I passed a room with an open door, I saw a woman crying inside.

When the concierge let me in, the first thing I saw was the image on the TV screen of the marathon finish line, smoke, and people on the ground. My legs went out from under me as I realized what was happening. My husband must have raced out to try to find me. Cell-phone service wasn't working, so it took us a horribly long half-hour to connect. When he returned to the room, we just held each other and cried tears of gratitude, but also of horror, shock and fear. Boston would never be the same again.

The next few hours were a mad scramble to decipher and digest news, reassure friends and relatives, and try to account for friends still on the course. My new friend Susan had been stopped at mile 25. She didn't finish her race, but she was safe.

I spent a good part of the following 12 months debating whether I wanted to return or not. I felt a lot of frustration at the loss of innocence and the new normal of terrorism that had shaken our running community. In the end, I did go back, to honour those lost and to show and feel my solidarity with Bostonians and their wonderful, magical marathon. I cried many tears that day—cleansing ones. We'd taken back Patriots' Day.

—Paula Roberts-Banks—

Wheeling

Always trying new things is always more fun, and it can be scary, but it's always more fun in the end.
~John Krasinski

Laura had recently discovered 5K events, and she wanted me to go with her. That was great for her, but I was in a wheelchair. Why would I want to go sit in the cold and watch people do something I couldn't?

"I'll push you," she said. That sounded like even less fun. In fact, the idea of having my ungainly older sister push my wheelchair through a sea of bodies while running seemed more like a recipe for disaster than a bonding moment.

"No, thanks," I said firmly.

"Bethany will do it with me," she grinned, "and I bet Mom will, too. We could all do it together!"

The thing about loving your sisters is that you want to make them happy, so almost before I understood what was happening, Laura had signed me up for Denver's annual Hot Chocolate 5K for the Make-A-Wish Foundation. Mom and Bethany signed up that same day. I resigned myself to being pushed through the streets of Denver amidst a mass of runners.

Parts of the race sounded good. They were going to have a fondue party at the finish line, and we received really cool hooded zip-up sweatshirts with our registrations. Mom and Laura bought us Buffs with funny sayings like "Will run for chocolate!" and "WTF? Where's the finish?"

On race day, it was very, very cold, and we had to make it to the start line before the sun rose. We bundled ourselves up as best we could and drove to Denver. "Remind me why we're doing this?" I asked as we unloaded my wheelchair from the car and set it up.

"It'll be fun," my sisters and mom insisted.

The three of them had enough energy for everyone attending the race, so we spent the next half-hour laughing and waiting for the first wave of runners to begin the course. It wasn't long before it was our turn, and off we went.

The Hot Chocolate 5K is popular, and the excitement is contagious. People line up along the course to cheer on the runners and shout encouragement. As far as I knew, I was the only person participating in the race in a wheelchair, and people gave me an extra wave whenever we passed a water station.

"This is awesome!" my family laughed when they saw people waving at me.

"I feel kind of bad. I'm not even pushing myself," I said, prompting my sister Bethany to ask, "Do you want to?"

It seemed like a good idea to wheel myself for a stretch, so when we rounded the next block, I put my freezing hands on my wheels and set to it. The cheers from the crowd lining the course spurred me on. It didn't take long before my arms were burning and Mom took over, but the experience made me think, *You know, with some practice, I think I could do this.*

I considered the idea during the fondue party and as we drove home. I knew nothing about wheelchair racing, but figured I could take the same approach to it as anything else — practice, and then get better. Plus, as a handicapped person, I am constantly faced with all the things I can't do (like running), and I was excited by the prospect of doing something that would keep me active, even in a wheelchair. After all, the 5Ks are often on streets, sidewalks, or through parks, and they all include both runners and walkers, so why not people in wheelchairs, too?

It was no surprise that my family was supportive about the idea.

We did a few more 5Ks to support a variety of topics, such as local charities, childhood literacy, cancer, disaster relief, and Alzheimer's. During those 5Ks, we learned that I could consistently push myself for about a mile before my arms got tired. Over the next year, my family helped me work up to being able to do a 5K without help on a flat course. The next year, I did several 5Ks on varied courses.

This year, I received a real racing wheelchair and have plans to begin doing 10Ks. Eventually, I think I want to do a half marathon!

I enjoy the racing, but more than anything, I love the memories I have of wheeling with my family walking next to me. We've done over a dozen 5Ks together, including a 5K in a blizzard, and one where I was so tired and took so long to finish that they actually took down the finish line before I could cross it. We've done them when people stop me every half-mile to shake my hand, and we've done ones when no one talks to us at all. We've done them together and virtually when we're apart. We've supported some amazing causes and met a lot of really cool people. I never would've started racing if they hadn't insisted that doing a 5K would be fun. You know what? They were right!

— Amy Anderson —

It's Therapy and More

Just Show Up

When life gives you a hundred reasons to cry,
show life that you have a thousand reasons to smile.
~Author Unknown

I was only two miles into my 14-mile run when I saw a ghost. Halfway between the Lincoln Memorial and the U.S. Capitol Building, my ex-girlfriend and I shared an uncomfortable nod as we sprinted past each other. A single "Hey" echoed in my mind as our shoes slapped pavement, adding distance to freshly opened wounds.

We met when we were young, fresh out of college and dropped in the middle of a city that promised exciting career opportunities in exchange for souls and firstborn children. She introduced herself to me as a university track enthusiast, and I quickly bought my first pair of running shoes to make a good impression.

Our relationship was marked by workouts. There was the run when we randomly bumped into each other on the National Mall and ended up going to dinner. There was the sunset run when I asked her to be my girlfriend by the Potomac River. There was the marathon in Philadelphia that we signed up for together and completed, falling asleep in each other's arms on the bus ride back to D.C.

We ran to other countries, and we ran to family vacations. We ran to different hobbies and late nights at the office. We ran to long business trips and separate dinners. We ran to tough conversations about changing expectations. We had always run at different speeds, but we had started running in different directions. Eventually, we ran away from each other.

After the breakup, I kept running. Putting one foot in front of the other allowed me to leave my problems behind. With my neon laces, I could run away from anything.

One morning, I was running by the Lincoln Memorial steps when I heard someone shouting at the top of his lungs, "Bring it in, bring it in! Get closer, get closer, make it tight!"

A man dressed in a neon green shirt, surrounded by a sea of oranges, yellows, and blues, commanded an audience like an orchestra conductor, "We're gonna start this workout with a little bounce!"

And as soon as the word "bounce" was uttered, the sea of neon began jumping up and down, chanting in unison with the man at its center. When the climactic "Good morning!" screams were exchanged, the group revealed itself to be a running group with an above-average enthusiasm for running up stairs.

Over the next few weeks, these people became my new family, a support group for the emotionally scarred. Everyone was made of hugs and friendships, name recognition and happy-hour invitations. Their motto was, "Just show up," and it wasn't only about showing up to workouts, but showing up for each other in life, too.

When I ran away from the neighborhoods my ex-girlfriend and I had frequented, they joined me in rediscovering a city I had lived in for the past six years. When I ran away from a job that had become stale, they advised me, giving me escape options. When I ran from the city and moved back to my parents' home in Massachusetts, they were there to catch me, with new faces and names but the same "Just show up" attitude at Harvard Stadium instead of the Lincoln Memorial. And when I ran away from the country to start an overseas adventure, they were there to send me off.

I ran to volunteer projects and expat communities. I visited islands, beaches, mountains, and cities in different countries, with my laces tied tight to keep me moving. If I was moving, I had no time to be sad about everything I had given up.

One evening, I found myself at a campsite with volunteers from over 15 different countries, gathered on a mountainside to build a school for the local community. Someone had designated it "culture night," and brave volunteers were sharing different traditions, demonstrating Chinese calligraphy, Latin dancing, and Australian folk songs around our campfire. Until this point in my travels, I had been a silent observer, seeing the sights and taking photographs. But on this particular night, something inside urged me to step up.

I looked out at the daring volunteers who had gone before me, admiring the way the firelight danced across their faces, searching for a smile to give me confidence. I was met with pure adrenaline, a series of steps appearing in front of me that no one else could see, so I cleared my throat and began.

"Bring it in, bring it in! Get closer, get closer, make it tight!" I paused, breathing in deeply. "We're gonna start this workout with a little bounce!"

On that day, I began running toward life instead of away from it.

— Brian Wong —

Tiny Sanctuary

I go to nature to be soothed and healed,
and to have my senses put in order.
~John Burroughs

I stared at the trailhead knowing exactly what I wanted from my hike before I embarked. I wanted a beautiful challenge, the sort of hiking experience that was brutal on the muscles yet breathtaking in its beauty. I needed steep elevations winding through forested area so canopied by trees that it changed the light of the blazing summer sun. I needed a cold creek to temper the Texas heat, for the humidity to drape itself over me. I needed to sweat out the sadness, worry, stress-eating, secret crying, and sleepless nights that come with mothering a child who is on the autism spectrum.

"Why don't you take a long break for yourself and go on a real hike, like the Appalachian Trail or camp at Big Bend?" a friend asked me when I told her about my plan.

"Because that's not how motherhood works," I said.

I needed a quick dose of peace, a trail that could be hiked in the few hours my son spent in his new autism therapy clinic 16 miles up the road. It was less romantic than sleeping beneath the stars, but healing for both of us would have to be done in smaller increments.

It had been two years since I last hiked the River Place Nature Trail, but it remained my favorite in Austin, a city full of beautiful nature preserves. I considered hiking all of them on my son's therapy days, feeling productive by covering the most territory, but healing doesn't work that way. I needed to be nurtured by the familiar, to walk the same paths each time and get lost in the sort of meditative trance that comes with repetition. Only this trail, an oasis protected and maintained by volunteers from the surrounding neighborhood, would do. Perhaps the love the trail received from its caretakers would soothe me, too.

I knew we couldn't undo the autism, and there are so many beautiful things about his unusual mind that we wouldn't want to. His autism affords him a near-photographic memory, a love of math I cannot comprehend, and an ability to create art with advanced perspective. We do, however, want a life for him with fewer stresses or dangers caused by autism triggers and sensory overstimulation. Like all parents, we want our child to have a life filled with love, independence and self-created happiness.

I looked back down the street and said, "I love you," sending the words out over the wind to my boy on this important day. While he took his first steps toward a different life, I moved forward and took the first steps toward mine.

The first hike was brutal and beautiful. Accidentally, I took the longest part of the trail. It boasted the highest elevation change in the Austin area — 1,700 feet in just a few miles. I needed breaks, several of them. Despite the heat and my dangerously high heart rate from the climb, I felt relief by wading in a stream so clear and cold that I was certain it had been consecrated. I half-expected a vision of a saint to appear.

Instead, I saw a cardinal. It perched for a moment on a large rock facing me, its deep red color a complement to the rich greens that surrounded us. I looked up and saw its partner on a branch, less red but still beautiful. Cardinals are rather common in Austin, but the birds still felt like little guardians along the path, rooting me on as I persevered. They are said to symbolize wisdom and living life with confidence and grace. They were the sort of cheerleaders I needed.

As I approached the end of my hike, I noticed the smooth and heavy rocking chairs that awaited hikers at the end of their journeys. I drank my last drops of water as I allowed the heavy motion of the rocking chairs to soothe my tired body. A breeze picked up from the nearby pond, cooling me off as I rocked back and forth, the trail nurturing me to the very end. Then I took a deep breath and went to pick up my son.

He looked forward to his therapy sessions each week, evolving in a way that gave him visible confidence and happiness. My slivers of time in this tiny sanctuary did the same for me. It wasn't a grandiose journey, but it was ours. At the end of each day, my boy ran toward me, undeterred by my sweat and disheveled hair, with smiles and hugs and some new project to show me. I always waited with my arms open, ready to embrace him with love, joy and the newfound sensation of hope.

— Tanya Estes —

Finding My Peace

On your good days, run hard. On your bad days,
run as long as you need.
~Author Unknown

"Don't forget to breathe." My cross-country coach's voice echoed in my head. "Look straight ahead. Chin down. Don't have lazy arms."

I focused on the person in the red jersey running ahead of me, adopting her pace as my own and catching up to her.

"Pick up your legs. Don't twist your hips. Relax your shoulders." I could smell the autumn leaves in the air and feel them crunching underneath my sneakers. Then I passed her.

I loved racing. When I was racing, I ran as fast as I could. I ran as if I were being chased by more than just the opposing team's runners. I ran for my life. I ran *from* my life.

Actually, I was running long before I started running.

There are ways of running that aren't physical. Growing up, my family moved around a lot. We left most things unsaid, swept them under the proverbial rug. I never knew why my father went to jail, but I was grateful to be in a new town where no one would know, where I'd have a new chance to keep all the secrets inside, where I wouldn't have to face the truth.

When I ran the required mile for gym class in middle school, I unexpectedly got one of the fastest times. My name was written on the "leaderboard" in the girls' locker room where everyone would see it. All the other top runners were popular girls, skinny cross-country runners who wore coordinated outfits to school, girls whose fathers weren't in jail, girls I didn't relate to.

I joined the track team. I won medals running the 400- and 800-meter races. With growing confidence, I joined the cross-country team in high school, renowned for being the best in the district. We trained like Olympic athletes. I learned I needed the right running shoes and expensive orthopedic inserts because my arch-less feet made me over-pronate and caused excruciating shin splints. I needed a watch that could beep at repeated intervals. I needed to journal my water intake, lift weights and eat carbs like a mad woman.

I loved all the rituals. I felt like I was a part of something. It made me feel seen after a whole lifetime of hiding.

I ran every day after school and on Saturday mornings. The same girls who were "out of my league" became my best friends. I enjoyed a camaraderie that has yet to be matched, with pre-meet spaghetti dinners, routine sleepovers and collective ice baths. I belonged somewhere. I was our fifth best runner, but a crucial runner in the scoring of cross-country races.

"The fifth runner wins or loses the meet," my coach told me. "A lot of teams have a few all-star runners, but to have a solid fifth runner means you have five all-star runners." I had something to prove, and I welcomed the pressure. Running was my escape from everything that I didn't want to face.

I liked the teamwork, but the running itself was a more selfish endeavor, a strange mental game I'd play with myself. People always said that running is one percent physical and 99 percent mental. Training the body is the easy part because muscle memory was on my side. My body did a lot of work to be a successful runner, but finding the discipline to do it wasn't that difficult. Sitting with my own mind for three, five, ten miles—that's the challenge. My mind is a savage animal that manufactures disturbing thoughts that desperately taunt me into attaching value to them, into believing them. When I'm running, my only defense is my own breath. Can I just keep breathing? Sometimes, my mind convinces me I can't.

Running is how I figured things out — things I didn't even know needed to be figured out. In that way, running has always functioned a lot like writing. It's how I've gotten through the worst times. It's the way I accessed that typically inaccessible part of my mind, the buried feelings in my heart. Running let me get to those parts of myself that I hid from the world — the ugly parts, the parts I felt ashamed to acknowledge. Running was always there at the end of a bad day, waiting for me like an old friend with a secret to share. When I was angry, I especially loved to run. I felt as if I was stomping all over whomever I was angry at, like I was running *at* them.

I learned in graduate school that sometimes my best insights come to me around mile 3. Every breakthrough I had in my master's thesis came after I'd stomped out three miles of self-doubt. Running was the ultimate freedom. For the duration of a run, nothing else mattered. It was just me and my thoughts. Passersby may see me running, but they have no idea if I'm ruminating over how my boss interrupted me three times, why my last boyfriend told me he loved me and then abruptly disappeared, or why my father had to die. Or perhaps I'm just blissfully unaware of any buried pain, jogging casually, taking in the jasmine and the honeysuckle blossoms, the cars honking at each other, and the sun on my face.

Running is a breeding ground. I can obsess over something that's happened, all the things I could have said or wish I'd said differently, or something that's not happened yet and probably won't ever happen. Running helps me gain perspective, clarity, and objectivity. It helps me become right-sized again. Maybe that's why runners always look so deep in thought. We're preoccupied. I can run to Ocean Beach, through Golden Gate Park, or into a busy city intersection, but I can never run away from myself, from my thoughts, from me. My mind goes with me wherever I run.

Sometimes, I am just taking in the scenery, filling my lungs with fresh air and running on autopilot in a blissful, Zen state. My mind takes a vacation, and my body thinks it can run forever. Sometimes, I can get to that place in a few miles; sometimes, it takes 10 miles; sometimes, I never get there. Runners call it the elusive "runner's high," when the brain is flooded with endorphins. That's a freedom, too.

Running is a paradox. I run to get away from it all, but I run to get closer, too. Now, running is how I lean into myself, how I call myself back to myself.

Running gave me friends; it gave me a community, a way to belong and a way to improve my health. But running gave me the greatest gift of all — the ability to be with myself. I don't have to run away anymore.

All I have to do is breathe.

— Niko Bellott —

Our First 5K

Unity is strength… When there is teamwork and collaboration, wonderful things can be achieved.
~Mattie Stepanek

I warned my husband that something crazy was about to come out of my mouth. "I think we need to run a 5K."

I was not a runner. I was a stay-at-home mom still carrying double-digit baby weight from two pregnancies in the last three years. With my husband in graduate school, and a toddler and a baby in the house, exercise hadn't been a priority. Running was just about the last thing I ever thought I would do for fun.

But it was an idea I hadn't been able to shake for a couple of days. A friend had posted something on Facebook about a program that would take people from no exercise to running a 5K in nine weeks, and I was intrigued.

My husband, who had been to Army boot camp and served eight years in the Reserves, was all in from the start. He started researching running gear, jogging strollers and a 5K we could register for a few months later. Me? Even though it was technically my idea, I was hesitant. In high school, one of the physical-education requirements was to run a mile-and-a-half every year. I dreaded it and always came in near last. I remembered how slow I was. How I would sweat and feel like I was going to faint as my face turned deep shades of red. How I had to walk part of the way. I was literally in no shape to be running.

Sometimes, I joked that the only time I would ever run after high school was if I needed to save my life. In a sense, I did. Our marriage was only three years old at this point and had been dealt a serious blow. My husband had recently confessed to infidelity. While we were both committed to healing and keeping our marriage together, it was going to take work. We needed a lot of help to restore our relationship, and for some reason I thought running would be part of the solution.

I was desperate enough to think that training for a 5K would benefit our marriage. For one, we'd have to spend time together several days a week. We had registered for a 5K that was exactly nine weeks from when we started the training program, so we had to keep to a strict schedule. Quality time as a couple was something we lacked, what with two small kids and no family within 800 miles. During our training, we had a few offers from friends to watch the kids, but buying a jogging stroller was our guarantee that we wouldn't miss a workout.

Second, I needed to accomplish something difficult—to push myself beyond what was easy and comfortable. I wasn't sure if I could run a 5K or save my marriage, but I knew I couldn't do either if I didn't try. I hoped that training for my first-ever 5K would help me develop the kind of discipline and perseverance I would need to face difficult circumstances of all kinds.

Third, I wanted the physical act of striving toward a common goal to inspire us to do the same for our relationship. I wasn't sure which would be harder.

Nothing dramatic happened in those nine weeks. I didn't lose a bunch of weight. Our marriage didn't heal automatically. But, week by week, we stuck to the plan and gave it our best effort.

The morning of the race, I was up with the kids before dawn, as usual. Their grandparents came to town to watch them (and us) during the run. It was a cold November morning and I questioned our sanity. This idea had always been crazy to me, but now that the reality of it had arrived, I was even more sure that this unconventional plan was not something normal people did.

My body practically hummed with adrenaline and nervousness as we gathered with hundreds of runners at the start line. And then we were off—putting our training to the test on the actual race route.

It was an emotional 36 minutes. The first mile passed quickly. The second mile dragged. We saw our kids a couple of times on the route, and I blinked back the tears. As we neared the end, people we'd never met — fellow runners — shouted encouragement.

When the finish line came into view, my husband, who was slightly ahead of me, reached back toward me to take my hand. I couldn't hold back the tears any longer. That one gesture symbolized so much of what we had been through in the past months. After all that had happened, he was still reaching for me. We were still in it together.

We finished the race holding hands and sobbing. Running a 5K hadn't made our marriage perfect, but it had changed something in us, something I hoped would last.

That was eight years ago. We're still married. We've run a few 5Ks since then, and we've had more than a few challenges in that time. But the lessons from that 5K remain. We make time for each other. We push ourselves to do and say what is difficult because we know it will be good for us. And we keep our goals in front of us, working together as a team.

I can't say I love running yet, but I love how running makes me feel. Strong. Confident. Accomplished. All because I took a chance on a crazy-for-me idea.

— Lisa M. Bartelt —

Pounding Out the Stress

Running is one of the best solutions to a clear mind.
~Sasha Azevedo

I couldn't stop my mind from cataloguing every ache in my body as I lay prone on that hill in Afghanistan. Rocks pressed into my knees and shins, my eyes burnt from the dust, and my feet and back were both screaming at me after the week of abuse. I was hungry, tired and ready to go back to base, but the mission was not yet complete. So, I lay there watching an empty stretch of dirt that wound into the mountains.

"Hey, Sarge," I said. "Is that a group of people coming our way or just some goats?" The ever-present dust hanging in the air made it nearly impossible to identify anything clearly. All I could really see was movement.

"Goats… I think." He paused and squinted down the path. "Yeah, definitely goats. People would ha…"

His words were cut short by an unexpected squawk from the radio at his side. I couldn't hear what was being said, but the look on Sarge's face told me that we were about to get moving. In anticipation of the instructions, I rolled onto my side, slid my arms through my rucksack straps, and struggled to my feet like an overturned turtle.

"We gotta move… now!" Sarge said as he stood up. Before I knew it, we were running down the hill and onto the winding trail behind us that we had used days earlier to get to the hilltop.

Running. Always running. No time to breathe. Just pounding the dust and dirt and rocks as fast as my short legs would take me.

My body isn't meant for running. I am short, stout, and slow. My body heaves itself around like an elephant. I may be built to carry heavy things, but those heavy things are going to move to their destination at a slow pace. But on that hilltop, I ran because I had to. Each step caused the muscles in my calves and thighs to burn. I gasped for breath as my lungs tried to suck in the thin air. Instead of expanding freely, my lungs found my armor pressed tightly against my body. I hated it, but I pressed on because that was the mission.

Then, I saw flashes and heard explosions. My world lit up. I looked everywhere, but couldn't figure out what was happening. Then I stopped running and started falling.

***

Frantically, I awoke, cold sweat pouring down my face.

It was the same dream again, a dream that I couldn't outrun. Or was it a memory? No, that didn't really happen, at least not like that. As my conscious mind took hold, I realized that the dream was a mixture of memories, fantasies, and fears. Missions merged and swirled into each other to form a dream that wouldn't let me forget Afghanistan, that wouldn't let me move on. It had been over five years, but the dreams never stopped, the memories never stopped. Nearly every night, I found myself running… running… running…

It was driving me mad. I needed to make it stop, by any means necessary.

An old friend knew I was lost and confused. I had confided in her before. And when I was at my worst, she offered up a piece of advice: buy some running shoes and go for a run. She rattled off the science and research, but I continued to doubt. At my best, I wasn't a runner, and after five years of post-military gluttony, I had gained 60 pounds. I wasn't stocky anymore. I was fat and heavy.

I was skeptical, but I was also desperate. I bought a pair of running shoes and went for a run. After a half-mile, I was winded, sweating, and exhausted. I walked back home, feeling defeated.

That night, I collapsed into my bed, and the dreams didn't come.

***

It was too late to stop running. I had come too far. The woods seemed to flow by me like a river, blurred by the sweat in my eyes. My ankles, knees and muscles ached. Each running step on the trail required concentration. Any distraction would lead to a root or a branch tripping me up.

Ahead of me, I saw other runners. Like me, they had a slight smile that looked a little odd on a sweaty, red face. They had a glow about them. I passed the nine-mile marker and knew the finish was around the next bend. I increased my pace.

As I approached the finish line, strangers started to cheer for me. Music and the buzzing of conversation filled the air. I wasn't finishing ahead of the pack, but I was finishing. And finishing was the only requirement to receive support.

I crossed the finish line a few feet behind another runner. He turned around and gave me a hug. We were both beaming from our success and newfound camaraderie. I never saw him again, but I counted him among my friends that day. I'd run hundreds of miles since putting on those running shoes years earlier, and I was thrilled to log another nine.

As I got my bearings, I saw my wife standing nearby, trying to take a picture. She was failing because our dog was doing all he could to run to me. He pulled on the leash, desperate to make sure I was safe after my absence in the woods. I gave him a hug, kissed my wife, and cheered on the others as they crossed the finish line.

That night, I was asleep before my head hit the pillow, and my dreams were happy.

— Peter J. Neiger —

Running Full Circle

Movement is a medicine for creating change in a person's physical, emotional, and mental states.
~Carol Welch

On a chilly October morning, I found myself riding the school bus that shuttled the runners to our leg of the Baltimore Marathon relay race. I was nervous about disappointing my more seasoned teammates. I had just started running, and on a whim I joined a relay team made up of my husband's family members. Being neither fast nor fit, I was rather intimidated by the brother-in-law who ran an annual seven-miler in the beginning of the summer in Baltimore, a cousin who had recently completed the hilly Baltimore marathon, and her husband who found running an easy pastime.

My adrenaline was already pumping when my brother-in-law came running toward me at the relay exchange point to hand off the running chip. It was surreal; I couldn't believe I was running in this race. Even though it was sunny and cold, the streets were filled with marathoners, half marathoners, and relay runners. The sidewalks were lined with spectators shouting encouragement, and a high-school rock band's music pushed us forward with their heart-pumping jam. I was in awe of the sheer number of people who showed up on a chilly October morning to either run or cheer on runners when they could have been sleeping in or enjoying a hot breakfast.

It was the first and only time I ever ran seven miles without walking.

By the time I finished my leg, tired and elated, I had fallen in love with running. For the first time in a long while, I was proud of myself and the hard training that brought me to the starting line. Unbeknownst to me at the time, running not only brought me to the starting line of that race, but it brought me to the starting line of claiming a healthier perspective. This perspective moved me away from depression and the insecurity of motherhood. During this training cycle, running became my armor against depression.

I suffered postpartum depression after having my first baby. I was overwhelmed with exhaustion, loneliness, and self-doubt. The depression was so intense that my husband did not recognize the wife he married. More than a few times, I considered that maybe I wasn't cut out for motherhood or life in general. My mood spiraled, and I went to counseling.

I was conflicted about leaving my son in the care of my mother while I went to work and taught other people's children. In school, I felt guilty that I was not giving enough time to my students — because I was longing to be home with my son. I could not find balance and reconcile the two. Finally, I gave up teaching to stay home full-time with our son.

It was then that I lost my identity. I didn't know who I was anymore. Teaching was second nature, and I was confident in my skills in the classroom. Motherhood was an unknown, and I was insecure in that new role. My therapist and I discovered that running was a mood lifter for me, and that I should continue running and increase my distance. In the beginning, I was running a mile a day, and it took longer for me to prepare for my run than to actually run.

By the time I ran the Baltimore Marathon, I had three children. I had finally gotten over the loneliness of being a stay-at-home mom while all my friends went back to work. Motherhood became easier when I started taking an hour for myself every day at the gym while someone else cared for my kids in childcare. By taking care of myself, I acknowledged that I was as important as my children, and that I deserved care, too.

After I took up running, my husband noticed a positive change in me. I was no longer sad, angry, or insecure. Running provided me with confidence, which translated into overall happiness. I signed up for races to keep me motivated to run. Over time, I found pleasure in my role as a mother. Motherhood was hard, but I could do this. This was my true vocation.

As luck would have it, on that fateful race day that would change my life, I sat on the shuttle bus next to a woman who was a seasoned runner. We chatted about the race and my concerns, and then she planted the idea in my head that I could run a local half marathon six months later. That just seemed crazy to me. Who? Me? A runner? Run more than seven miles?

As we filed off the bus, I thanked her and never saw her again, but that seed was planted.

This year, I revisited the race that started my passion for running seven years earlier. Gone were the cotton workout pants and shirts of yesteryear that chafed and irritated. Gone was the anxiety that I couldn't run my leg of the relay. Gone was the idea that I didn't know who I was or what I could be. Gone was the intimidation of running with more seasoned runners. I traded all of that for runner-friendly technical clothes, training plans that prepared me for my races, and confidence. I am a wife. I am a mother. I am a runner.

—Heather Martin Jauquet—

The Marathon Finish Line

Being a daddy's girl is like having permanent armor for the rest of your life.
~Marinela Reka

In the 1980s, someone dared my husband to run the Shamrock Marathon without any serious training or preparation. Always up for a challenge, he accepted. He didn't set any great records, but he did finish that race. He even had the runner's patch to prove it. Now here I was, 25 years later, clutching that faded patch in my hands as I searched among a new generation of marathon runners for my daughter.

Six months earlier, my husband had been diagnosed with cancer. Our daughter Jacquelyn signed up to run that year's Shamrock Marathon in his honor. She joined the Livestrong Foundation team and raised more money than anyone on her team except for the CEO of the foundation. She was even the featured runner for the marathon's publicity newsletter. Sadly, she was now running the race in her dad's memory. Although she wasn't quite as unprepared as he once was, her training schedule fizzled down to an occasional walk in the last weeks of her dad's life.

The morning of the race, we both felt raw and anxious. My head whirled with mixed emotions. I was proud of her for wanting to run, but sad by what had prompted it.

"Dad will be with me this way," she said of her poignant plan to carry her dad's patch. It was easy to see in her eyes how important it was. She was too nervous to eat, so we packed some power snacks in her layered clothes. I dropped her off near the corral where her pace group was assigned to gather.

I mapped and timed the route of the race, planning to cheer at three intersections where I could easily spot her. As I waited at the first corner, I watched lots of different speeds, strides and outfits, until I finally saw the sideways kick of her heels in the crowd. I jumped, waved and clicked photos as she ran by, my throat so tight I feared my heart would burst. The second time I saw her, she was smiling. She'd found her groove and speed, eaten her power snacks, and shed a few layers of clothes. She waved happily as she trotted by, and I silently thanked the unknown runners around her for encouraging each other.

Because the route eventually traveled deep into Seashore State Park, the third time I saw her was the last. By then, she looked a little tired and had a vague limp, but she was positive and excited, pleased with her pace and progress. I smiled and started the walk back to the car.

I put my hands in my pocket and was shocked to find Neil's patch. *What is this doing in my coat?* That patch meant more to her than crossing the finish, and now I had missed my last chance to give it to her. "This is so unfair, God," I complained angrily as I stood in the middle of the road. "First, her dad, and now this?" Stomping through a few puddles, I came to my senses. I had found her three times already; how hard could it be to do it one more time?

I headed off toward the finish line, only to discover that the route was densely crowded with onlookers. Even standing sideways, the mob squished me, without any clear path to the front. Even the runners crammed into thick groups, and it was hard to tell them apart.

I estimated Jackie's finish time based on her earlier progress and prayed she'd stayed at that pace. As the projected time came closer, I gradually pushed my way through the thick crowd. My head twisted at a painful angle, and I stretched my neck to see the approaching runners.

I knew not to look for her clothes; she would undoubtedly have shed more layers. Instead, I looked for her feet using the zoom lens on my cell phone. And then, there she was: those blue Nike-clad feet kicking out sideways as black-blue leggings shifted above them. I disregarded all the ropes, barricades, police and other observers, and jumped into the fray of runners.

"Jackie, here's Dad's patch!" I yelled. Surprised to see me but quick to understand, she grabbed the patch and shot me a huge smile of gratitude. Off she sped with renewed energy and a fresh reminder of her purpose. Within a minute, I heard her name announced over the loudspeaker as she crossed the finish line.

When I finally caught up with her a half-hour later, she was floating on her runner's high, but her tear-streaked face matched mine. Isn't it funny how things become so important? Four months earlier, I had prayed for a miracle cure. Two months earlier, I had prayed for Neil's suffering to end. And that day, I prayed with all my heart that a daughter could carry her dad's ancient marathon patch across the finish line of a 26.2-mile adventure. That tiny piece of fabric meant nothing to others, but it meant everything to my daughter. And in my heart, I knew Neil was smiling.

— Colleen M. Arnold —

Running in Sickness and in Health

That's what is incredible about human beings,
is the choice to keep going.
~Jack Antonoff

Runners run for many reasons. I began to run to help cope with a broken heart after a break-up during my sophomore year of college. With every step, through sweat and tears, I began to heal.

I kept running recreationally. Years later, I started running road races — more than 25 marathons, half marathons, and 5Ks. I also got married and gave birth to my daughter Jonna and my son Sebastian. Running kept me physically fit and healthy. I ran through the fourth month of each pregnancy. I ran my first 5K race when my daughter was two, and my first half marathon when my son was six months old.

Running also helped me survive the trauma of workplace bullying and harassment. To help me cope, I tackled my first 50-mile ultramarathon. That was 14 years ago.

Running has always been my medicine. It saved me after a laparoscopic hysterectomy that went haywire and left me with sepsis. My strong physical condition helped me endure three more major abdominal surgeries in ten weeks, a 26-day hospital stay, cipro toxicity, and a rheumatoid arthritis diagnosis. Running helped me to endure more workplace bullying and harassment after I returned from a six-month medical leave, and it helped me when I lost my job.

Twenty-one ultramarathons later and six years after surviving my medical nightmare, running came to my rescue again when my husband was diagnosed with rectal cancer that metastasized to his left lung. Running has helped me with becoming a cancer caregiver, and Jon has stayed with me as I've continued to run. He's been pacing me and crewing me since I began running ultramarathons. Now he can't pace me at 100-mile ultramarathons, so I stick to 50-mile, 50K and 24-hour ultra events close to home. My next ultramarathon — my 26th ultra and my seventh 24-hour ultra — is on a 400-meter track not far from home. Jon won't need to pace me or worry about me taking a tumble in the trails. I'll be in plain sight on the track. He will sleep in our tent in the dead of night while I chug alongside fellow ultra runners.

Running has a new meaning — a new purpose for me and for us. We now pace each other in the world of cancer care and treatment. As an ultra runner, I have endured falls and bloody injuries. I have endured loss of cognitive functioning and hallucinations. Jon's body has endured radiation and will endure life-long chemotherapy. His hair is starting to fall out. Jon is running an ultramarathon of a different kind.

We'll continue to run, walk, and move together in sickness and in health. Now I train and run to be strong for Jon. Running will help me to be a healthy caregiver. An unhealthy caregiver is good to no one.

Jon keeps moving on his ElliptiGO and joins me on my short training runs when he can. Movement is so important for mind, body, spirit and all-around health.

In a couple of weeks, I will celebrate my 60th birthday. I hope to run 60 birthday miles to celebrate 60 years and 60 blessings. The aid station will be our home. Jon will be there to feed me and encourage me to keep going. And he'll pace me on his ElliptiGO for a few laps if he can.

We met 38 years ago in a college history class, and we have been at each other's side ever since. As he tackles his cancer, I remain by his side and pace him along his journey to healing.

Running has been good to us. Running continues to be part of our journey—in sickness and in health.

—Miriam Díaz-Gilbert—

I Faced My Divorce at the Finish Line

Life throws challenges and every challenge comes with rainbows and lights to conquer it.
~*Amit Ray,* World Peace: The Voice of a Mountain Bird

It took weeks for my toes to stop hurting. But at least something was finally hurting worse than my heart. That's when I knew I was going to be okay.

I had no idea that long-distance running could literally leave one with blackened toenails. If I had, I might have chosen something else to distract myself from the end of my marriage.

I had been a wife for almost two decades. Now I wasn't sure what I was. My brain was working overtime, and I needed a distraction. I needed something to keep me busy when my daughter went to visit her father. I needed to fill my time with something healthier than "another glass of wine." So I picked a half marathon.

I called my go-to friend for adventure and asked if she wanted to run it with me. The race was at Disney World. I thought it was ironic to run at the happiest place on earth given my state of mind. I also thought it was ironic the race was called "The Dark Side" half marathon. You have to find the humor in life. It's my number-one rule in dealing with a crisis.

I trained to the soundtrack of inspirational songs. My mantra became a country song called "Dance in the Rain" by Jana Kramer. My other favorite track was the conversation between my friend and me as we rounded corners and ascended hills. Well, truth be told, my friend did most of the talking uphill. I mostly listened. It was so nice to listen to something other than the thoughts whirling inside my head.

Running was hard, but I figured if I could gut out 13.1 miles straight without stopping, I could gut out anything. Mostly, I was just happy to have some control at a time when the rest of my life felt so out of control.

The morning of the race, we met up with a few other friends who were running. As we stood in our starting gate in the dark, I wondered what had brought these tens of thousands of people here. Did they have something to prove, too? What personal bests were they trying to reach? What demons were they fighting?

Until that day, I hadn't run more than 11 miles. Finishing what I started was going to take the same thinking that had got me this far. I was going to have to focus on the positive.

I wasn't sure how I was going to get through the last two miles. Fortunately, by that time, I had learned to just take it one mile at a time. Worrying about the next one did me no good. It's an approach I now apply to other parts of my life.

I had quite a band of cheerleaders rooting for me. My daughter, my mom, two sisters, an aunt, a niece, and a cousin traveled miles and multiple states to be there. They wore bright yellow shirts that said "Dancing in the Rain," umbrella hats, and rainbow-striped socks to remind me there is always a rainbow after the storm. They were loud and perfect. It was quite a sight to see in the stands. The experience was a beautiful reminder to me that people are willing to encourage, support and love unconditionally, even in our toughest times. I really needed to believe that.

My body was exhausted when I crossed the finish line. I didn't even have the energy to fake it.

I couldn't seem to find my breath, but I had no problem finding my tears. Loss, pain, and grief fell down my face, making room for hope inside. Steadying myself on the shoulders of my mom at the finish line, I faced my divorce and braced myself for the next chapter in my life.

I was going to get my rainbow. I felt it.

— Allison Andrews —

Running Through Life

I'll be happy if running and I can grow old together.
~Haruki Murakami

I've been running my whole life. At first, it was to escape the Pirates in Neverland, or to tell on my brother for stealing cookies before dinner—and then running to escape the cookie stealer as he stormed toward me in retaliation. I ran through my teenage years and college as an easy and cost-effective way to stay fit. I continued to run through adulthood as motherhood, career and hobbies kept me in constant motion. Running was a fun hobby—something to be done quickly and efficiently so I could get back to my busy life.

Despite my perseverance, running never became more than a hobby for me. Never running more than three miles at a time, I couldn't fathom enduring anything more than a 5K. It wasn't until I was overcome with temporary insanity that I was forced to step outside of my comfort zone and sign up to run a half marathon.

The majority of my life was spent in a small town in the Deep South. I left for college, but soon transferred back to a university in my home state to marry the love of my life. Turns out this "love of my life" had ambitions of adventure beyond the Mason-Dixon, and he eventually moved our family away from the comforts of family, friends, grits and front porch sittin'.

Excited as I was to be in a new city, with new food, places, people and adventures to be had, I was also lonely, and desperate to make friends and form connections. I joined a book club, quilting club, moms' group and dinner group. Months passed, and I still felt I hadn't developed meaningful relationships with anyone.

I blame what happened next on pure desperation. It's all that could explain my enthusiastic "Sounds great, count me in!" when approached about participating in an upcoming half marathon. A half marathon! 13.1 miles. I must have been insane. Reflecting back on my usual three miles, 13 miles was an unfathomable distance.

After the initial shock wore off, I found comfort in burying myself in research. My research led me to buy my first pair of what I could only assume were gold-lined running shoes. Comforted in knowing I was outfitted for the upcoming task, I laced the most expensive shoes I'd ever bought and thought myself ready for my first day of training.

My running partners picked me up at my door, and we fell into a steady jog. I took it slow. One mile, then two. They coached me on form and proper hydration. Words like "chafing," "carb loading," "strides" and "electrolytes" became part of my regular vocabulary. I built slowly to three, four and five miles. Seven straight miles felt akin to climbing Everest in my eyes, and I soon became addicted to the high I'd grown accustomed to after a long run.

Mile after mile, I fell in step beside my new friends. We talked about our favorite music and restaurants, and exchanged funny stories about our children. At about mile 10, the conversations deepened. We confided in each other about our past and hopes for our future. We discussed our fears and disappointments. Breaking for hydration and quick gooey fuel, we'd lean on each other to stretch our quivering legs.

By the time we were running 12-mile legs, I knew I'd made lifelong friends.

The day of the race finally arrived. Adorned in gold-lined shoes, waistband of water and goo, with my sweatband in place, I finally felt like a bona fide runner. At the start line, armed with my friends, I already felt like a champion.

My time training had paid off. I felt capable and strong. I held a steady pace and kept up with my companions as long as I could. By mile 10, I began to slow and told my trusty running mates to go on without me. As predicted, they gently slowed their pace to fall in line with me. Legs shaking and knees buckling, we crossed the finish line together.

What began as a need to fill a social void in my life became a skill that would be vital in the years to come. At the age of 31, I was diagnosed with a rare form of cancer. Not minutes after the diagnosis was confirmed, I had on my trusty running shoes and was soon miles away from home. I ran until the tears came, and I kept running. I ran until the panic set in, and I kept running. I ran until my husband caught up with me and let me fall tear-stricken into his arms. As the endorphins and adrenaline wore off, we walked home arm and arm to tell our children. But now I was ready. I'd left my fears on the trail, and what remained were the will and determination to fight.

Throughout treatment, I continued to run when I could (and was permitted to by my doctor). Running became my drug like never before. At times, I needed to release stress and anxiety, and do something that felt normal. I would strap on my shoes and leave it all on the road. Though there would come a time when I couldn't get out of bed, let alone walk, I still dreamed of the day when I could step out of my house and feel free.

We had our moments of doubt that those days would ever come, but come they did. Not long after my treatment ended and recovery began, I let the tears of gratitude fall down my face as I half-jogged, half-walked around my old trail. Still bald and frail, it was liberating to do something that meant I was still me.

I've participated in multiple races, relays and team obstacle courses since. Even still, when my head is blurred or burdened, I release the tension with my shoes on the pavement. Step after step, my heart pumps, and my breath quickens. I listen to the sounds of the world around me and let my mind wander to wherever it needs to go.

Although it started as a means to social inclusion, running not only provided me with friendships, but with a skill that would aid me the rest of my life. Though that first pair of shiny shoes is long forgotten, running will never be replaced. It's safe to say I'm an addict for life. I hope in the years to come that my running will include scoring the winning touchdown at our family's Thanksgiving Turkey Bowl, catching the Frisbee my son throws to me across the beach, and racing for the last cookie or to catch the mailman before he leaves. And after running all the marathons of life, I hope to continue running, even when my strides shorten and my pace slows so that I can play Captain Hook and chase a new little Indian across Neverland.

— Emily Rusch —

Meet Our Contributors

Amy Anderson worked as a chef before her invisible disability caused her to pursue a writing career instead. She's worked with *The Sacrifice* anthology, *Aelurus*, *Wild Photon*, and *The Bird and Dog*. E-mail her at contactamyanderson@gmail.com or follow her on Facebook at ShadowLinesWriting.

Kate E. Anderson is a three-time contributor to the *Chicken Soup for the Soul* series. Mother of five, she runs for health and sanity. In recent years, her amazing niece Sariah has been her running partner, motivation, and inspiration. Kate shares her Northern Utah home with her breathtaking husband, their kids, and two precocious Beagles.

Michelle Anderson lives in the Midwest with her husband and two cats. She runs as much as she can when the icy sidewalks allow. Her best racing memory was beating her goal at the Twin Cities Marathon and bursting into tears as she crossed the finish line. This year, she's planning to give triathlons a try.

Allison Andrews is an Emmy Award-winning television producer who is working on her first children's book. She loves adventure, which is good considering she's a single mom of a teenager. She's planning to visit 50 places the year she turns 50 and is tracking all the crazy on Twitter @milemarker_50.

Dr. Colleen M. Arnold is a writer and family physician in Lexington, VA. She is a widow and mother of three young adult daughters. She enjoys hanging out with family, taking care of her patients, writing, walking, and working on her blog, "Living and Loss: Learning Lessons, Finding Joy." Learn more at colleenarnold.org.

Dana Ayers accidentally became a runner more than 10 years ago and has logged a vast array of average finish times since. Read more of her (mis)adventures in *Confessions of an Unlikely Runner: A Guide to Racing and Obstacle Courses for the Averagely Fit and Halfway Dedicated.*

James Barrera was a soldier in the Canadian Armed Forces from 1997 to 2014 with several deployments to Kandahar, Afghanistan. He plans to write a book about his experiences.

Lisa M. Bartelt has an incurable case of curiosity, loves a good story and won't start her morning without a cup of coffee. She lives in Pennsylvania with her husband and two kids, and writes about life's unexpected turns on her blog, "Beauty on the Backroads" at lisabartelt.com. This is her second story published in the *Chicken Soup for the Soul* series.

Michelle Barton is an ultrarunner. She has won over 80 races in 14 years and holds over two dozen course records. She has competed in some of the toughest races on the planet. Michelle loves to mountain bike, road bike and swim. She loves Yosemite and the Canadian Rockies. Michelle has a daughter and lives in Laguna Niguel, CA.

Niko Bellott is a San Francisco-based writer and traveler who writes about the tenderness of the human experience. She stays up at night thinking about chance encounters, irrevocable memories, liminal spaces, subverting the status quo, and what it means to love and be loved. Her first manuscript is a work in progress.

Helen Boulos is a mother to three children, four cats, and two very naughty dogs. She received her Master's of Education from the University of Virginia. She uses her degree to try to understand the secret language of teens and husbands. She is a writer for a local magazine in Delaware and is working on short stories.

D.E. Brigham is a retired educator who lives and writes in Tellico Village in Eastern Tennessee. He enjoys pickleball, kayaking, bridge, and hiking. E-mail him at davidebrigham@gmail.com.

After a lifetime of being inactive and overweight, **Elizabeth Calcutt**, made it her goal to get fit and help others do the same. She is a certified personal trainer and fitness blogger for FireYourTrainer.net. Her life's mission is now to empower individuals to embark on their own fitness journey confidently and competently.

Lorraine Cannistra is a writer, speaker, blogger, and wheelchair ballroom dancer. Her first book, *More the Same than Different: What I Wish People Knew About Respecting and Including People with Disabilities*, is available online. She shares her home with her fabulous and phenomenal service dog, Leah.

Eva Carter is a freelance writer and amateur photographer. Her background is in telecommunications where she spent 23 years in finance. She and her husband live in Dallas, TX. E-mail her at evacarter@sbcglobal.net.

Jen Chapman has a Bachelor of Arts in Print Journalism from Marshall University. She and her husband Shawn have been married for 21 years and have an 18-year-old son, Noah. Jen is a freelance writer, blogger, and church secretary in Huntington, WV. Her ideal day would include pajamas, books and *Gilmore Girls*.

Darin Cook is a freelance writer based in Chatham, Ontario who draws material for his travel essays and works of nonfiction from all of life's experiences, whether traveling the globe, journeying into his past, or exploring the mundane aspects of daily life.

Tracy Crump has eagerly anticipated the release of each of her 21 stories in the *Chicken Soup for the Soul* series but not as much as the arrival of her third perfect grandchild (with whom she will walk, not run). Visit her at TracyCrump.com or find her course on writing at SeriousWriterAcademy.com.

Billy Cuchens is the father of five through transracial foster and domestic newborn adoption. He lives with his family in Texas.

Karyn Curtis is a lifelong runner, writer and avid chocolate fan. It is claimed by some that she ran her first ultramarathon solely to avail herself of the chips and cookies at the aid stations. She has run numerous marathons with her friend, Karen. She lives in Ottawa with her husband, two boys and two cats.

Nancy Lee Davis has been a writer since the times of the big black typewriters. She wrote her first play at age 12, and later had a small column in a small town weekly newspaper. Mother, grandmother and now, great-grandmother, Nancy draws on plenty of past experiences and hopes, bits of wisdom and humor to pass on.

Jill Diaz is a seasoned runner who resides in the Chicagoland area with her husband and two young children. To date, she has run seven marathons, one of which she qualified for was Boston, and 16 half marathons. She works in higher education doing college counseling. In addition to staying active she loves to write.

Miriam Díaz-Gilbert has an M.A. in Theology and is an adjunct professor. She has been running 30-plus years and has run ultramarathons since 2005. She and her husband are avid gardeners and love to hike in national parks. She is working on her memoir, *Come What May; I Want to Run*.

A native of Cleveland, OH, **Joan Donnelly-Emery** earned a BFA in Musical Theatre from Syracuse University and performed both regionally and nationally following graduation. Her cancer is now in remission, and she enjoys a quiet writing life in Franklin, TN along with her husband, Alan, and Terrier, Dottie.

R. A. Douthitt is an award-winning author of books for middle grade readers and writes inspirational fiction for women. She resides in Phoenix, AZ with her husband and two little dogs. She enjoys running marathons, traveling, painting, drawing, and volunteering, and plans to write more inspirational fiction.

Denise Murphy Drespling received her MFA in creative writing from Carlow University. She lives in western Pennsylvania with her husband, two daughters, three cats, and vast book collection. When she's not writing, editing, or reading, she can be found exploring nature or remodeling her house. Learn more at www.DeniseDrespling.com.

Melissa Edmondson is thrilled to have her seventh story published in the *Chicken Soup for the Soul* series. She is the author of her own collection of stories, *Lessons Abound*, which is available online. She is a real estate paralegal in North Carolina and a wife and mother of four great kids. Read her blog at missyspublicjunk.wordpress.com.

Shawnelle Eliasen is married to her husband Lonny and is the mother of five sons. She home teaches the youngest two, and they live near the Iowa banks of the Mississippi River with a yellow Labrador named Rugby.

Tanya Estes spent most of her career as a librarian and bookseller. Now she is a writer who delights in experiencing her son's enchanted world each time he says "Fee Fi Fo Fum" while climbing a tree. You can find her little family hiking through the woods of central Texas.

A teacher's unexpected whisper, "You've got writing talent," ignited **Sara Etgen-Baker's** writing desire. Sara ignored that whisper and pursued a different career; upon retirement, she returned to writing.

Her manuscripts have been published in a host of anthologies and magazines including the *Chicken Soup for the Soul* series and *Guideposts*.

Shaun P. Evans, a Physical Therapist, lives in New York with his wife, Nichole, and sons Shamus and Simon. He is VP of Education for Ainsley's Angels, an organization advocating inclusion for individuals with disabilities. In 2015 he and Shamus ran 3,200 miles across America promoting inclusion. Follow him @power2push.

Melissa Face lives in Prince George County, VA, with her family. Her essays and articles have appeared in local and national publications, including *Richmond Family Magazine*, *Sasee*, and *Farm and Ranch Living*, as well as in 20 *Chicken Soup for the Soul* books. Learn more at melissaface.com.

Kristi Cocchiarella FitzGerald is a Willamette Writer's member and a four-time NaNoWriMo finisher. She has had articles in *Renaissance* magazine and five stories published in the *Chicken Soup for the Soul* series. She has also had poems, stories and essays published in *Fine Lines*, a creative journal where she is an online editor.

Millicent Flake is a retired school media specialist who lives with her husband in an old farmhouse in the country. Her son, daughter-in-law and granddog Molly live in Atlanta. She loves reading all kinds of books, working in her flower garden, and running. Read her blog at maflake.com.

Marianne Fosnow lives in Fort Mill, SC. The mild climate allows for walks and runs year round. It's hard not to feel happy under a Carolina blue sky. She also enjoys reading and jigsaw puzzles.

Patricia A. Gavin received her Bachelor of Arts in Russian, *magna cum laude*, from Emmanuel College in 1966. She has six sons, two daughters and 25 grandchildren. She works in elder services and is an active volunteer in her community.

Karl W. Gruber is an avid, life-long runner and running coach. He has a Bachelor's in Communications from Ohio State. Most of Gruber's adult life has been spent as a professional radio disc jockey; now he does freelance writing and life coaching. Most of his time is spent in Ohio, and the rest in the sunshine of Hawaii.

Kenneth Heckard is a graduate of Seattle University. He enjoyed 35 years in the newspaper industry, mostly in the Seattle area. Retired, Kenneth enjoys spending time with his wife Gale and running. He competes in races from 5Ks to marathons and in 2017 crossed the Boston Marathon off his "bucket list."

Ruth Heidrich, Ph.D. is an author, speaker, nutritionist, triathlete, and now a "movie star." She's starred in the ground-breaking documentary, *Forks Over Knives*. Still competing at the age of 84, she's won over 900 medals and was named "One of the Ten Fittest Women in North America." Learn more at www.ruthheidrich.com.

Eileen Melia Hession lives in Long Beach, NY, and enjoys daily runs (or walks) on the boardwalk. She has been published in many periodicals and has one published book of poems, *Vittles in Verse*. She enjoys visiting her daughter's home in Maine where they hike and ski and eat in fabulous restaurants.

Tracy Chamberlain Higginbotham is a 24-year woman entrepreneur and public speaker. She is the Founder of Women TIES, LLC and the Women's Athletic Network. She promotes women in business, sports, and politics. She is a feminist at heart. She has a husband Scott and two sons, Thomas and Adam, who love her "pink" spirit.

Kristin Baldwin Homsi lives in Houston, TX with her husband and three children. Kristin began writing after the premature birth of her twins drastically altered the trajectory of her life. She chronicles her attempts to manage life with three babies at raisingtrinity.com and on her Facebook page, Raising Trinity.

When not writing, **Larry Hoy** can be found on the back of his motorcycle. If you are fortunate enough to see him out and about, please wave him down and tell him how much you loved his story. E-mail him at LarryHoy@att.net.

Heather Martin Jauquet is a school reading specialist turned stay-at-home mom who lives in the suburbs of D.C. with her husband and four children. She tries to live by her favorite sentiment and parenting practice: "We are called to serve one another." She can often be found reading, writing, running, and crocheting.

Rene Jordan is a 54-year-old runner, married to Mike and mother to 13-year-old Macy and two vivacious Boxers. She loves the beach, photography, and is an avid reader. She is a seasoned cosmetologist of 36 years, owning two hair salons. She spends her off time running around their 1,200-acre farm that produces peanuts, cotton, and cucumbers.

Tammi Keen is an Army National Guard Officer, a leadership development coach and analyst for the federal government. A lifelong learner, she holds bachelor's degrees in music education and English, master's degrees in music and emergency management, and plans to pursue a Ph.D. in strategic leadership.

Heidi Kling-Newnam received a Doctor of Nursing Practice from West Chester University in 2017. She is employed as a nurse practitioner in Pennsylvania. Heidi enjoys writing, hiking, and camping.

Kristen Knott holds a University of Toronto creative writing certificate and posts at www.kristenknott.com. She lives in Oakville with her family and two fat cats. She has written her first fictional novel, *Cawaja Roots*, about love and a family secret. Kristen is a believer in all things female and a Wonder Woman want-to-be!

Lisa Leshaw divides her time between conducting empowerment groups for women, motivational seminars for seniors, and freelance writing. Her favorite pastimes are meeting new people and cuddling with those she already loves.

Robert Allen Lupton is a commercial balloon pilot in New Mexico. He runs and writes every day, but not necessarily in that order. Over 100 of his stories have been published in anthologies and online. His novels, *Foxborn* and *Dragonborn*, and his collection, *Running Into Trouble*, are available online and in finer bookstores.

Susan Lynn is a consultant and former adjunct professor. Throughout her career, she has held positions in finance, strategic planning, organizational development, and human resources. Susan is an author and frequent contributor to articles, blogs, and books. She resides in the Northeast with her husband.

Doug Malewicki of Irvine, CA has a Masters of Science degree from Stanford University and is the author of *Fit at 75!* Doug turned 80 this year. He is doing a year-long series of trail running, hiking and cycling challenges meant to inspire others that they too can retain their physical powers into their elder years. See his 80th year challenge list at www.InventorDoug.com.

A.J. Martin is an amateur author with a passion for crafting stories that stick with readers. He is Ohio born and raised, and aims to publish novels of the fantasy fiction variety.

"Barefoot Ted" McDonald is a primal lifestyle pioneer living in Santa Barbara, CA. He is recognized as an independent athlete committed to encouraging the rediscovery of natural human movement capacities for health and happiness. These days he is mostly occupied with the role of spokesperson for his award-winning sandal company, LUNA Sandals.

Dimity McDowell founded Another Mother Runner in 2010 with Sarah Bowen Shea, a fellow freelance writer and runner. The duo has written three books: *Run Like a Mother*, *Train Like a Mother*, *Tales from*

Another Mother Runner, hosts a weekly podcast, and offers training programs in the Train Like a Mother Club.

Angela McRae can't remember a time when she wasn't writing. A former newspaper reporter and magazine editor, she now edits books and recently published her first cozy mystery, *Emeralds and Envy*. She and her husband live in Georgia, and when she isn't writing and editing, she enjoys cooking, quilting, and junking.

Ed Meek writes poetry, fiction, articles and book reviews. His most recent book of poems is *Spy Pond* and his collection of short stories is entitled *Luck*. He lives in Somerville, MA with his wife Elizabeth. Ed is working on another book of poems. Follow him on Twitter @emeek.

Jen A. Miller is the author of *Running: A Love Story*. She lives in Audubon, NJ with her dog Annie Oakley Tater Tot.

Kathy Lynn Miller is a writer of poetry and fiction and resides in Allison Park, PA.

Connie Biddle Morrison grew up near the Eastern Shore of Delaware, delighting in the smells of the salty marshes. She attended the University of Delaware, and with her husband and two children, moved to north central Florida in 1978. She has stories published in e-zines, magazines, and the *Chicken Soup for the Soul* series.

Ann Morrow is a writer, photographer and frequent contributor to the *Chicken Soup for the Soul* series. She lives in the Black Hills of South Dakota, where she consults the trail often. Read more of Ann's work, and see her trail photos at annmorrow.net.

Diane Morrow-Kondos writes a weekly blog about grandparenting at www.tulsakids.com/Grand-Life/. Her book, *The Road to Happy: A Sister's Struggles Through her Brother's Disabilities*, will be released in

September 2019. Diane is also a triathlete and open water swimmer. Learn more at www.dianemorrowkondos.com.

Peter J. Neiger is a combat veteran of the United States Army who was raised in Oregon. After his service he earned a B.S. in Economics from the College of Charleston. He now lives in Wilmington, NC, where he works with local governments on affordable housing issues and is currently training for his first triathlon and marathon.

Kimberly Nichelle, an author and filmmaker in Atlanta, owns Kimberly Nichelle Entertainment (www.snackratproductions.com) and has several film and television projects on the horizon. Her short film, *Exposed Destiny*, will be screened at several film festivals in 2019.

Risa Nye co-edited the anthology *Writin' on Empty: Parents Reveal the Upside, Downside, and Everything in Between When Children Leave the Nest*. She writes as Ms. Barstool for berkeleyside.com. Her memoir, *There Was a Fire Here* (She Writes Press) was published in 2016. Learn more at www.risanye.com.

While **Olivia O'Toole** hasn't received any formal writing education, she likes to think of herself as somewhat of a wordsmith. She has been running competitively for five cross-country seasons and plans to keep at it until her knees give out. She aspires to travel the world, and hopes to one day weave her own world with words.

Jon Penfold is the author of *The Last Indians*, a novel, and *The Road and the River: An American Adventure*, which tells his true story of traveling across the United States by bicycle and down the Mississippi River by canoe. Jon currently lives and writes in the Pacific Northwest.

Francesca Peppiatt is a writer and actor living in Chicago, IL. Her theater company, Stockyards Theatre Project's mission statement is "giving volume to the voices of women." She continues writing her blog, books, plays, a musical adaptation of *Treasure Island* and developing inspirational books to enhance her speaking career.

Perry P. Perkins is a writer and professional blogger whose work has been published in magazines from *Guideposts* and *Writer's Digest* to *Bass Master* and *Bible Advocate*. Perry's essays have been included in 16 *Chicken Soup for the Soul* books. Learn more at www.perryperkinsbooks.com.

Burr Purnell is a creative director, with nearly 25 years in the advertising industry. He received his Bachelor's degree, with honors, from Northeastern University in 1994. Burr has lived in the San Francisco Bay Area for 20 years with his wife and two daughters.

Annie Randall is a wife and mother of four. She is also a university student, pursuing a B.A. at Concordia University of Edmonton in Alberta, Canada. In her free time, she enjoys spending time with family and hanging out with friends.

Carol Randolph's first story appeared in *Chicken Soup for the Soul: Divorce and Recovery*. She is the Founder of New Beginnings, a Washington, D.C. nonprofit for separation/divorce since 1979 (www.newbeginningsusa.org). She believes that the quality of our relationships gives our lives meaning and can be our greatest legacy.

Brian Reynolds is an elite bilateral below the knee amputee distance runner. He has set the world record for bilateral below the knee amputees in the marathon multiple times. He lives in Northern New Jersey with his wife and two children. He plans to continue racing at an elite level both in marathons and the paratriathlon.

Sarah A. Richardson is a running enthusiast, "back of the packer," certified coach of frustrated runners, and author of *From Side Lines to Start Lines*. She has made it her mission to help runners ditch self-doubt, fall in love with running, and to do it safely, with confidence, and from the heart. E-mail her at sarah@riseandshine.run.

Paula Roberts-Banks is a former academic turned translator, photographer and artist, based in Muskoka, Ontario. She obtained her B.A., M.A. and Ph.D. at the University of Toronto. She enjoys being outdoors running, playing with her dogs, or taking pictures. She is writing and illustrating her first children's book.

Patricia Ann Rossi has served as a volunteer running coach for the Leukemia & Lymphoma Society's "Team in Training" program. Patricia is a volunteer facilitator for "Writing to Heal" workshops for breast cancer survivors. Patricia also volunteers weekly as a writing club instructor at a local library for developmentally challenged adults.

Ruth Roy loves to write! She has had stories previously published in *Chicken Soup for the Soul: Angels Among Us* and *Chicken Soup for the Soul: The Dog Did What?* She lives on a farm with her husband and has accumulated many more ideas from which to write as she tends to her animals and recognizes their inspiring uniqueness.

Carolyn Roy-Bornstein's nonfiction stories have appeared in *The New York Times*, *The Boston Globe*, *Poets & Writers*, and *The Writer* magazine. Her memoir *Crash: A Mother, a Son, and the Journey from Grief to Gratitude* was published in 2012. She just finished a new memoir titled *Last Stop on the Struggle Bus: A Memoir of Love*.

Emily Rusch is the mother to three active boys. She works as a holistic health practitioner, a health and wellness advocate and fitness instructor. She lives with her family in beautiful Northern Virginia.

Yasir Salem is a man on a mission. Starting with the 2018 New York City marathon, he will run 50 marathons in 50 states in one year. Yasir is taking on this feat to honor his late wife, Gweneviere, who passed in July 2018 from lung cancer. Through the Gweneviere Mann Foundation he is spreading awareness for early detection. His story was written with Dawn Sheggeby.

S. Scott Sanderson grew up in Kentucky and is proud to be a country boy from Appalachia. Now married and living in the sunshine of Florida with his wife and dog (queen of the house), S. Scott is a scholar with advanced degrees in Geography and Religion. His inspiration comes from the beauty and uniqueness in the world around him.

John M. Scanlan is a 1983 graduate of the United States Naval Academy, and retired from the Marine Corps as a Lieutenant Colonel aviator. He currently resides on Hilton Head Island, SC, and is pursuing a second career as a writer. E-mail John at ping1@hargray.com.

Sherrod C. Schuler is a motivational speaker and author. He received his BBA from Grand Valley State University and MBA from Spring Arbor University. He lives in Michigan with his wife, Bridgette, and is the proud father of a remarkable daughter, Autumn. E-mail him at info@sherrodspeaks.com or on Instagram/Twitter @sherrodspeaks.

Deb Sinness lives in Michigan with her life partner Annie and their two Australian Shepherds: Petunia and Buddy. She is a proud veteran of the Army Reserve, Marine Corps, and Air Force Reserve. Deb is a published poet and is currently writing a memoir. Learn more at DebSinness.com or on Twitter @DebSinness.

Andrew Todd Smith received his B.S. in Journalism (basically a redundancy) from Texas A&M University in 1993. He and his wife, Lisa, have four children and live in north Houston. He enjoys running, writing, and helping others attain their goals.

Ruchi Sneha is an ambitious 18-year-old writer, who likes to read, play video games and find new music.

Michele Sprague, a Michigan-based writer, is the author of the book *Single Again 101* and has written hundreds of stories for corporate magazines and newsletters. Her pieces have also been published in many online publications. Learn more at portfolio.michelesprague.com.

Diane Stark is a wife and mother of five. She is a frequent contributor to the *Chicken Soup for the Soul* series. She loves to write about the important things in life: her family and her faith.

Kelly L. Swan Taylor is a Boston-based Business/Intellectual Property attorney, who lives in Providence, RI with her husband, Jonathan. As an avid runner and traveler, Kelly has run races all over the world, from Iceland to Hawaii. Her proudest running achievements include completing the Boston, New York City, and Chicago Marathons.

Ingrid Tomey wrote for several magazines and several Detroit papers for 10 years, then turned to writing books for children and teens. She has five published books. She no longer runs but bikes, hikes and does yoga. She grew up in Michigan but now lives in Florida on an island near St. Petersburg.

Erika Tremper's twin girls are almost grown now, and she devotes her non-working hours to meditation, swimming, reading, traveling, and hiking. Goals, ambitions, aspirations? No, thank you. Something always presents itself. E-mail her at erikatremper@comcast.net.

Heather Truckenmiller is a farm wife in central Pennsylvania. Recent empty nesters after raising and homeschooling four children, including twins, she and her husband enjoy geocaching and exploring local small towns and their unique restaurants. Heather runs a blog for crafters, and is currently writing a book about the empty nest years.

Diana L. Walters is the administrator of an assisted living facility in Chattanooga and part-time writer who has been published in the

Chicken Soup for the Soul series, *Upper Room*, and *Purpose* magazine. She and her husband develop material for ministry to people in care facilities. E-mail her at dianalwalters@comcast.net.

Mild-mannered librarian, humor writer and writing coach **Roz Warren** writes for everyone from the *Funny Times* to *The New York Times* and has appeared on both the *Today Show* and *Morning Edition*. Roz is the author of *Our Bodies, Our Shelves: Library Humor*. E-mail her at roswarren@gmail.com.

Mary Z. Whitney has contributed to over 30 *Chicken for the Soul* books. She also contributes to *Angels on Earth*, a Guideposts publication. Mary enjoys walking with her husband John and their little dog Max. Max has his children's book entitled, *Max's Morning Watch*.

Brian Wong is a traveling teacher and aspiring digital nomad with a background in technology and business. In 2015, he left his city job to pursue a sustainable life abroad. He has many stories to tell about his experiences.

Rebecca Wood is a freelance writer in Zionsville, IN. She's in a mixed-marriage (runner and non-runner) with her husband Chris. Together, they parent four boys. Rebecca's work has been included in numerous publications and blogs, including *Runner's World* online. She's run 12 marathons, including four Boston Marathons.

Susan Yanguas is a repeat contributor to the *Chicken Soup for the Soul* series. Her short stories have appeared in regional magazines and her novel *Bluff* was awarded a BRAG Medallion. She is also an editor and teaches a writing workshop at a local prison, when not walking around her neighborhood.

Meet Amy Newmark

Amy Newmark is the bestselling author, editor-in-chief, and publisher of the *Chicken Soup for the Soul* book series. Since 2008, she has published more than 155 new books, most of them national bestsellers in the U.S. and Canada, more than doubling the number of Chicken Soup for the Soul titles in print today. She is also the author of *Simply Happy*, a crash course in Chicken Soup for the Soul advice and wisdom that is filled with easy-to-implement, practical tips for enjoying a better life.

Amy is credited with revitalizing the Chicken Soup for the Soul brand, which has been a publishing industry phenomenon since the first book came out in 1993. By compiling inspirational and aspirational true stories curated from ordinary people who have had extraordinary experiences, Amy has kept the twenty-six-year-old Chicken Soup for the Soul brand fresh and relevant.

Amy graduated *magna cum laude* from Harvard University where she majored in Portuguese and minored in French. She then embarked on a three-decade career as a Wall Street analyst, a hedge fund manager, and a corporate executive in the technology field. She is a Chartered Financial Analyst.

Her return to literary pursuits was inevitable, as her honors thesis in college involved traveling throughout Brazil's impoverished northeast region, collecting stories from regular people. She is delighted to have come full circle in her writing career — from collecting stories "from the people" in Brazil as a twenty-year-old to, three decades later, collecting stories "from the people" for Chicken Soup for the Soul.

When Amy and her husband Bill, the CEO of Chicken Soup for the Soul, are not working, they are visiting their four grown children and their first grandchild.

Follow Amy on Twitter@amynewmark. Listen to her free podcast — "Chicken Soup for the Soul with Amy Newmark" — on Apple Podcasts, Google Play, the Podcasts app on iPhone, or by using your favorite podcast app on other devices.

Meet Dean Karnazes

TIME magazine named him one of the "Top 100 Most Influential People in the World." *Men's Fitness* hailed him as one of the fittest men on the planet. Stan Lee, of Marvel Comics fame, called him, "A real superhuman."

An acclaimed endurance athlete and *NY Times* bestselling author, Dean Karnazes has pushed his body and mind to inconceivable limits. Among his many accomplishments, he has run 350 continuous miles, foregoing sleep for three nights. He's run across the Sahara Desert in 120-degree temperatures, and he's run a marathon to the South Pole in negative 40 degrees. On 10 different occasions he's run a 200-mile relay race solo, racing alongside teams of 12. His long list of competitive achievements includes winning the World's Toughest Foot Race, the Badwater Ultramarathon, running 135 miles nonstop across Death Valley during the middle of summer. He has raced and competed on all seven continents of the planet, twice over.

In 2006 he accomplished the seemingly impossible by running 50 marathons, in all 50 US states, in 50 consecutive days, finishing with the NYC Marathon, which he ran in three hours flat! In 2011 Dean ran 3,000 miles from the coast of California to New York City, averaging 40 to 50 miles per day (one day covering more than 70!). Along the way he stopped at schools to speak to students about the importance of exercise and healthy eating. When passing through Washington D.C., he was invited to run through the White House to meet with First Lady Michelle Obama and be honored for his tireless commitment to helping the country get back in shape.

Dean and his incredible adventures have been featured on *The Today Show, 60 Minutes, The Late Show with David Letterman, CBS News, CNN, ESPN, The Howard Stern Show, NPR's Morning Edition, Late Night with Conan O'Brien, the BBC*, and many others. He has appeared on the cover of *Runner's World, Outside*, and *Wired* magazines, and has been featured in *TIME, Newsweek, People, GQ, The New York Times, USA TODAY,* the *Washington Post, Men's Journal, Forbes, The Chicago Tribune,* the *Los Angeles Times*, and the *London Telegraph*, to mention a few. Dean is the winner of an *ESPN* ESPY and a three-time recipient of *Competitor Magazine's* Endurance Athlete of the Year award. He serves as a US Athlete Ambassador and has traveled to Central Asia and South America as a Sports Diplomacy envoy. He's twice carried the Olympic Torch (2008 and 2018 Olympic Games).

Beyond being a celebrated endurance athlete, philanthropist, and bestselling author, Dean is an accomplished businessman with a notable professional career working for several Fortune 500 companies and startups alike. A graduate of the USF McLaren School of Business & Management, he is uniquely able to demonstrate how the lessons learned from athletics can be applied to business, and he is able to convey, with authenticity, the many insights he has gleaned along the way as a record-setting athlete and professional businessman.

Thank You

We owe huge thanks to all of our contributors and fans. We were overwhelmed by the thousands of stories you submitted about how running and walking have changed your lives. It takes a large team to turn all those submissions into a *Chicken Soup for the Soul* book: Our VP & Associate Publisher D'ette Corona, our Senior Editor Barbara LoMonaco, and our editors Susan Heim, Laura Dean, and Crescent LoMonaco made sure they read and graded every single one. After that, Dean Karnazes and Amy Newmark made their final selections for this new collection.

Susan Heim did the first round of editing, D'ette Corona chose the perfect quotations to put at the beginning of each story, and editor-in-chief Amy Newmark edited the stories and shaped the final manuscript.

As we finished our work, D'ette Corona continued to be Amy's right-hand woman in creating the final manuscript and working with all our wonderful writers. Barbara LoMonaco, Kristiana Pastir and Elaine Kimbler jumped in at the end to proof, proof, proof. And, yes, there will always be typos anyway, so feel free to let us know about them at webmaster@chickensoupforthesoul.com, and we will correct them in future printings.

The whole publishing team deserves a hand, including Executive Assistant Mary Fisher, Senior Director of Marketing Maureen Peltier, VP of Production & Special Projects Victor Cataldo, and our graphic designer Daniel Zaccari, who turned our manuscript into this beautiful book.

Sharing Happiness, Inspiration, and Hope

Real people sharing real stories, every day, all over the world. In 2007, *USA Today* named *Chicken Soup for the Soul* one of the five most memorable books in the last quarter-century. With over 100 million books sold to date in the U.S. and Canada alone, more than 250 titles in print, and translations into nearly fifty languages, "chicken soup for the soul®" is one of the world's best-known phrases.

Today, twenty-six years after we first began sharing happiness, inspiration and hope through our books, we continue to delight our readers with new titles, but have also evolved beyond the bookstore with super premium pet food, television shows, a podcast, video journalism from aplus.com, movies and TV shows on the Popcornflix app, and licensed products, all revolving around true stories, as we continue "changing the world one story at a time®." Thanks for reading!

Share with Us

We all have had Chicken Soup for the Soul moments in our lives. If you would like to share your story or poem with millions of people around the world, go to chickensoup.com and click on "Submit Your Story." You may be able to help another reader and become a published author at the same time. Some of our past contributors have launched writing and speaking careers from the publication of their stories in our books!

We only accept story submissions via our website. They are no longer accepted via mail or fax. Visit our website, www.chickensoup.com, and click on Submit Your Story for our writing guidelines and a list of topics we are working on.

To contact us regarding other matters, please send us an e-mail through webmaster@chickensoupforthesoul.com, or fax or write us at:

Chicken Soup for the Soul
P.O. Box 700
Cos Cob, CT 06807-0700
Fax: 203-861-7194

One more note from your friends at Chicken Soup for the Soul: Occasionally, we receive an unsolicited book manuscript from one of our readers, and we would like to respectfully inform you that we do not accept unsolicited manuscripts, and we must discard the ones that appear.

Changing your life one story at a time®
www.chickensoup.com